The Nature of Things

Emptiness and Essence in the Geluk World

The Nature of Things

Emptiness and Essence in the Geluk World

by
William Magee

Snow Lion Publications
Ithaca, New York, USA

Snow Lion Publications
P.O. Box 6483
Ithaca, New York 14851 U.S.A.
Telephone: 607-273-8519

www.snowlionpub.com

Printed in Canada on acid free recycled paper.

ISBN 1-55939-145-6

Library of Congress Cataloging-in-Publication Data

Magee, William A.
The nature of things: emptiness and essence in the Geluk World / by William Magee.
p. cm.
Includes bibliographical references and index.
ISBN 1-55939-145-6
1. Sunyata. 2. Dge-lugs-pa (Sect) -- Doctrines. 3. Mādhyamika (Buddhim) 4. Tsoṇ-kha-pa Blo-bzaṇ-grags-pa, 1357-1419. 5. Nāgārjuna, 2nd cent. I. Title.

BQ4275. M34 2000
294.3'420423--dc21 00-022590

CONTENTS

CONVENTIONS

Tibetan and Sanskrit words for technical terms translated into English are given parenthetically upon their first occurrence. Although proper names and place names are capitalized, there is no capitalization of book titles in Sanskrit citations. I give translation equivalents for all Buddhological terms (including the names of philosophical schools) and book titles; however, some Sanskrit words are used as if they were English words: Buddha, Bodhisattva, karma, nirvāṇa, sūtra, tantra, vajra, and yogi, among others.

Since Tibetan proper names and place names for the most part do not translate well, these are left in Tibetan, having been rendered into a rough system of essay phonetics devised by Jeffrey Hopkins.[1] Essay phonetics are useful when Tibetan words are required in the text, since they free the reader from impenetrable and unpronounceable transliterations such as *'jam dbyangs bzhad pa'i rdo rje ngag dbang brston grus.* The essay phonetics system renders this name more sensibly as Jam-ȳang-shay-b̄ay-dor-jay Nga-w̄ang-dzön-drü. The long marks over the consonants indicate Tibetan high tones.

The following table gives Tibetan consonants in the classical script called Ū-Chen,[2] Wylie transcription,[3] and Hopkins' essay phonetics:

---

[1] See Jeffrey Hopkins, *Meditation on Emptiness* (Boston: Wisdom Publications, 1983), 19-22.

[2] *dbu chen.*

[3] Turrel V. Wylie, "A Standard System of Tibetan Transcription," *Harvard Journal of Asiatic Studies*, Vol. 22 (1959), 261-267.

ཀ་	ka	ḡa	ཁ་	kha	ka	ག་	ga	ga	ང་	nga	nga/n̄ga
ཅ་	ca	j̄a	ཆ་	cha	cha	ཇ་	ja	ja	ཉ་	nya	nya/n̄ya
ཏ་	ta	d̄a	ཐ་	tha	ta	ད་	da	da	ན་	na	na/n̄a
པ་	pa	b̄a	ཕ་	pha	pa	བ་	ba	ba	མ་	ma	ma/m̄a
ཙ་	tsa	d̄za	ཚ་	tsha	tsa	ཛ་	dza	dza	ཝ་	wa	wa
ཞ་	zha	sha	ཟ་	za	sa	འ་	’a	a	ཡ་	ya	ya
ར་	ra	ra	ལ་	la	la	ཤ་	sha	s̄ha	ས་	sa	s̄a
ཧ་	ha	ha	ཨ་	a	a						

The essay phonetics system gives Tibetan high tones with a line above a consonant (for instance, "s̄hay"). Nasal consonants are sometimes high in tone (for instance, "n̄gak"). The semi-vowel *la* is sometimes high in tone. As suffixes, the consonants *ga* and *ba* are given as *–k* and *–p.* The Tibetan vowel *a* narrowed by a *da* or *sa* suffix is pronounced and spelled "e," as in "d̄en." When a consonant is followed by concluding suffix *sa* or *da* the resultant sound is rendered as "ay." Also, in phoneticizing the sound of *a'i,* the letters "ay" are used for clarity. The syllables of Tibetan names are separated by hyphens, but the different names comprising one person's name are separated by spaces and each begins with a capital.

ABBREVIATIONS

In citing the following Sanskrit, Tibetan, or English language works in the text, abbreviations are used. All other works — less frequently cited — are referred to in English first by their complete name, thereafter by a brief version of that name if such an abbreviation is possible and desirable. See Bibliography for full citations.

DAE	Elizabeth Napper, *Dependent-Arising and Emptiness* (London: Wisdom Publications, 1989).
DBU	*Treatise on the Middle / Fundamental Treatise Called "Wisdom" (dbu ma rtsa ba'i tshig le'ur byas pa shes rab ces bya ba)*, Tibetan edition, P5224, Vol. 95.
D-TSHIG	*Clear Words Commentary on (Nāgārjuna's) "Treatise on the Middle" (dbu ma rtsa ba'i 'grel pa tshig gsal ba)* by Candrakīrti, Tibetan language edition (Dharamsala: Tibetan Publishing House, 1968).
GRS	*Illumination of the Thought (dbu ma la 'jug pa'i rgya cher bshad pa dgongs pa rab gsal)* by D̄zong-ka-b̄a, P6143 (Dharamsala: 'Bras spungs blo gsal gling dpe mdzod khang, 1973).
LRC	*Great Exposition of the Stages of the Path (lam rim chen mo / skyes bu gsum gyi rnyams su blang ba'i rim pa thams cad tshang bar ston pa'i byang chub lam gyi rim pa)* by D̄zong-ka-b̄a, P6001 (Dharamsala: Shes rig par khang, no date).
MAB	*Madhyamakāvatāra par Candrakīrti.* Tibetan edition of the *madhyamakāvatārabhāṣya* by Louis de la Val-

lée Poussin, Bibliotheca Buddhica IX (Osnabrück: Biblio Verlag, 1970).

MCHAN *Four Interwoven Annotations* (*lam rim mchan bzhi sbrags ma / mnyam med rje btsun tsong kha pa chen pos mdzad pa'i byang chub lam rim chen mo'i dka' ba'i gnad rnams mchan bu bzhi'i sgo nas legs par bshad pa theg chen lam gyi gsal sgron*) with the interlineal notes of Jam-ȳang-shay-b̄a[4] (1648-1721), Ba-so Chö-gyi-gyel-tsen[5] (1402-1473), De-druk-ken-chen Nga-w̄ang-rap-den[6] (17th century), and Dra-d̄i Ge-shay Rin-chen-dön-drup[7] (17th century); (New Delhi: Chos-'phel-legs-ldan, 1972).

MED Jeffrey Hopkins, *Meditation on Emptiness* (London: Wisdom Publications, 1983; 2nd edition, 1996).

MMK *Nāgārjuna Mūlamadhyamikakārikāḥ.* Sanskrit edition by J.W. de Jong (Adyar: The Adyar Library and Research Centre, 1977).

P *The Tibetan Tripiṭaka,* Peking Edition, edited by Daisetz T. Suzuki (Tokyo-Kyoto: Tibetan Tripitika Research Institute, 1961).

PP *Clear Words, Mūlamadhyamikakakārikās de Nāgārjuna avec la Prasannapadā Commentaire de Candrakīrti.* Sanskrit edition by Louis de la Vallée Poussin, Bibliotheca Buddhica IV (Osnabrück: Biblio Verlag, 1970).

---

4 *'jam dbyangs bzhad pa.*

5 *ba so chos kyi rgyal mtshan.*

6 *sde drug mkhan chen ngag dbang rab rten.*

7 *bra sti dge bshes rin chen don grub.*

RGT	*Ocean of Reasonings* (*dbu ma rtsa ba'i tshig le'ur byas pa shes rab ces bya ba'i rnam bshad rigs pa'i rgya mtsho*) by Ḏzong-ka-ḇa, P6153 (Sarnath: Pleasure of Elegant Sayings Printing Press, 1973).
TSHIG	*Clear Words Commentary on* (*Nāgārjuna's*) *"Treatise on the Middle," dbu ma rtsa ba'i 'grel pa tshig gsal ba*, P5260, Vol. 98.

1 *EMPTINESS AND ESSENCE*

> Then Mañjuśrī propounded to Je Ḏzong-ka-ḇa a penetrating analysis of the view of the Consequence and Autonomy schools.[8]
>
> —*The Secret Biography*

INTRODUCTION

This book investigates emptiness[9] and nature[10] according to three Buddhist philosophers of the Middle Way School:[11] Nāgārjuna[12] (1st–2nd C.E.), Candrakīrti[13] (6th–7th C.E.[14]), and Je Ḏzong-ka-ḇa Ḻo-sang-drak-ḇa[15] (1359–1417), founder of the Tibetan Geluk lineage. In order to provide textual support for Ḏzong-ka-ḇa's discussion of nature, Part Two of this book provides translations of portions of five texts important to this lineage: (1) Nāgārjuna's

---

8 *rje rin po che'i gsang ba'i rnam thar rgya mtso lta bu las cha shas nyung ngu zhig yongs su brjod pa'i gtam rin po che'i snye ma*. From *The Collected Works of Rje Tson-kha-pa Blo-bzan-grags-pa*, Vol. 1 (Delhi: Ngawang Gelek Demo, 1979), 184.5.

9 *stong pa nyid, śūnyatā.*

10 *rang bzhin, svabhāva.*

11 *dbu ma pa, mādhyamika.*

12 *klu grup.*

13 *zla ba grags pa.*

14 Date according to David Seyfort Ruegg, *Literature of the Madhyamaka School of Philosophy in India* (Wiesbaden: Otto Harrassowitz, 1981), 71.

15 *tsong kha pa blo bzang grags pa.*

Fundamental Treatise on the Middle,[16] Chapter XV: "The Analysis of Nature," (2) Candrakīrti's commentary on Chapter XV in the *Clear Words,*[17] (3) Dzong-ka-ba's *Ocean of Reasonings*[18] on Chapter XV, (4) Dzong-ka-ba's *Great Exposition of the Stages of the Path*[19] section entitled "The Refutation of an Identification of the Object-to-be-negated That Is Too Narrow," and (5) an interwoven commentary — entitled *Four Interwoven Annotations* — on Dzong-ka-ba's *Great Exposition of the Stages of the Path.*[20]

---

[16] *Fundamental Treatise Called "Wisdom"* (*dbu ma rtsa ba'i tshig le'ur byas pa shes rab ces bya ba, prajñānāmamūlamadyamakakārikā madhyamakaśāstra*). P5224, Vol. 95. Edited Sanskrit: *Nāgārjuna, Mūlamadhyamakakārikāḥ.* J.W. de Jong, ed. (Adyar: Adyar Library and Research Centre, 1977).

[17] *Clear Words Commentary on (Nāgārjuna's) "Treatise on the Middle"* (*dbu ma rtsa ba'i 'grel pa tshig gsal ba, mulamadhyamikavṛtti prasannapadā*). P5260, Vol. 98; cited as *TSHIG.* Tibetan edition: Dharamsala, Tibetan Publishing House, 1968, cited as *D-TSHIG.*

[18] *Ocean of Reasonings, Explanation of (Nāgārjuna's) "Treatise on the Middle"* (*dbu ma rtsa ba'i tshig le'ur byas pa shes rab ces bya ba'i rnam bshad rigs pa'i rgya mtsho*). P6153, Vol. 156. Drashi-hlun-bo edition, Vol. ba, 316.5-333-6. Also: Sarnath, India: Pleasure of Elegant Sayings Printing Press, 1973.

[19] *Great Exposition of the Stages of the Path / Stages of the Path to Enlightenment Thoroughly Teaching All the Stages of Practice of the Three Types of Beings* (*lam rim chen mo; skyes bu gsum gyi rnyams su blang ba'i rim pa thams cad tshang bar ston pa'i byang chub lam gyi rim pa*). P6001, Vol. 152. Also: Dharamsala: Shes rig par khang, no date.

[20] *Four Interwoven Annotations on (Dzong-ka-ba's) "Great Exposition of the Stages of the Path," The Lam Rim Chen Mo of the Incomparable Tsong-kha-pa* (*lam rim mchan bzhi sbrags ma / mnyam med rje btsun tsong kha pa chen pos mdzad pa'i byang chub lam rim chen mo'i dka' ba'i gnad rnams mchan bu bzhi'i sgo nas legs par bshad pa theg chen lam gyi*

The Middle Way School is a Great Vehicle[21] Buddhist tenet system that purports to describe how phenomena exist, just as they are, avoiding the two extremes of true establishment and non-existence. In this school, each material and mental phenomenon in the universe is said to exist conventionally, as a mere designation. Things do not exist by way of their own entity, but only as terms and names.

While things exist conventionally as names, their ultimate truth is an *emptiness of a nature that is established by way of its own entity*. Such a nature established by way of its own entity does not exist, but is only imagined to exist by innate ignorance conceiving of a self.

The Middle Way School holds that realization of emptiness yields the wisdom that acts as an antidote to the ignorance that binds us in cyclic existence. Complete familiarity with emptiness leads to the omniscient consciousness of enlightenment. Without the correct view of emptiness, one is not released from bondage in cyclic existence.

D̄zong-ka-b̄a L̄o-sang-drak-b̄a established a logically structured, methodical approach to establishing a view that upholds conventional existence and conventionally existent causes and effects, while rejecting any sort of existence that exists by way of its own side or nature. He called this approach the Path of Reasoning.[22] One of the purposes of this study is to determine the extent of D̄zong-ka-b̄a's contribution to the topic of nature.

---

gsal sgron), With the Interlineal Notes of Ba-so Chos-kyi-rgyal-mtshan, Sde-drug Mkhan-chen, Ngag-dbang-rab-rtan, 'Jam-dbyangs-bshad-pa'i-rdo-rje, and Bra-sti Dge-bshes Rin-chen-don-grub. New Delhi: Chos-'phel-legs-ldan, 1972 [386.6-408.1].

21 *theg chen, mahāyāna.*

22 *rigs lam.*

The Path of Reasoning gives each practitioner a large measure of responsibility, since the inferential reasoning process must take place within each individual. Nevertheless, the view realizing emptiness is said to be difficult to realize. The correct view is as narrow as a razor's edge. One can judge the narrowness of the edge by seeing how the mind rebels from the idea that nominal existence is existence, and how the mind clings to the notion that existent things must be established from their own side.

Due to the philosophical and psychological difficulties involved (to say nothing of the social and economic problems posed by a contemplative path), the correct view of emptiness is not often achieved. In order to ease this difficulty, D̄zong-ka-b̄a urges practitioners to rely on one of the two great Indian commentators prophesied by the Buddha: Asaṅga (4th century C.E.) and Nāgārjuna. Asaṅga was the Chariot Way Opener of the Mind Only School and Nāgārjuna was the Chariot Way Opener of the Middle Way School. This work is limited to a consideration of Nāgārjuna, but without relying on one of these philosophical guides, the seeker after reality is "like a blind person without a guide fleeing in fright."[23]

Nāgārjuna is held to be the Chariot Way Opener of the Middle Way School because in the *Treatise on the Middle* he explained the teachings on emptiness in the Buddha's Perfection of Wisdom Sūtras.[24] Nāgārjuna propagated Great Vehicle teachings two millenia ago at Nālanda Monastic University in Magadha. Although little is known of his life or times, it seems likely that he was a seminal figure in the emergence of the Mahāyāna, and is considered the earliest of the Mahāyāna treatise authors. An extensive

---

[23] *LRC*, 367.a.1. Reported in *DAE*, 25.

[24] *pha rol du phyin pa'i mdo, prajñāpāramitāsūtra.*

mythology surrounds Nāgārjuna, and this also indicates his importance for the Mahāyāna.[25]

For later followers of the Middle Way School, one of the most highly valued aspects of the *Treatise on the Middle* is Nāgārjuna's investigative method. Nāgārjuna employs ultimate analysis to determine the ontological status of things. Ultimate analysis searches for a findable mode of subsistence. Such analysis seeks an inherently existent essence or nature through examining material objects or mental events for evidence of inherent existence. Thus, the sphere of an ultimate analysis is limited to determining the presence or absence of inherent existence. In practice, it always finds nothing, confirming the presence of emptiness.

Since Nāgārjuna's *Treatise* is extremely terse and difficult to unpack, Tibetan exegetes usually do not approach it without a commentary. For Geluks, the preferred commentary is Candrakīrti's *Clear Words*. In the *Clear Words*, Candrakīrti describes the purpose of Nāgārjuna's treatise as being a hermeneutical one. The *Clear Words* says:

> This *Treatise on the Middle* was composed by the master [Nāgārjuna] for the sake of showing the difference between that requiring interpretation and the definitive.[26]

Thus, the purpose of the *Treatise* is not so much to establish the mode of subsistence of phenomena (although it does so) as it is to determine the interpretable and the definitive among passages of

---

25 Two recent publications have included parts of Nāgārjuna's legend: (1) Jeffrey Hopkins, *Buddhist Advice for Living and Liberation* (Ithaca: Snow Lion Publications, 1998), 9-21 and (2) Gyel-tsap, *Yogic Deeds of Bodhisattvas,* commentary by Geshe Sonam Rinchen, translated and edited by Ruth Sonam (Ithaca: Snow Lion Publications, 1994), 11-15.

26 P5260, 7.5.7; Poussin, 40.7-2.8. This is partially quoted by Dzong-ka-ba in *RGT* 64.2.3.

scripture. It does this through providing numerous examples of ultimate analysis proving that phenomena are empty of true establishment.

Although the purpose of the *Treatise* is to determine the interpretable and the definitive, the subject matter of the *Treatise* is extensive, covering many topics, especially emptiness:

> The *Treatise* extensively sets forth the suitability of conventional phenomena within an emptiness of inherent existence as well as the four truths, actions and their effects, the Three Jewels, the eight levels of approaching and abiding in the fruits of Stream Enterer, Once Returner, Never Returner, and Foe Destroyer, and so forth...Still...these varieties are not the principal object of discourse in the *Treatise;* the profound emptiness is.[27]

Dzong-ka-ba agrees that, in order to attain their goal, Mahāyāna practitioners must depend on discriminating between the interpretable and definitive. Unfortunately, discriminating between the two is not possible just through hearing scriptural passages saying, "this is interpretable," or "this is definitive." He gives three reasons for this:

(1) If it were otherwise, the commentary authors composing commentaries differentiating the interpretable and the definitive would be senseless.
(2) Sūtras relate numerous different ways of positing the interpretable and the definitive.
(3) Sūtra statements that "this is definitive" are insufficient to establish the interpretable and the definitive.

---

[27] *MED*, 403-404.

Since sūtras alone are insufficient to determine definitiveness, D̄zong-ka-b̄a recommends relying on those commentarial authors who "settle [suchness] well with reasonings that (1) fault interpreting definitive scriptures as having some other meaning and (2) prove the definitive meaning as unsuitable to be interpreted otherwise."

Nāgārjuna fulfills both these criteria for being a reliable commentarial author. The *Treatise* is a repository of reasonings to help meditators refute inherent existence with respect to persons and other phenomena. The syllogistic reasonings employed in meditations on emptiness are designed to generate a valid cognition of the definitive meaning. As Āryadeva's *Four Hundred* says:

> When selflessness is seen in objects,
> The seeds of cyclic existence are destroyed.[28]

The seeds of cyclic existence are the actions and afflictive emotions caused by the root, ignorance. These ignorance-inspired actions and emotions keep beings revolving in cyclic existence. Meditation on emptiness destroys ignorance and thus is one of the principal aspects of the path as described by Je D̄zong-ka-b̄a.

EMPTINESS IN THE MIDDLE WAY SCHOOL

According to D̄zong-ka-b̄a, and to the many Geluk thinkers who have followed in D̄zong-ka-b̄a's path, an emptiness is a thing's absence of inherent existence. The thing (a conventional truth) and its emptiness (an ultimate truth) are one entity but differentiable to thought. This means that although a jar and its emptiness exist in the same time and space, thought can differentiate them. The emptiness of a thing such as a jar can be considered in isolation

---

[28] *MED*, 556.

from the jar itself. This isolating process is called a reverse.[29] When one reverses a jar and its emptiness — approaching them in reverse as (1) not not jar and (2) not not emptiness of jar — it can be seen that they appear very differently to the mind. In this way, using the conceptual mind as an isolator, one is able to meditate on the emptiness of a jar without engaging the jar itself as an object of meditation.

Let us continue to discuss the jar and its emptiness by saying that a jar is a positive phenomenon,[30] manufactured and having causes and conditions. The emptiness of a jar is a negative phenomenon,[31] like all emptinesses.

For Geluk philosophers, both positive phenomena and negative phenomena are existent because they are observed by valid cognitions. All phenomena, positive and negative, are equal ontologically in being empty. The differentiation between positives and negatives does not lie in their mode of subsistence. Rather, the division is made by way of how these objects appear to the conceptual mind. Negatives are cognized through explicitly eliminating an object-to-be-negated.[32] Hopkins makes the point that "to realize non-cow, cow must be openly eliminated, but to realize cow, non-cow does not have to be *explicitly* eliminated though indeed it is *implicitly* eliminated. Thus, non-cow is a negative phenomenon and cow is a positive phenomenon."[33]

---

[29] *ldog pa.*

[30] *sgrup pa, vidhi.*

[31] *dgag pa, pratiṣedha.*

[32] For some Tibetan scholars, "eliminate" means "not focus upon."

[33] *MED,* 722. It is a good thing that implicit elimination is not enough to make a phenomenon negative, else all phenomena would be negative.

Emptiness is a negative phenomenon because it is an absence of *svabhāva* that is cognized through the explicit elimination of an object-to-be-negated. Within being a negative, emptiness is said to be a non-affirming negative because nothing remains following the refutation of the object-to-be-negated.

Negatives can be divided into affirming negatives and non-affirming negatives. An affirming negative leaves something after the elimination. For instance, the affirming negative "the fat Devadatta does not eat during the day" affirms that he eats during the night. Non-affirming negatives leave nothing to be affirmed after the negation. Emptiness is a non-affirming negative because it is a mere elimination of inherent existence in a thing.

This is an important point for the Consequence School, because Consequentialists use reasoning to eliminate inherent existence; when all trace of *svabhāva* has been eliminated by reasoning, emptiness can be realized. If emptiness were an affirming negative, something would always be left over to be investigated, and there would never be a point at which the meditator could be realizing emptiness. Moreover, if jar were to remain after determining the nature of jar (which might happen if emptiness was an affirming negative), then jar would be its own nature and would truly exist. The ultimate analysis would have yielded a truly existent jar.

Due to these problems, Consequentialists are firm in saying that emptiness is a non-affirming negative. As long as emptiness is non-affirming, it follows that there is a point when emptiness can be realized by reasoning. This is because emptiness is the mere elimination of the object-to-be-negated, *svabhāva.*

Every emptiness of inherent existence is a mere absence of the object-to-be-negated nature. This non-existent object-to-be-negated nature is only one type of *svabhāva.* D̄zong-ka-b̄a describes this type of *svabhāva* as "a thing's establishment by way of its own entity."[34] The *Great Exposition of the Stages of the Path* states:

> There does not exist in phenomena even a particle of the nature that is establishment by way of a thing's own entity.[35]

The object-to-be-negated nature does not exist as an external reality. Nothing is established by way of its own entity, and this nature is a thing's establishment by way of its own entity. Nevertheless, the object-to-be-negated nature is seen to exist by ignorant consciousnesses, and we assent to its existence implicitly in all we think, say, and do.

The absence of the object-to-be-negated nature does exist. This is called the emptiness nature. Thus, it is important to note that there are opposing usages of the term *svabhāva*:

(1) A non-existent, object-to-be-negated nature (*dgag bya'i rang bzhin*) that is an object's establishment by way of its own entity (*rang gi ngo bos grub pa*).

(2) An existent, reality nature (*rang bzhin chos nyid*) that is a phenomenon's ultimate truth (*don dam bden pa*) or emptiness (*stong pa nyid*).

As we shall see, there are also other usages of *svabhāva.*

Speaking of these two *svabhāva* in terms of whether they exist or not, the *svabhāva* that is imagined to exist and that is the object of innate ignorance is itself non-existent. Although an ignorant consciousness fashions an appearance of it, that appearance has no existent referent in reality, because nothing is established by way of its own entity.

---

[34] *rang gi ngo bos grub pa.*

[35] *LRC*, 864.5:

> *chos rnams la rang gi ngo bos grub pa'i rang bzhin ni rdul tsam yang med do //*

Things are empty of an object-to-be-negated nature. This means things are not established by way of their own entity. This does not imply that things do not exist. Things do not have to be established by way of their own entity in order to exist. Instead, Geluks argue that they can and do exist imputedly, through dependence on names and mental imputations. All phenomena are merely imputed by thought and empty of inherent existence.

Thus, the Geluks are saying that we live in a world of entities that appear to exist by way of their own nature, and yet are merely imputations. All these entities function and yet are empty of inherent existence. They fall under the category of conventional truths.[36] Things that exist conventionally, such as tables, jars, mental events, and so forth, are all said to be conventional truths.

Each phenomena also has an ultimate truth,[37] an emptiness of inherent existence. The conventional truth, the table, and the ultimate truth, the emptiness of the table, are related as one entity, but different isolates[38] (i.e., isolatable by thought). In this way there are two truths for each phenomenon.

Emptiness is also empty. However, it is an ultimate rather than a conventional truth because it exists the way it appears to an ultimate consciousness.

An ultimate consciousness does not cognize conventionalities but instead is a reasoning consciousness realizing emptiness. Ultimate consciousnesses can be conceptual and non-conceptual. A non-conceptual ultimate consciousness is a meditative equipoise directly realizing emptiness. A conceptual ultimate consciousness realizes emptiness through a conceptual image. Since emptiness is a slightly hidden phenomenon (like impermanence), it can be

---

36 *kun rdzob bden pa, saṃvṛtisatya.*

37 *don dam bden pa, paramārthasatya.*

38 *ngo bo gcig ldog pa tha dad.*

brought to mind indirectly at first through an inference and then, eventually, directly in meditation. Perception of the emptiness of any phenomenon leads to a realization of the emptiness of all phenomena.

Just as there exist ultimate and conventional consciousnesses capable of certifying the two truths for a phenomenon, so too there are conventional and ultimate analyses. Conventional analysis is any type of logical process that inquires into conventionalities to determine facts. We perform conventional analysis when we inquire into the facts of ordinary matters: medicinal questions, the temperature of the stars, how to stop war, and so forth.

Ultimate analysis, on the other hand, attempts to determine the ontological status of things. Ultimate analysis searches for a mode of subsistence that is findable. Such analysis seeks an inherently existent essence or nature through examining material objects or mental events for evidence of inherent existence. Thus, the sphere of an ultimate analysis is limited to determining the presence or absence of inherent existence. In practice, ultimate analysis always finds nothing — no evidence of *svabhāva.* This non-finding confirms the presence of emptiness, which is the absence of *svabhāva.* In the face of the ultimate analyses of Nāgārjuna, the non-finding of inherent existence is the finding of emptiness.

Emptiness is an absence of inherent existence; but what is inherent existence, and what is its relation to nature? The next chapter begins our discussion of *svabhāva,* the essential nature.

2 NATURE IN THE CONSEQUENCE SCHOOL

How could the world exist in fact,
With a nature passed beyond the three
times?
Not going when destroyed, not coming,
And not staying even for an instant?[39]

—*The Precious Garland*

THE MEANINGS OF NATURE

"Nature" does not have a fixed meaning in Indian and Tibetan philosophical literature. There are a variety of natures. A glance at Sanskrit and Tibetan sources reveals at least twelve different meanings of nature from Buddhist and non-Buddhist scriptures and commentaries. These meanings vary from the divine to the fabricated:

(1) Nature (*prakṛti*) in the *Kāṭha* Upaniṣad: the underlying principle of the universe; an aspect of *ātman.*[40]

(2) Nature (*svabhāva*) in the *Śvetāśvatara* Upaniṣad: one of five principles that are involved in the workings of causality.[41]

---

[39] *rgyal po la gtam bya ba zrin po che'i phreng ba'i rgya cher bshad pa, rājaparikathāratnāvalī;* P5658, 183.2.

[40] See the Sanskrit text of *Kāṭhopaniśad,* II.1.6-8, from Swami Kriyananda Saraswati's translated edition, *Nine Principal Upanishads* (Bihar School of Yoga Press, 1975). See also Deussen's translation of Rāmāyaṇa's commentary in his *Sixty Upaniṣads of the Veda* (Delhi: Motilal Banarsidass, 1980), 291.

[41] Saraswati, *Nine Principal Upanishads,* "Śvetāśvatara" (I.2), 120:

kālaḥ svabhāvo niyatiryadṛcchā //

(3) Nature (*prakṛti*) in the *Bhagavat Gītā:* the universe's fundamental essence; aspect of the god Kṛṣṇa.[42]

(4) Nature (*svabhāva*) in the *Bhagavat Gītā:* the nature of persons that is their uncommon character in accordance with their caste (*varṇa*) and qualities (*guṇa*).[43]

(5) For the Nihilists, a nature that allows a thing to arise causelessly.[44]

(6) The fundamental nature (*rtsa ba'i rang bzhin, prakṛti / mūlaprakṛti*) in Sāṃkhya; a basic principle of the universe, unmanifest but present in all phenomena.[45]

(7) Nature in the context of three-nature (*ngo bo nyid gsum, trisvabhāva*) doctrines found in a variety of Buddhist scriptures and treatises.[46]

---

bhūtāni yoniḥ puruṣa iti chintyā //
samyoga eṣāṃ na tvātmabhāva //
ātmāpyanīśaḥ sukhaduḥkhahetoḥ //

[42] The *Bhagavat Gītā,* IX.7, 88:

sarvabhūtānikaunteya prakṛti yānti māmikām //
kalpakṣaye punastāni kalpādau visujāmyaham //

[43] The *Bhagavat Gītā,* XVIII.40, 168:

brāhmaṇakṣatriyaviśāṃ śūdrānāṃ ca parantapa //
karmāṇi pravibhaktāni svabhāvaprabhavair guṇaiḥ //

[44] Jang-ḡya's *Presentation of Tenets,* 23.4-5:

dngos po rnams rgyu med par ngo bo nyid las byung bar smra bas ngo bo nyid smra ba'am rang bzhin smra ba zhes zer //

[45] Larson and Bhattacharya, editors, *Sāṃkhya: a Dualist Tradition in Indian Philosophy,* volume 4 of the *Encyclopedia of Indian Philosophies* (Princeton University Press, 1987), 190.

[46] *mdo sde dgongs 'grel / dgongs pa nges par 'grel pa'i mdo, saṃdinirmocanasūtra,* P774. For a discussion of the three natures in the Mind Only

(8) The fabricated nature, i.e., the heat of fire (see page 79).
(9) A non-existent object-to-be-negated nature (*dgag bya'i rang bzhin*. See page 39).
(10) an existent reality nature (*rang bzhin chos nyid*) endowed with the three features of emptiness (see page 37).
(11) The conventional nature of a phenomenon (*tha snyad pa'i rang bzhin*. See page 143).
(12) A positive and independent nature: the Nature Body (*rang bzhin gyi sku*) asserted by Döl-b̄o S̄hay-rap-gyel-tsen[47] (see page 108).

Within these various meanings of nature, Nāgārjuna and Candrakīrti mainly concentrate on refuting (8) the fabricated nature, while D̄zong-ka-b̄a and his followers also refute (9) the object-to-be-negated nature and (12) a positive and independent nature. Both Indian and Tibetan authors also concentrate on asserting (10) an existent reality nature that is emptiness. Although this emptiness is the ultimate, it is itself empty.

In the Middle Way School, the term "nature" (like the term "thing") is given a number of different meanings and is used for different purposes. Candrakīrti and Je D̄zong-ka-b̄a concur in identifying three meanings of nature:

(1) A non-existent, object-to-be-negated nature (*dgag bya'i rang bzhin*) that is an object's establishment by way of its own entity (*rang gi ngo bos grub pa*).
(2) An existent, reality nature (*rang bzhin chos nyid*)

School in India, see Ake Boquist, "Trisvabhāva: A Study of the Development of the Three-nature-theory in Yogācāra Buddhism," Tord Olsson, ed., *Lund Studies in African and Asian Religions*, Vol. 8 (Lund: University of Lund, 1993).

[47] *dol po pa, shes rab rgyal mtshan.*

that is a phenomenon's ultimate truth (*don dam bden pa*) or emptiness (*stong pa nyid*).

(3) The conventional nature of a phenomenon (*tha snyad pa'i rang bzhin*).

Writing in the *Four Interwoven Annotations,* Jam-ȳang-shay-b̄a provides advice to dispell confusion over these various meanings:

> Moreover, in general, just as one must understand "thing" (*dngos po, bhāva*) as having two meanings — one as able to perform a function and the other as the nature that is the object-to-be-negated — so there are many usages of "nature":
>
> (1) the mode of subsistence of objects [emptiness],
> (2) the conventional nature of forms and so forth,
> (3) establishment from an object's own side, the [non-existent] object-to-be-negated.
>
> Thus there are many meanings of nature. One should know which meaning by way of the context. [48]

When the nature of things being spoken of is reality — the ultimate truth of an object — then that nature exists in fact. However, when the nature of things being spoken of is the object-to-be-negated in the view of selflessness, that nature is only imagined to exist. Je D̄zong-ka-b̄a's *Illumination of the Thought* confirms the two main meanings of nature in texts of the Consequence School when he speaks of a nature to be negated and a nature to be asserted:

---

[48] *MCHAN,* 387.2-387.4:

> *de yang spyir dngos po zhes pa la yang don byed nus pa la byas pa dang dgag bya'i dngos po chos rnams kyi rang bzhin la bshad pa gnyis su go dgos pa ltar rang bzhin la yang gnas lugs la der gsungs pa dang gzugs sogs kyi kun rdzob pa'i rang bzhin dang rang ngos nas grub pa'i dgag bya la der gsungs pa sogs du ma 'byung bas skabs ltobs kyis shes dgos so //*

> The nature that is refuted is a refutation of [its] being the basic disposition of eyes, etc. The nature that is asserted is that negative which is accepted as a nature called "the reality of eyes, etc."[49]

According to Je D̄zong-ka-b̄a, only the second of these two types of nature exists. Although they are both called "nature," they have nothing in common, except perhaps that the former is hypothetically non-fabricated and the latter is actually non-fabricated.

THE SCRIPTURAL SOURCES FOR NATURE

Middle Way School scriptural sources for discussions involving nature are passages in the Perfection of Wisdom Sūtras, the *Descent into Laṅkā Sūtra,* and Nāgārjuna's *Treatise on the Middle.* Most later discussions of nature in the Consequence School are derived from these sources.

The importance of the *Descent into Laṅkā Sūtra* to the study of nature in the Consequence School is shown in the fact that it is quoted by Candrakīrti during his discussion of nature in the *Clear Words* (XV):

> Just as those having opthomalia wrongly apprehend falling hairs,
> So this imputation as thing (*dngos por brtag pa, bhāvavikalpa*) is a wrong imputation by childish beings.
>
> There is no nature (*rang bzhin med, na svabhāva*), no consciousness, no basis-of-all, and no things (*dngos med, na svabhāva*),

[49] *GRS,* 426.11-426.13:

> *rang bzhin bkag pa ni mig sogs gshis lugs yin pa bkag pa yin la rang bzhin khas blangs pa ni bkag pa de mig sogs kyi chos nyid ces pa'i rang bzhin du 'dod pa yin //*

> But children, bad logicians, and those like corpses impute them.[50]

In this passage the sūtra presents a refutation of "imputation as thing." The "thing" imputed to exist refers to the nature mentioned in the next line — "there is no nature." This nature does not exist but is conceived to exist by children, and so forth.

Buddhist scriptures also mention an "emptiness of nature"[51] and an "emptiness of entityness/nature"[52] as two of the divisions of emptiness into twenty.[53] Although these divisions occur in a

---

[50] *LAS*, 19, quoted in *PP*, 262.2-5:

keshoṇḍukaṃ yathā midhyā gṛhyate taimirivairjñanaiḥ //
tathā bhāvavikalpo 'yaṃ midhyā balairvikalpyate //
na svabhāvo vijñaptirna ca vastu na kālpa //
balairvikalpitā hyetu svabhūtaiḥ kutārkikaiḥ iti //

TSHIG, 42.4.7-42.4.8; *D-TSHIG*, 226.3-7:

ji ltar rab rib can dag gi //
skra shad log par 'dzin pa ltar //
de bzhin dngos por brtag pa 'di //
byis pas log par rnam par brtags //
rang bzhin med cing rnam rig med //
kun gzhi med cing dngos med na //
byis pa ngan pa rtog gi ba //
ro dang 'dra bas 'di dag brtags //

[51] *rang bzhin stong pa nyid, prakṛti-śūnyatā.*

[52] *ngo bo nyid stong pa nyid, svabhāva-śūnyatā.*

[53] The twenty aspects of emptiness (*stong pa nyid kyi bye brag gis rnam pa nyi shu*) appear in the *Perfection of Wisdom Sūtra in Twenty-Five Thousand Lines* (*pañcaviṃśatisāhasrikā*). See T. R. V. Murti, *The Central Philosophy of Buddhism* (London: Unwin Publishers, 1980), 351.

variety of classical sources, the Perfection of Wisdom Sūtras are the most significant.[54]

The origins of these sūtras are obscure. Williams says, "It is not possible at the present stage of our knowledge to make many very certain statements regarding the origins and development of the Prajñāpāramitā literature."[55] Buddhist tradition traces the Perfection of Wisdom Sūtras to the Buddha, but some recent scholarship places their composition at a variety of later dates. Conze gives a range from 100 B.C.E. to 1200 C.E. and places the *Eight Thousand Stanza Perfection of Wisdom Sūtra*[56] as the oldest of the texts.[57] Lancaster confirms this in his report that the *Eight Thousand Stanza Perfection of Wisdom Sūtra* was the first of the Mahāyāna sūtras to appear in China, around 180 C.E.[58]

Nature is discussed in a number of the Perfection of Wisdom Sūtras. The *Eight Thousand Stanza Perfection of Wisdom Sūtra* brings up nature (*svabhāva*) in its discussion of the emptiness of the five aggregates.[59] The *Eight Thousand Stanza Perfection of Wisdom Sūtra* states:

---

[54] See Edward Conze, *Materials for a Dictionary of the Prajñāpāramitā Literature* (Tokyo: Suzuki Research Foundation, 1973), 438.

[55] Paul Williams, *Mahāyāna Buddhism* (London: Routledge, 1989), 40.

[56] *shes rab kyi pha rol tu phyin pa brgyad stong pa'i mdo, aṣṭasāhasrikā-prajñāpāramitā-sūtra*, P734.

[57] See Edward Conze, *The Prajñāpāramitā Literature* (London: 1960).

[58] Lewis Lancaster, "The Oldest Mahāyāna Sūtra: Its Significance for the Study of Buddhist Development," *The Eastern Buddhist* (Vol. 8, 1975), 30-35.

[59] *phung po lnga, pañca skandhāḥ.*

> Subhūti, since the five aggregates are without nature, they have a nature of emptiness.[60]

The five aggregates are often spoken of in Perfection of Wisdom Sūtras in terms of being empty, and in this passage we are told that their emptiness is due to their lack of nature. The passage speaks of nature in two senses: the imagined nature that the aggregates are without is the object-to-be-negated. Their nature of emptiness is their reality nature.

The *Eight Thousand Stanza Perfection of Wisdom Sūtra* also offers the argument that a lack of own-entity[61] is the reason that the form[62] aggregate is neither bound nor freed through the three times:[63]

> Form is neither bound nor freed, because form has no own-being. The past starting point of a material process [=form] is neither bound nor freed, because the past starting point of a material process is without own-being. The end of a material process, in the future, is neither bound nor freed, because the future end of a material process is without own-being. A present material process is neither bound nor freed, because

---

[60] *Eight Thousand Stanza Perfection of Wisdom Sūtra,* P734, Vol. 21, [XII.256] 118.4.6-118.4.7:

> *rab 'byor phung po lnga rnams ni ngo bo nyid med pas na stong pa nyid kyi ngo bo nyid do //*

Ed. P.L.Vaidya (Darbhanga: Mithila Institute, 1963), Buddhist Sanskrit Texts No. 4, *Aṣṭasāhasrikā Prajñāpāramitā with Haribhadra's Commentary called Āloka*, 125.18-19:

> *śūnyatāsvabhāvā hi subhūte pañca skandhāḥ asvabhāvatvāt //*

[61] *ngo bo nyid med pa, asvabhāvatā.*

[62] *gzugs, rūpa.*

[63] Conze, *Literature*, 142.

> the fact of being present is not part of the own-being of a present form. And so for the remaining skandhas.[64]

Forms, and so forth, are beyond bondage and liberation because they are empty. The terms "bondage" and "liberation" only apply to those who conceive of forms as possessing an object-to-be-negated nature.

The *Eight Thousand Stanza Perfection of Wisdom Sūtra* shows the early usage of "nature" in the two senses of the reality nature and the object-to-be-negated nature. The Perfection of Wisdom Sūtras are also a source for the assertion that emptiness itself is devoid of nature. Thus, although the object-to-be-negated nature becomes more important for Geluk exegetes than it originally appears to be in sūtras and Indian commentaries, it is not entirely a later Geluk innovation.

NĀGĀRJUNA: THE ART OF THE TREATISE

Nāgārjuna is considered by his followers to have expressed the essence of the Perfection of Wisdom Sūtras in his seven treatises:

(1) *Fundamental Treatise Called "Wisdom" (dbu ma'i bstan bcos / dbu ma rtsa ba'i tshig le'ur byas pa shes rab ces bya ba, madhyamakaśāstra prajñānāmamūla-madyamakakārikā).*[65]

(2) *Essay on the Mind of Enlightenment (byang chub sems kyi 'grel pa, bodhicittavivaraṇa).*

(3) *Refutation of Objections (rtsod pa bzlog pa'i tshig le'ur byas pa, vigrahavyāvartanīkārikā).*

---

[64] *Eight Thousand Stanza Perfection of Wisdom Sūtra,* P734, Vol. 21, 93.7-16.

[65] P5224, Vol. 95. Edited Sanskrit: Nāgārjuna, *Mūlamadhymakakārikāḥ.* J.W. de Jong, ed. (Adyar: Adyar Library and Research Centre, 1977). See Bibliography for translations.

(4) *Seventy Stanzas on Emptiness* (*stong pa nyid bdun cu pa'i tshig le'ur byas pa, śūnyatāsaptatikārikā*).
(5) *Sixty Stanzas of Reasoning* (*rigs pa drug cu pa'i tshig le'ur byas pa, yuktiṣaṣṭikākārikā*).
(6) *Treatise Called "The Finely Woven"* (*zhib mo rnam par 'thag pa zhes bya ba'i mdo, vaidalyasūtranāma*).
(7) *Precious Garland of Advice for the King* (*rgyal po la gtam bya rin po che'i phreng ba, rājaparikathāratnāvalī*).

From among these, Nāgārjuna's *Treatise on the Middle* is the central treatise of the Middle Way Consequence tradition. Geluk exegetes usually approach Nāgārjuna's *Treatise* through Candrakīrti's *Clear Words* commentary. Candrakīrti describes the purpose of Nāgārjuna's treatise as being a hermeneutical one, to determine the interpretable and the definitive amongst passages of scripture. As mentioned earlier, it does this through providing examples of ultimate analysis proving that phenomena are empty of true establishment. Although the purpose of the *Treatise* is to determine the interpretable and the definitive amongst passages of scripture, the subject matter of the *Treatise* is extensive, covering many topics regarding emptiness, and not just emptiness. Hopkins states a number of these other topics:[66]

> The *Treatise* extensively sets forth the suitability of conventional phenomena within an emptiness of inherent existence as well as the four truths, actions and their effects, the Three Jewels, the eight levels of approaching and abiding in the fruits of Stream Enterer, Once Returner, Never Returner and Foe Destroyer, and so forth...Still...these varieties are not the principal object of discourse in the *Treatise;* the profound emptiness is.

---

[66] *MED*, 403-404.

TREATISE ON THE MIDDLE *CHAPTER XV*

Nāgārjuna's *Treatise on the Middle* (XV), "The Analysis of Nature,"[67] investigates and refutes a nature that is fabricated. One of the important projects of Chapter XV is to discredit the possibility that an ultimate nature of things is caused (see the complete treatment of this topic, page 79). The *Treatise on the Middle* states:

> The arising of nature due to causes and conditions (*rgyu dang rkyen, hetupratyaya*) is not reasonable.[68]

Nāgārjuna mounts his argument on the maxim that the nature of something must be non-fabricated.[69] In the *Treatise* he says:

> Nature is non-fabricated...[70]

Being non-fabricated, nature cannot be a product of causes and conditions. This means that a nature cannot be, for instance, the heat of fire.

Not only does Nāgārjuna reject a fabricated nature that is produced by causes and conditions, but — as D̄zong-ka-b̄a points out in the *Great Exposition* (see page 185) — he also maintains that a nature must be endowed with the three attributes of being non-fabricated, immutable, and independent. Two of these at-

---

67 *rang bzhin brtag pa, svabhāvaparīkṣā.*

68 *MMK,* XV.1ab, 19:

> *na saṃbhavaḥ svabhāvasya yuktaḥ pratyayahetubhiḥ* //

DBU, 6.3.1:

> *rang bzhin rgyu dang rkyen las ni* //
> *'byung bar rigs pa ma yin no* //

69 *bcos ma min pa, akṛtaka.*

70 *MMK,* XV.2cd, 19.

tributes — independence and non-fabrication — are mentioned at the beginning of Chapter XV of the *Treatise* (XV.2cd):

> Nature is non-fabricated and does not depend on another.[71]

The third attribute of a nature — its unchanging state, its immutability — is mentioned in the *Treatise* (XV. 8cd):

> Change of a nature is never feasible.[72]

In these stanzas, Nāgārjuna refutes a nature arisen from causes and conditions. He also points out that a nature of things (1) must not be dependent and (2) must be unchanging. The existence of a causally arisen nature of things, such as the heat of fire, is contradictory with the necessity that a nature be non-fabricated, immutable, and independent. In this way, Nāgārjuna's Chapter XV refutes the possibility of a fabricated nature and instead makes the point that an essential nature must be non-fabricated, immutable, and independent.

Interpretations of this assertion vary. Some Tibetans have felt that Nāgārjuna is describing the putative qualities of a non-existent *svabhāva.* Some modern scholars have taken Nāgārjuna to mean that there is no possibility of a nature existing anywhere. In the Middle Way tradition of Candrakīrti, Nāgārjuna is said to be describing the reality nature, emptiness.

---

71 *MMK,* XV.2cd, 19.

72 *MMK,* XV.8cd, 19:

> *prakṛter anyathābhāvo na hi jātūpapadyate //*

DBU, 6.3.5-6:

> *rang bzhin gzhan du 'gyur ba ni //*
> *nam yang 'thad par mi 'gyur ro //*

3 EXISTENT NATURES

> Subhūti, since the five aggregates are without nature, they have a nature of emptiness.[73]
>
> — *Eight Thousand Stanza Perfection of Wisdom Sūtra*

DOES THE TRIPLY-QUALIFIED NATURE EXIST?

Although the *Treatise on the Middle* indicates non-fabrication, independence, and immutability to be three features of a nature, it does not explicitly mention whether a nature possessing these three features exists or not. If it exists, Nāgārjuna does not explain how this nature can be said to possess these three attributes. On the other hand, if the nature possessing the three attributes is meant to be identified as the object-to-be-negated, Nāgārjuna does not explain if the three attributes are to be taken hypothetically as *being* the object-to-be-negated or as logical implications of a more subtle object-to-be-negated. Although Nāgārjuna does not address these issues, Candrakīrti, D̄zong-ka-b̄a, and their followers address all of them in their commentaries on the *Treatise's* crucial yet mercurial analysis of nature.

Candrakīrti assumes that Nāgārjuna is referring to an existent nature and also explicitly identifies Nāgārjuna's triply-qualified nature as emptiness (see page 147). This is interesting, since Nāgārjuna himself does not actually say here in the *Treatise* that such a triply-qualified nature exists.

---

[73] *Eight Thousant Stanza Perfection of Wisdom Sūtra*, P734, Vol. 21, [XII.256] 118.4.6-118.4.7

Still, Nāgārjuna does speak elsewhere of an existent nature. For instance, the *Precious Garland*[74] implies that things have a nature, and speaks in stanza LXIII of such a nature as "passed beyond the three times." The *Precious Garland* states:

> How could the world exist in fact,
> With a nature passed beyond the three times,
> Not going when destroyed, not coming,
> And not staying even for an instant?[75]

Such brief statements are all that Nāgārjuna has to say about the

---

[74] *rgyal po la gtam bya ba zrin po che'i phreng ba'i rgya cher bshad pa, rājaparikathāratnāvalī;* P5658, 183.2.4-201.4.7; sde dge bstan-'gyur series (Karmapa edition) Vol. 172, 251.4-329.5. Sanskrit, Tibetan, and Chinese in: Michael Hahn, *Nāgārjuna's Ratnāvalī, Vol. 1, The Basic Texts* (Bonn: Indica et Tibetica Verlag, 1982).

[75] Jeffrey Hopkins, *Buddhist Advice*, 36. Sanskrit from Hahn, 26:

> *vibhavaṃ naiti nāyāti* //
> *na tiṣṭhaty api ca kṣaṇam* //
> *tarikālyavyativṛttātmā* //
> *loka evam kuto 'rthataḥ* //

Tibetan from Hahn, 27:

> *zhig gnas 'gro med 'ong med cing* //
> *skad cig kyang ni mi gnas pa* //
> *de ltar dus gsum 'das pa'i bdag* //
> *'jig rten don du ci yod dam* //

Here Hopkins translates *ātmā* and *bdag* as "nature" instead of the more usual "self." In defense of this translation, I submit a similar usage in the *Clear Words* of the Sankrit term *ātmaka* translated into Tibetan as *rang bzhin:* "Just this lack of production, which is the nature of things" (*dngos po rnams kyi rang bzhin du gyur pa skye ba med pa* [*TSHIG*, 43.1.8-43.2.1; *bhāvānāmanutpādātmakaḥ* [*PP*, 265.7-8] *D-TSHIG*, 228.13-15]). See note 93.

triply-qualified nature. Due to this absence of an explicit description of the triply-qualified nature, at least two contradictory schools of thought have arisen regarding the meaning of Nāgārjuna's triply-qualified nature:

(1) *The triply qualified nature is emptiness.* Candrakīrti and Dzong-ka-ba explicitly identify Nāgārjuna's triply-qualified nature as emptiness, the reality nature.

(2) *The triply qualified nature is a non-existent object-to-be-negated nature.* Some Tibetans hold the three attributes to be features of a non-existent object-to-be-negated nature.

The identity of those Tibetans who held the second position remains obscured. Here is Dzong-ka-ba's *Great Exposition* (with some bracketed material from Jam-yang-shay-ba) discussing these unnamed Tibetans:

> Some [Tibetans] say:
>
> > [On the occasion of this Consequence School] that which is to be refuted is nature and that [object-to-be-negated nature] has the three attributes which are (1) an entity attribute, that it is not produced by causes and conditions, (2) a state attribute, that it is immutable, and (3) a certification attribute, that it does not depend on another.[76]

These unnamed Tibetans interpret Chapter XV very differently from Candrakīrti and Dzong-ka-ba. They do not follow Candrakīrti's understanding that Nāgārjuna is speaking of the reality nature. Instead, they understand Nāgārjuna to be speaking of a nature that does not exist but is only imagined to exist by ignorance, but which would be triply qualified *if it did exist.*

---

76 See page 87 for a discussion of the three attributes.

Ḏzong-ka-ḇa does not identify these Tibetans explicitly, but he does strenuously object to their belief that the Consequence School asserts such an object-to-be-negated. His objection is based on the grounds that the triply-qualified nature is *too narrow*[77] to be the object to be negated by a wisdom consciousness negating inherent existence and realizing emptiness.

In Je Ḏzong-ka-ḇa's view, simply negating the false belief that things have a nature of being non-fabricated, immutable, and independent is insufficient to break the bonds of cyclic existence. One must also negate the false belief that things are established by way of their own entities, which is more subtle and broader in scope. Only this is the object of innate ignorance in the Consequence school.

Who were these Tibetans with their divergent opinion about the Consequentialists' identification of the triply-qualified nature? Possible candidates to be the referent of "some Tibetans" are the Ka-dam-pa lineage of Ngok-lo-tsā-wa Lo-den-shay-rap[78] (1059-1109) and the abbots of Sang-pu Monastery. This group included Cha-ba[79] (1109-1169). The scholarly abbots of Sang-pu maintained a Yogic Practice Autonomy (Yogācāra Svātantrika) view prior to their order's conversion to the Consequentialist view. Tibetan historians relate that their conversion to Consequentialism was the result of B̄a-tsap Nyi-ma-drak[80] (b. 1055) translating and disseminating Candrakīrti's Consequentialist texts in the early 12th century. Thus, it was not until B̄a-tsap that Candrakīrti's

---

77 *khyab chung ba.*

78 *rngog lo tsha ba blo ldan shes rab.*

79 *phywa ba.*

80 *spa tshabs nyi ma grags.*

commentaries on Nāgārjuna and Āryadeva became popular in the Ka-dam-pa lineage.

Karen Lang traces this development:

> Nyi-ma-grag's excellent translations and his skill in teaching Mādhyamika texts in the light of Candrakīrti's Prāsaṅgika viewpoint led the bKa'-dam-pa school to adopt this interpretation, so that it prevailed over the Svātantrika interpretation from the 12th century onwards.[81]

N̄ya-cha-wa Tsön-drü-s̄eng-gay — author of one of the only available texts of the Sang-pu lineage — studied the commentaries of Candrakīrti with B̄a-tsap Nyi-ma-drak. He and Tsang Nag-pa, among others, were influential in disseminating Candrakīrti's interpretation of Nāgārjuna and Āryadeva throughout central Tibet.[82] There is no mention of confusing the nature having the three attributes with the object-to-be-negated in N̄ya-cha-wa Tsön-drü-s̄eng-gay's extant 12th-century commentary on the *Treatise.* Instead, N̄ya-cha-wa speaks of Nāgārjuna's discussion of nature in the *Treatise* (XV) in terms of an existent nature that is emptiness, the "suchness nature"[83] having the three attributes; he does not discuss an object-to-be-negated that possesses the three attributes.

DOES THE REALITY NATURE EXIST?

Nāgārjuna does not explicitly and clearly mention a reality nature in the *Treatise* (XV). He merely mentions that nature must be non-fabricated, and so forth, without further explanation. Never-

---

[81] Karen Lang, "A Dialogue on Death," in *Tibetan Buddhism: Revelation and Reason*, ed. Steven Goodman and Ronald Davidson (Albany: SUNY Press, 1992), 46.

[82] I have not located any of B̄a-tsap's commentaries.

[83] *de kho na nyid gyi rang bzhin.*

theless, Candrakīrti and Ḏzong-ka-ḇa confidently identify Nāgārjuna to be referring to a reality nature that is the ultimate truth, emptiness.

In the Consequence School, the process of liberation involves realizing emptiness with reasoning. For Geluks, it follows that emptiness must exist in order for it to be realizable, since only an emptiness that is an object of knowledge[84] can be realized with a reasoning consciousness. Geluk exegetes following Ḏzong-ka-ḇa point to the *Treatise on the Middle* (XV) — as well as Candrakīrti's commentary on that text in the *Auto-Commentary* (quoted below) which supplies a scriptural source — as a *locus classicus* for the assertion that emptiness exists.

Candrakīrti's *Auto-Commentary* presents a question and answer section addressing the issue of whether the nature exists. In this passage (cited in the *Great Exposition of the Stages of the Path*), Candrakīrti claims that an existent nature is the thought of Nāgārjuna:

> *Objection:* Does the master Nāgārjuna assert that a nature qualified in such a way exists or not?
>
> *Response:* That reality in terms of which the Supramundane Victor says in the Perfection of Wisdom Sūtras, "Whether the Tathāgatas appear or not, the reality of phenomena just abides," exists.
>
> *Objection:* What is this reality?
>
> *Response:* It is the final mode of abiding of these phenomena, eyes, and so forth.
>
> *Objection:* What is the nature that is the mode of abiding of these like?
>
> *Response:* It is their non-fabricatedness, i.e., non-falsity, their mode of subsistence which does not depend on other causes and conditions and is the entity realized by a Supe-

---

[84] *shes bya, jñeya.*

rior's knowledge [of meditative equipoise] free from the visual dimness of ignorance and its predispositions by way of not being polluted by those.

Objection: Does that nature exist?

Response: Who could say that it does not exist? If it did not exist, for what purpose would Bodhisattvas cultivate the path of the perfections? Bodhisattvas initiate hundreds of efforts for the sake of realizing such a reality.[85]

Here, Candrakīrti gives reasons that the nature does exist, and he quotes a Perfection of Wisdom Sūtra to the effect that "Whether the Tathāgatas appear or not, the reality of phenomena just abides." This quote serves as a scriptural source to establish that the Consequence School posits an existent reality nature. It is a non-fabricated mode of subsistence that does not depend on causes and conditions and is the entity realized by the wisdom of meditative equipoise.

The *Clear Words* provides Candrakīrti with another opportunity to embellish his discussion of an existent reality nature. The

---

[85] *LRC,* 863.6-864.4:

khyad par gsum du mdzad pa rnam pa de ltar ba'i rang bzhin slob dpon gyis zhal kyis bzhes pa zhig yod dam zhe na gang gi dbang du mdzad nas bcom ldan 'das kyis de bzhin shegs pa rnams byung yang rung ma byung yang rung chos rnams kyi chos nyid 'di ni gnas pa nyid do zhes rgyas par gsungs pa chos nyid ces bya ba ni yod do chos nyid ces bya ba 'di yang ci zhig // mig la sogs pa 'di dag gi rang bzhin no // de dag gi rang bzhin yang gang zhig ce na de dag gi bcos ma ma yin pa nyid dang gzhan la ltos pa med pa gang yin pa ste ma rig pa'i rab rib dang bral ba'i shes pas rtogs par bya ba'i rang gi ngo bo'o // ji di yod dam med do zhes de skad su smra // gal te med na ni ci'i don du byang chub sems dpa' rnams pha rol tu phyin pa'i lam sgom par 'gyur te gang gi phyir chos nyid rtogs par bya ba'i phyir byang chub sems dpa' rnams de ltar dka' ba brgya phrag rtsom pa yin no //

Clear Words describes an existent entity that is "an entity of suchness[86] that always abides":

> What is this suchness? It is that entity of suchness that does not change and always abides. For, that which is not produced in any way, because of not being fabricated and because of not relying on another, is called the nature (*rang bzhin, svabhāva*) of fire and so forth.[87]

Candrakīrti's assertions of an existent nature show that even though Nāgārjuna does not explicitly refer to an existent reality nature, it is traditional for the Consequence School to assert an existent reality nature, based on scriptural sources.

In his discussion of the reality nature, Candrakīrti equates reality, emptiness, and suchness and refers to nature in terms of the three attributes. Candrakīrti and D̄zong-ka-b̄a agree that Nāgārjuna speaks of a reality nature and that this reality nature exists. D̄zong-ka-b̄a identifies emptiness not as nothingness or as a mere linguistic convention but as a phenomenon. This opinion is at odds with the opinion of many non-traditional scholars who hold emptiness to be a non-entity or a mere linguistic convention.[88]

---

[86] *de bzhin nyid kyi ngo bo, tathābhāva.*

[87] *PP*, 265.1-265.2:

> *keyam tathatā tathābhāvo 'vikāritvam sadaiva svāyitā // sarvadānutpāda eva hi agnyādīnām paranirapekṣatvād akṛtrimatvāt svabhāva //*

TSHIG, 43.1.5-43.1.6; *D-TSHIG*, 228.3-228.7:

> *de bzhin nyid 'di yang gang zhig ce na de bzhin nyid kyi ngo bo 'gyur ba med pa nyid dang rtag tu gnas pa nyid de rnam pa thams cad du skye ba med pa nyid ni bcos ma ma yin pa'i phyir dang gzhan la bltos pa med pa'i phyir me la sogs pa rnams kyi rang bzhin yin no //*

[88] Lamotte, May, Streng, and Sprung, among others. *DAE*, 126-133.

Within the broad perspective of Tibetan Buddhism, D̄zong-ka-b̄a's assertion that emptiness exists is by no means normative. Discussing this, Jam-ȳang-shay-b̄a laments that in Tibet "few have wished to meditate on emptiness and have called meditation on a vacuity of nothingness meditation on emptiness."[89] Ngok-lo-tsā-wa Lo-den-shay-rap is an early example of a Tibetan scholar who held the position that emptiness does not exist. Ngok asserted that the ultimate truth is not an object of knowledge because no thing can withstand reasoned analysis.[90]

Though Candrakīrti's texts present evidence for a Middle Way tradition asserting an existent reality nature, the situation is not quite so simple. Candrakīrti also makes statements that provide evidence that he holds a more nihilistic view. Regarding the non-existence of change, the *Clear Words* states:

> Also, the explanation, "Because change is seen, there is no nature," is said in the context of a seeing of change that is renowned to others. We do not assert ever anywhere that change exists. Therefore, in this way, nature does not exist at all, and all phenomena are that of which nature does not exist, and also change of those does not exist.[91]

---

[89] Jam-ȳang-shay-b̄a's *Great Exposition* (and Nga-w̄ang-b̄el-den's *Annotations,* note *cha* 32b.5), quoted in *MED*, 409.

[90] *DAE,* 713 n. 241. Quoting Sha-mar-den-dzin's *Difficult Points of (D̄zong-ka-b̄a's) "Great Exposition of Special Insight"* (76.1-76.4).

[91] *PP,* 272.9-11:

> *yaccāpyuktamanyathātvasya darśanānāsti prakṛtiriti // tadapi paraprasiddhānyathātvadarśanamadhikṛtyoktaṃ // na tvasmābhiḥ kadā cidapi kasya cidanyathātvamabhyupetaṃ // tadevamatyantataḥ prakṛtāvasaṃvidhyamānāyāṃ sarvadharmeṣvasaṃvidhyamāneṣvasvabhāveṣu //*

TSHIG, 44.3.1-43.3.4; *D-TSHIG,* 235.2-8:

Ḏzong-ka-ḇa addresses the first two sentences of this quotation in the *Ocean of Reasonings*, where he argues that Candrakīrti is discussing nature in the context of there being "change of that which exists by way of its nature." That which exists by way of its nature is that which exists inherently. Candrakīrti is denying that inherently existent things have change, he is not refuting "mere change." The *Ocean of Reasonings* states:

> Here in the [*Clear Words*] commentary Candrakīrti says:
>
> > Also, the explanation, "Because change is seen, there is no nature," is said in the context of a seeing of change that is renowned to others. We do not assert ever anywhere that change exists.
>
> This is said with respect to explaining the statements made earlier, above, "Even you observe change of that which exists by way of its nature, fire and so forth," [and] since nature is seen to change, there is no existence by way of [something's] nature; [Candrakīrti] is not saying that he does not assert mere change.[92]

---

gang yang gzhan du 'gyur pa mthong ba'i phyir rang bzhin yod pa ma yin no zhes bshad pa de yang gzhan la grags pa'i gzhan du 'gyur pa mthong ba'i dbang du byas nas brjod pa yin gyi kho bo cag gis nam yang gang la yang gzhan du 'gyur pa yod par khas ma blang so // de'i phir de ltar rang bzhin gtan yod pa ma yin dang chos thams cad yod pa ma yin pa'i rang bzhin can yin pa dang de dag la gzhan du 'gyur ba yang yod pa ma yin bzhin du... //

92 *RGT*, 738.3-10:

'dir 'grel pa las gzhan 'gyur mthong ba'i phyir rang bzhin yod ma yin no zhes pa yang gzhan la grags pa'i gzhan 'gyur mthong ba'i dbang du byas nas brjod kyi kho bo cag gis nam yang gang la yang gzhan 'gyur yod par khas ma blangs so zhes gsungs pa ni sngar gong du me la sogs pa rang bzhin gyis yod pa dag kyang gzhan du 'gyur ba khyed kyis dmigs pa yang yin no zhes rang bzhin gzhan du 'gyur ba mthong bas rang bzhin gyis yod pa min no zhes bshad

In other words, the opponent, who propounds that the nature of fire is heat, accepts that that nature is seen to change. The point is that the Consequentialists do not assert that the nature of fire — emptiness — ever changes. It is just this sort of change — change of an immutable nature — that Dzong-ka-ba says Candrakīrti never asserts, not mere change.

It is interesting that the *Ocean of Reasonings* does not address the following quotation that strongly suggests that Candrakīrti asserts a non-existent reality nature. In the context of a discussion of no production, the *Clear Words* states:

> You should [also] know that just this lack of production which is the nature of things, is just a non-thing due to not being anything at all, whereby...it is not the nature of things.[93]

Unlike the situation with Candrakīrti's statement about the non-existence of change, it is difficult to interpret this statement as referring to inherent production, and not mere production, since the subject is the "lack of production, which is the nature of

---

pa la zer ba yin gyi gzhan 'gyur tsam khas mi len par smra ba min no //

93 *PP*, 265.7-8:

sa caiṣa bhāvānāmanutpādātmakaḥ svabhāvo 'kiṃcittvenābhāvamātratvādasvabhāva eveti kṛtvā nāsti bhāvasvabhāva iti vijñeyaṃ //

TSHIG, 43.1.8-43.2.1; *D-TSHIG*, 228.13-15:

dngos po rnams kyi rang bzhin du gyur pa skye ba med pa de yang ci yang ma yin pa nyid kyis dngos po med pa tsam yin pas ngo bo med pa'i phyir dngos po'i rang bzhin du yod pa ma yin no shes par bya'o //

things." Candrakīrti clearly predicates this lack with the phrase, "just a non-thing due to not being anything at all."[94]

This would seem to be a clear statement that the negative of true production is a non-existent. However, Dra-d̄i Ge-shay, writing in the *Four Interwoven Annotations,* cleverly interprets the words "is not anything at all"[95] to mean "not anything at all" in the sense of "not explicitly provable to others." The *Four Interwoven Annotations* says:

> The emptiness which is the lack of production by nature and which is the final nature that is the mode of subsistence of things such as forms — as it appears in meditative equipoise devoid of all the two elaborations[96] — is not anything at all in the sense that it is not explicitly provable to others — in accordance with how it appears — through analyses, verbalizations, examples, and reasons and hence it is just a non-thing in that it is the vanishing of things such as forms. Therefore in the face of that meditative equipoise, its entity is not apprehendable.[97] Hence, that nature of things abides in this way, and that nature does not exist in the face of that meditative equipoise in the manner of things such as forms being the support and the nature being the supported.[98]

---

94 *ci yang ma yin pa nyid kyis dngos po med pa tsam yin pa; akiṃcittvena abhāvamātratvā.*

95 *ci yang ma yin pa nyid.*

96 The elaborations of true existence (*dgag bya'i spros pa*) and the elaborations of mistaken appearances (*'khrul snang gi spros pa*).

97 That is, it cannot be explained to others through analyses, verbalizations, and so forth.

98 *MCHAN*, 404.4-6:

> *gzugs sogs dngos po rnams kyi sdod lugs kyi rang bzhin mthar thug du gyur pa rang bzhin gyis skye ba med pa'i stong nyid spros pa gnyis po thams cad dang bral ba mnyam gzhag la ji ltar shar ba*

That is, since the things that are empty do not appear, that emptiness in the face of that meditative equipoise does not appear in the aspect of being the nature of those things. It cannot, since appearing in the aspect of being the nature of things involves the necessary appearance of things.

Dra-d̄i Ge-shay's commentary is ingenious, and although it may seem forced, it is a necessary commentarial "patch" to preserve the Geluk presentation of Candrakīrti as asserting an existent emptiness. In favor of this reading of Candrakīrti, we shall see in the next section that he also explicitly makes the case that the reality nature exists conventionally.

THE REALITY NATURE EXISTS CONVENTIONALLY

Even though emptiness is the ultimate, the reality nature, its mode of subsistence is not different from that of other phenomena. This is because, according to Nāgārjuna, all phenomena — conventional and ultimate — are dependent-arisings. The *Treatise on the Middle* (XXIV.19) states:

> Because there are no phenomena
> That are not dependent-arisings,
> There are no phenomena that are not
> Empty [of inherent existence].[99]

> *de yang ni de la shar ba ltar gzhan la brtags pa dang brjod pa dang dpe dang gtan tshigs kyis dngos su bsgrub tu med pas na ci yang ma yin pa nyid kyis gzugs sogs su snang ba ltar gyi dngos po log pa'i sgo nas dngos po med pa tsam zhig yin pas mnyam gzhag de'i ngor ngo bo bzung du med pa'i phyir dngos po'i rang bzhin de ltar gnas kyi rang bzhin de ni gzugs sogs kyi dngos po'i rang bzhin du ste dngos po rten dang rang bzhin brten pa'i tshul du mnyam gzhag gi ngo na yod pa ma yin no zhes gsungs so //*

[99] *MMK,* XXIV.19, 35:

> *apratītya samutpanno dharmaḥ kaścin na vidyate //*

Having no nature of their own that exists by way of its own nature, phenomena are merely imputed through superimposition. Candrakīrti explains that this does not mean they are non-existent. When an opponent in the *Clear Words* asks Candrakīrti if the emptiness of such a phenomenon exists, Candrakīrti says "It exists conventionally."[100] The *Clear Words* states:

> *Objection:* Does there exist such a non-fabricated and non-relative entity of fire?
>
> *Response:* Such a nature is not existent by way of its own entity and is not [utterly] non-existent either. Though it is so, in order to get rid of the fear of the listeners, when this is taught, it is said upon making a superimposition that it exists conventionally.[101]

Although the reality nature does not possess an ontological status that privileges it in some way "above" conventional truths, that

---

> *yasmāt tasmāt aśūnyo hi dharmaḥ kaścin na vidyate //*

DBU, 9.3.5-9.3.6:

> *gang phyir rten 'byung ma yin pa'i // chos 'ga' yod pa ma yin pa //*
> *de phir stong pa ma yin pa'i // chos 'ga' yod pa ma yin no //*

100 *kun rdzob tu de yod; samāropya tadasti.*

101 *PP*, 264.2-4 [brackets added by Poussin from the Tibetan]:

> *kim khalu [agneḥ] tadithaṃ svarūpamasti // na tadasti na cāpi nāsti svarūpataḥ // yadhyapyevaṃ tathāpi śrotṛṇāmuttrāsaparivarjñanārthaṃ saṃvṛtyā samāropya tadastīti brūmaḥ //*

TSHIG, 42.5.8-43.1.1; *D-TSHIG*, 227.9-12:

> *ci me'i rang gi ngo bo de lta bur gyur pa yod dam zhe na // de ni rang gi ngo bos yod pa ma yin pa med pa yang ma yin no // de lta yin mod kyi 'on kyang nyan pa po rnams kyi skrag pa sbang bar bya ba'i phyir sgro btags nas kun rdzob tu de yod do zhes bya bar smra'o //*

nature also does not utterly not exist. As Candrakīrti says, "it exists conventionally."

D̄zong-ka-b̄a explains that the meaning of this statement is that emptiness is a conventionally existent phenomenon like all dependent-arisings. The *Ocean of Reasonings* addresses the qualm that a nature that exists "upon superimposition" does not exist. There, D̄zong-ka-b̄a asserts that even a conventionally existent reality nature exists:

> Also propounding that since [Candrakīrti] says "upon superimposition," the ultimate truth is not an object of knowledge, is not reasonable. For, as a source for the statement that it exists upon superimposition, [Candrakīrti] cites a verse from the *King of Meditative Stabilizations Sūtra,* which states:
>
> > What hearing, what teaching is there
> > Of the inexpressible doctrine?
> > The inexpressible is heard and taught
> > Upon superimposition.
>
> In this, the hearers, explainers, and doctrines to be explained are all said to be done upon superimposition, whereby these too would come not to be objects of knowledge.
>
> Therefore, since even with regard to teachings upon imputation by the mind, it is often said, "upon superimposition," this need not be something like the superimposition of the two selves.[102]

---

[102] *RGT,* 732.19-733.6:

sgro btags nas zhes gsungs pas don dam bden pa shes bya min no zhes pa yang mi rigs te sgro btags nas yod par gsungs pa'i shes byed du yi ge med pa'i chos la ni nyan pa gang yin ston pa gang sgro btags pa la yi ge med de ni nyan zhing ston pa'ang yin zhes ting 'dzin rgyal po drangs pa las nyan mkhan dang bshad bya'i chos rnams kyang sgro btags nas byed par gsungs pas de rnams kyang shes bya ma yin par 'gyur ba'i phyir ro // des na blos btags nas ston pa la yang sgro btags nas zhes gsungs pa mang po yod pas bdag

The two selves spoken of here are the self of persons[103] and the self of phenomena other than persons.[104] The coarse and subtle aspects of the two selves are variously described in the Mind Only and Middle Way Schools — the Great Exposition and Sūtra Schools do not assert a putative self of phenomena — but in D̄zong-ka-b̄a's interpretation of the Consequence School, the object-to-be-negated nature is the subtle self of persons and of phenomena. These two selves do not exist, and thus they are only superimposed on persons and phenomena.

In the statement above, when it is said that all phenomena are superimposed, including ultimate truth, this does not mean that phenomena do not actually exist. The ultimate truth, for instance, is a superimposition that does exist — a non-erroneous superimposition. There are, however, superimpositions that do not exist: the two selves are superimpositions that do not exist — erroneous superimpositions.

D̄zong-ka-b̄a reaffirms Candrakīrti's view that the reality nature is not an absolute in the sense that it is not established by way of its own entity. The *Great Exposition of the Stages of the Path* states:

> Thus Candrakīrti refutes that a nature is established by way of its own entity and says that it exists conventionally.[105]

Emptiness exists, and is the ultimate, but it is not an absolute. It just exists conventionally, upon imputation, as do all phenomena

---

gnyis sgro brtags pa 'dra ba yin mi dgos so //

[103] *gang zag gi bdag.*

[104] *chos kyi bdag.*

[105] *LRC*, 865.2:

rang bzhin de yang rang gi ngo bos grub pa bkag nas tha snyad du yod par gsung //

according to the Consequentialist system. Dzong-ka-ba provides a further explanation of why ultimates are conventionally existent: they are posited by way of the two "positors"[106] of non-fabrication and non-dependence on another. The *Great Exposition of the Stages of the Path* states:

> Although the ultimate truth is established [as the nature in the sense of] positing reality as nature, [an ultimate truth] is posited by way of its two positors, non-fabrication and non-dependence on another, and hence [the ultimate] does not at all come to be established by way of its own entity. Therefore [the ultimate] is only established conventionally.[107]

Nothing that is posited in dependence on other factors exists by way of its own entity, and the ultimate is posited by way of non-fabrication and non-dependence on another. As these quotations reveal, it is the thought of Candrakīrti and Dzong-ka-ba that it is not contradictory for an ultimate to exist conventionally.

We have seen Candrakīrti put forth his contention that the *Treatise on the Middle* (XV) speaks of the reality nature that possesses the three attributes. Dzong-ka-ba agrees with Candrakīrti, and criticizes those who identify Nāgārjuna's stanzas as referring to an object-to-be-negated nature. In Geluk soteriology, this wrong identification is a significant mistake, since it is the identification of an object-to-be-negated nature that is too narrow. Moreover, this object-to-be-negated is a learned ignorance, whereas the actual object-to-be-negated — a thing's establishment

---

106 *'jog byed.*

107 *LRC,* 866.2-866.3:

> *don dam pa'i bden pa ni chos nyid la rang bzhin du bzhag pa der grub kyang rang bzhin der 'jog byed bcos ma min pa dang gzhan la mi ltos pa ni rang gi ngo bos grub pa'i rang bzhin der cung zad kyang med pas tha snyad du grub pa tsam mo //*

by its own entity — (1) is more subtle than the three attributes and (2) conceiving of it is the innate ignorance that binds sentient beings in cyclic existence. The reality nature, on the other hand, which is the lack of the object-to-be-negated nature in a phenomenon, *does* possess the three attributes of non-fabrication, independence, and immutability.

THE REALITY NATURE ENDOWED WITH THE THREE ATTRIBUTES

The Consequence School describes emptiness as having the three attributes of non-fabrication, immutability, and independence. What exactly do the three attributes of the reality nature mean? The *Great Exposition of the Stages of the Path* provides a brief description of fabrication and dependence:

> Being fabricated means not existing earlier and being created as a new arising. Depending on another means depending on causes and conditions.[108]

The *Four Interwoven Annotations* slightly expands on this. Jam-ȳang-shay-b̄a's commentary states:

> Here, being fabricated means not existing earlier and being created later as a new arising, or being produced later contingently. Depending on another means depending on other causes and conditions.[109]

---

[108] *LRC,* 866.3:

bcos ma na sngar med gsar du 'byung ba'i byas pa dang gzhan la ltos pa ni rgyu rkyen la ltos pa'o //

[109] *MCHAN,* 399.2:

'dir bcos ma'i don ni kho rang sngar med pa la phyis gsar du 'byung ba'am phyis glo bur du skye ba'i byas pa dang gzhan la ltos pa'i don ni rgyu rkyen gzhan la ltos pa'o //

Here, Ḏzong-ka-ḇa says depending on another means depending on causes and conditions, and the *Four Interwoven Annotations* concurs. However, earlier in the *Great Exposition of the Stages of the Path,* Ḏzong-ka-ḇa speaks of the entity attribute (non-fabrication) as not being produced by causes and conditions and the certification attribute (independence) as "not depending on another."[110] This confuses the entity and certification attributes of non-fabrication and independence, since they both seem to mean not depending on causes and conditions. (See page 87 for a discussion of the three attributes.)

In order to differentiate the two, an exegetical patch is applied. This can be seen in Dra-ḏi Ge-shay's gloss in a note, where he qualifies "not depending" with "not depending on another *positing awareness.*"[111] Later in the *Great Exposition,*[112] Ḏzong-ka-ḇa states that non-dependence on a *positing consciousness* is the meaning Candrakīrti intends in his use of the term "non-dependence on another" in his commentary on Āryadeva's *Four Hundred* (see page 59).

"Non-fabricated" has the meaning "not existing earlier and being created later as a new arising." Non-fabrication is a feature of emptiness since emptiness — like all permanent phenomena —

---

110 *LRC,* 860.5; bracketed material from *MCHAN,* 387.5:

rnam 'jog [gyi khyad par] gzhan la mi bltos pa'o //

111 *MCHAN,* 388.2:

'jog byed kyi blo gzhan la bltos pa med pa //

112 Ḏzong-ka-ḇa discusses this meaning of no dependence on another in the section that follows "The Refutation of an Identification of the Object-to-be-negated That Is Too Narrow" [*LRC,* 860.4-870.1], called "The Identification of the Actual Meaning of the Object-to-be-negated" (*dngos kyi don dgag bya ngos bzung ba*) [*LRC,* 870.1-886.4].

is not created. The term "immutable" is not mentioned in this context but one assumes it means "permanent" in the sense of non-momentary. Immutability is also a feature of emptiness, just as it is a feature of all permanent phenomena.

The independence attribute is more problematic. How can the reality nature — emptiness, a dependent-arising like all phenomena — be endowed with an attribute of independence? After all, in D̄zong-ka-b̄a's own system, emptiness, although ultimate, is similar to all other phenomena in that it arises dependently. Is it not the case that being a dependent-arising is inconsistent with being independent?

The answer is that "independence" is given a variety of meanings in the Geluk system. Just in the context of speaking of dependent-arisings, Geluks discuss three types of dependence:

(1) arising through meeting (*'phrad 'byung, prāpyasamutpāda*),
(2) existing in reliance (*ltos grub, apekṣyasamutpāda*), and
(3) dependent-existence (*rten grub, pratītyasamutpāda*).[113]

Nga-w̄ang-b̄el-den[114] (born 1797 in Mongolia), in his *Annotations for (Jam-ȳang-shay-b̄a's) "Great Exposition of Tenets," Freeing the Knots of the Difficult Points, Precious Jewel of Clear Thought,*[115] discusses these three types of dependence as set forth in J̄ang-ḡya:

(1) "Arising through meeting" is held to refer to a

---

[113] See *MED*, 166-167.

[114] *ngag dbang dpal ldan.* Also known as B̄el-den-chö-jay (*dpal ldan chos rje*).

[115] *grub mtha' chen mo'i mchan 'grel dka' gnad mdud grol blo gsal gces nor* (Sarnath: Pleasure of Elegant Sayings Printing Press, 1964).

thing that is a dependent-arising that is produced by its causes. This is a lower school tenet and also a Consequentialist tenet.[116]

(2) "Existing in reliance" means phenomena — compounded and non-compounded — gain their own entity in reliance on their own parts...This is more pervasive than the earlier and just the meaning that is actually indicated is accepted by other [i.e., Autonomist] Proponents of the Middle and is also a Consequentialist tenet.[117]

(3) "Dependent-existence" refers to the fact that all phenomena are dependently imputed. They are established just as imputations on their own bases of imputation. This is a special feature of only the excellent [Consequentialist] system.[118]

"Arising through meeting." The dependence of compounded phenomena on their causes and conditions is called "mere condi-

---

[116] *Annotations*, 154.6-7:

> *'phrad ba zhes bya bas ni gtan tshigs kyi don dngos po rang gi rgyus bskyed pa'i rten 'brel 'dzin pa yin la 'di ni grub pa'i mtha' 'og ma dang yang thun mongs pa'o //*

[117] *Annotations*, 154.7:

> *ltos ba zhes bya bas ni 'du byas dang 'du ma byas kyi chos rnams rang rang gi cha shas la ltos nas rang gi bdag nyid rnyed...'di ni snga ma las khyab che zhing dngos bstan gyi don tsam dbu ma pa gzhan dang yang thun mongs pa'o //*

[118] *Annotations*, 154.8-155.1:

> *brten pa zhes bya bas ni 'chos thams cad brten nas btags pa'i gtan tshig kyi don bstan pa ste rang rang gi gtags gzhi la brten nas btags pa tsam du grub pa'o // 'di ni lugs mchog tu gyur ba 'di kho na'i khyad chos yin //*

tionality."[119] Nga-w̄ang-b̄el-den's *Annotations* states:

> "Mere conditionality" is a name for the dependent arising of compounded phenomena. It is explained that only Consequentialists assert causes as being dependent on effects and that all Buddhist proponents of tenets assert that effects depend on causes.[120]

Nga-w̄ang-b̄el-den's note makes the two points that (1) mere conditionality refers only to the dependent-arising of impermanent things and (2) whereas all Buddhist proponents of tenets assert that effects depend on causes, only Consequentialists assert causes as being dependent on effects.

"Existing in reliance." Permanent phenomena do not depend on causes and conditions. Instead, non-products such as space, emptiness, and so forth, "exist in reliance"; i.e., they gain their own entity in reliance on their own parts. Existing in reliance on a collection of parts is the second meaning of "dependence" in the context of discussing dependent-arisings that are both permanent and impermanent.

"Dependent-existence." Refers to the fact that all phenomena are dependently imputed. Permanent and impermanent phenomena arise in dependence on a conceptual consciousness that imputes them. Jam-ȳang-shay-b̄a's *Great Exposition of Tenets* quotes Candrakīrti as a source that the meaning of "no dependence on another" is that phenomena are not dependent on thought. Jam-ȳang-shay-b̄a states:

---

119 *rkyen nyid 'di pa tsam, idaṃpratyayatā.*

120 *Annotations*, 117.3-4:

> *rkyen nyid 'di ba tsam ni 'dus byas kyi rten 'byung gi ming yin la rgyu 'bras bu la ltos pa ni thal 'gyur ba kho nas 'dod cing 'bras bu rgyu la ltos pa ni nang ba'i grub mtha smra ba kun gyis 'dod par bshad do //*

> Candrakīrti's commentary [on Āryadeva's *Four Hundred*] says, "Here, that which has its own entity, has nature, has its own power, or has no dependence on another would exist by itself; therefore, it would not be a dependent-arising."[121]

Dzong-ka-ba takes this statement by Candrakīrti — that "no dependence on another" means the opposite of "dependent-arising" — to imply that independence and nature are equivalent. Therefore, independence must have a broader meaning than "non-dependence on causes and conditions," for such is too narrow an identification of nature. Geluk exegetes take Candrakīrti's statement about non-dependence to mean that an object is not posited through the power of a conventional consciousness. This is the third meaning of dependence in the context of dependent-arising: "dependent-existence" refers to the fact that all phenomena are dependently imputed.

From Dzong-ka-ba's point of view, the opposite of "dependent-existence" means a thing is not posited through the power of a conventional consciousness. In the absence of dependent-existence, things would not be dependent-arisings and thus things would be established by way of their nature. Nga-wang-bel-den's *Annotations* traces this opinion through Dzong-ka-ba to Candrakīrti:

> Dzong-ka-ba's "Great Exposition of Special Insight" states that this passage [i.e., Candrakīrti's commentary on Āry-

---

[121] Jam-yang-shay-ba's *Great Exposition of Tenets, MED*, Tibetan text section, 70.11-14:

> *'grel pa las // 'di na gang rang gi ngo bo dang rang bzhin dang rang dbang dang gzhan la rag ma las pa nyid yin pa de la ni rang las grub pas rten cing 'brel par 'byung ba yod pa min no zhes so //*

Candrakīrti's commentary on Āryadeva. P5266, Vol. 98, 270.3.6, commenting on XIV.23.

adeva's *Four Hundred*] states that own-entity, nature, own-power, and no dependence on another are equivalent:

> Here, "no dependence on another" is not no dependence on causes and conditions; rather, "other" refers to an object-possesor, a conventional consciousness, and not being posited through the power of that [object-possesor] is called "no dependence on another."
>
> Therefore, "independent existence" is an entity of these objects which has its own uncommon mode of subsistence or abiding. Just this is called own-entity and nature.[122]

This passage shows D̄zong-ka-b̄a defining "non-dependence on another" in a context where "other" refers to a conventional consciousness. He does so in commentary on Candrakīrti's statement that any phenomenon that exists by itself without the need of such positing would not be a dependent-arising.

D̄zong-ka-b̄a also employed a relative meaning of "independent" in his discussion of a thing's "mine" (see page 85). To exemplify the independence of "the mine," he gives "one's servant" and "one's wealth." One's servant and wealth do not depend on others in the sense that others do not control ones servant or wealth since oneself controls them. Thus, this fourth type

---

[122] Nga-w̄ang-b̄el-den's *Annotations,* 134.5-7 [see *LRC,* 882.4-883.1]:

lung 'dis rang gi ngo bo dang rang bzhin dang rang dbang dang gzhan la rag ma las pa zhes pa rnams ming gi rnam grang su gsung shing // de la gzhan la rag ma las zhes pa ni rgyu rkyen la rag ma las pa ma yin gyi yul can tha snyed pa'i shes pa la gzhan zhes bya ste de'i dbang gis bzhag pa min pas gzhan la rag ma las pa'o // des na rang dbang zhes bya ste yul de dag gi rang rang gi gnas lugs sam sdod lugs thun mong min pa'i ngo bo 'o // de nyid la rang gi ngo bo dang rang bzhin zhes bya'o zhes lhag mthong chen mor gsungs so //

of dependence has the meaning of "beyond one's control." The corollary, independence, has the meaning of "under one's control."

A fifth meaning of "dependence" — and therefore also its corollary, "independence" — surfaces on the occasion of explaining how a feature of emptiness is non-dependence on another, at which point both Candrakīrti and D̄zong-ka-b̄a employ a comparative meaning of "independent." This meaning explains how the reality nature is independent in the sense of not being a changeably relative phenomenon, like long and short or hot and cold. The *Clear Words* states:

> That which, even in all three times, is the non-fabricated fundamental entity non-mistaken in fire, that which is not the subsequent arising of something that did not arise previously, and that which does not have reliance on causes and conditions, as do the heat of water or near and far, or long and short, is said to be the nature [of fire].[123]

Candrakīrti employs a special meaning of "dependent" here — dependently comparative. Hot is only posited relative to cold, long is posited relative to short, and so forth. Using this identification of dependent, emptiness can be said not to be dependent

---

[123] *PP*, 263.5-264.2:

> *yadevāgneḥ kālatraye apyavyabhāri nijaṃ rūpamakṛtrimaṃ pūrvām abhūtvā paścādhyanna bhavati yacca hetupratyayasāpejñaṃ na bhavatyapāmauṣṇyavatpārāvāravadṛīrdhahrasvavavā tatsvabhāva iti vyapadiśyate //*

TSHIG, 42.5.6-42.5.8; *D-TSHIG*, 227.5-9;

> *de'i phyir dus gsum du yang me la mi 'khrul ba gnyug ma'i ngo bo ma bcos pa gang zhig sngar ma byung bas phyis 'byung ba ma yin pa gang zhig chu'i tsha ba 'am tshur rol dang pha rol lam ring po dang thung ngu ltar rgyu dang rkyen la bltos pa dang bcas par ma gyur pa gang yin pa de rang bzhin yin pa brjod do //*

in the sense that emptiness does not require a comparable phenomenon for its positing. That is to say, whereas a person's perception of a thing as hot may switch to a perception of that same thing as cold in the presence of something hotter, and the perception of long may become a perception of short in the presence of something longer, emptiness will never be perceived to switch to become something not empty.

In the *Great Exposition,* Dzong-ka-ba provides little gloss to Candrakīrti's usage of "dependent," and the *Four Interwoven Annotations* also presents an uninspired paraphrase. Neither commentarial source remarks upon Candrakīrti's unusual usage of dependent. However, in the *Four Interwoven Annotations,* Jam-yang-shay-ba speaks of nature in terms of a fundamental entity that existed from the start and is independent:

> [Nature] from the beginning does not depend on another — unlike the heat of water which depends on fire as a condition and does not depend on a positing factor because it does not pass beyond a natural emptiness from the very start, without being like positing here and there, long and short, and so forth, in dependence on any [comparative] basis.[124]

We have seen five meanings of "dependent" employed in Geluk commentary. The reality nature cannot be said to be independent in the first sense of "arising through meeting" since it does not depend on being produced by causes and conditions. It cannot be said to be independent in the senses of "existing in reliance" and "dependent-existence," since even emptiness depends on its parts

---

124 *MCHAN,* 394.3:

> *tsha ba rkyen me la ltos pa lta bu ma yin par dang po nyid nas gzhan la ma ltos par rang bzhin gyis stong pa tshu rol dang pha rol dang ring thung sogs gzhi 'ga' zhig la ltos nas bzhag pa ltar ma yin par gzhi gang la ltos kyang rang bzhin gyis stong pa las ma 'das pas 'jog byed gyi rgyu la ma ltos pa //*

for gaining its own entity and also is imputed onto its bases of imputation.

The reality nature is not independent according to the fourth type of dependence because issues pertaining to one's control of the reality nature do not apply. However, the reality nature *can* be said to be independent from comparisons, the corollary of the fifth meaning of dependence, because emptiness, unlike hot and cold, does not switch to something else following comparison.

In this way, through employing this narrow meaning of independent as "independence from comparisons," Candrakīrti, Ḏzong-ka-ḇa, and their Geluk followers are able to assert an independent reality nature without violating the central Consequence School premise that emptiness itself is a dependent-arising. Perhaps most importantly, they are able to contend that, in the *Treatise on the Middle* (XV.2), Nāgārjuna speaks of a reality nature endowed with the three features or attributes of emptiness.

4 NATURES THAT DO NOT EXIST

> When there is an apprehension of things existing as established by way of their nature, conceptions apprehending extremes arise.[125]
>
> — Dzong-ka-ba's *Illumination of the Thought*

WHAT IT MEANS TO EXIST

In previous chapters we looked into Dzong-ka-ba's identification of the reality nature. Now let us observe his refutation of natures that do not exist. From Dzong-ka-ba's point of view, natures that do not exist are:

(1) a fabricated nature, such as the heat of fire,
(2) the Consequence School's uncommon object-to-be-negated nature (a thing's establishment by way of its own entity),
(3) an object-to-be-negated nature possessing the three attributes that is mistakenly held to be the Consequence School's uncommon object-to-be-negated nature, and
(4) a nature that is positive and independent that is asserted by Döl-bo Shay-rap-gyel-tsen.

All of these natures are identified and refuted in the *Great Exposition's* delineation of the view of selflessness.

The identification of an object-to-be-negated that is refuted in the delineation of the view of selflessness is a topic that does not receive much attention in Consequentialist writings before Dzong-ka-ba, although it does originate in Indian Buddhism.

---

125 *GRS,* 351.16-352.1.

Since Ḏzong-ka-ḇa's development of the topic goes far beyond the mention it receives in India, his developed discussion of the object-to-be-negated deserves close scrutiny: is he elaborating upon a received tradition that implicitly describes an object-to-be-negated, or is he innovatively supplying an object-to-be-negated that goes beyond the thought of the Middle Way School's Indian forebears? To decide this question, let us first examine the role of the identification of the object-to-be-negated in the Consequence School.

One of the basic teachings of the Buddha is that suffering[126] is the result of activities[127] that are either virtuous or non-virtuous.[128] These activities occur because they are prompted at their root by an individual's innate ignorance.[129] This ignorance is the extreme conception of a self[130] of persons and phenomena. According to Ḏzong-ka-ḇa (see his commentary in the *Illumination of the Thought* below), Candrakīrti's *Introduction* (VI.116) refers to such conceptions when it states that conceptions arise in the presence of a view that things exist. Candrakīrti's stanza states:

> When things exist, conceptions arise.
> It has been analyzed how things do not exist.
> These do not arise without existent things,
> Just as without fuel fire does not exist.[131]

---

126 *sdug bsngal, duḥkha.*

127 *las, karma.*

128 *mi dge ba, akuśala.*

129 *ma rig pa lhan skyes.*

130 *bdag 'dzin.*

131 *MAB,* VI.116, 229:

> *rtogs rnams dngos po yod na 'gyur ba ste //*
> *dngos po ji ltar med par yongs dpyad zin //*

Candrakīrti's stanza says that when things are seen to be existent, conceptions arise. The opposite is also true: without seeing things as existent, such conceptions do not arise. Seeing things as existent is necessary to the conception of an extreme, just as fuel is necessary to fire.

It is crucial, here, to determine what is meant by existent. Candrakīrti does not explain whether the phrase "things exist"[132] in the stanza (VI.116) refers to existence in general, or to a superimposed inherent existence. D̄zong-ka-b̄a determines that it is the second interpretation that is true. His commentary in the *Illumination of the Thought* explains the meaning of "things existing" in Candrakīrti's stanza to be "things existing as established by way of their nature":[133]

> When there is an apprehension of things existing as established by way of their nature, conceptions apprehending extremes arise. It has been analyzed by reasoning just explained how things do not have establishment by way of their nature and these conceptions apprehending extremes do not arise without apprehending things to be established by way of their nature; for example, without the cause — fuel — the effect — fire — does not exist.[134]

---

dngos po med par 'di rnams mi 'byung dper //
bud shing med par me yod min de bzhin //

[132] *dngos po yod pa.*

[133] *dngos po rang bzhin gyis grub pa.*

[134] *GRS,* 351-16-352.1:

> *mthar 'dzin rtogs rnams dngos po rang bzhin gyis grub par 'dzin pa yod na 'byung bar 'gyur ba ste // ji skad bshad pa'i rigs pas dngos po rang bzhin gyis grub pa ji ltar yang med par yongs su dpyad zin la // dngos po rang bzhin gyis grub par 'dzin pa med par mthar 'dzin gyi rtog pa 'di rnams mi 'byung ste dper na rgyu bud shing med par 'bras bu me yod pa min pa de bzhin no //*

D̄zong-ka-b̄a's commentary modifies the *Introduction* stanza VI.116 so Candrakīrti's statement to the effect that seeing things as existent is ignorance becomes instead a statement that ignorance is seeing things as established by way of their own nature. In D̄zong-ka-b̄a's system, things appear to be established by way of their own nature, but this appearance is the object-to-be-negated, not the things' mode of subsistence. Seeing things to exist like this is to see them as existent *in the wrong way*, such that one is mistakenly assenting to the appearance of a thing's object-to-be-negated nature. When one understands that there is such an object-to-be-negated that is deceptive about things, then one can appreciate the need to differentiate between things existing in general and their existing inherently.

The need to differentiate between things existing in general and their existing inherently is the point of D̄zong-ka-b̄a's statement in the *Great Exposition of the Stages of the Path:*

> Therefore, it is clear that you who propound, "If there is no nature, that is to say, establishment by way of own-entity, then what else is there?" have unquestionably not differentiated the two, the lack of inherent existence of a sprout and the non-existence of a sprout, and, due to that, you have also not differentiated the existence of a sprout and the establishment of a sprout by way of its own entity.[135]

D̄zong-ka-b̄a criticizes those Proponents of the Middle who experience Nāgārjuna's dialectic as annihilation. Not understanding that inherent existence can be refuted without refuting existence in general, they believe an existent must be established by way of

---

135 *LRC*, 798.5-798.6:

> *des na rang gi ngo bos grub pa'i rang bzhin med na gzhan ci zhig yod ces smra ba 'dis ni // gdon mi za bar myu gu rang bzhin med pa dang myu gu med pa gnyis kyi khyad par ma phyed par gsal //*

its own entity. The correct position, according to Ḏzong-ka-ḇa, involves differentiating nominally existent phenomena from the appearances of inherent existence.

Ḏzong-ka-ḇa's statement that "exists" means "exists by way of its nature" is one of his most commonly used exegetical strategems. This strategem has its roots in Indian Buddhism. Candrakīrti's *Commentary on (Āryadeva's) "Four Hundred"* states:

> According to Proponents of [Truly] Existent Things, as long as there is an existence of things, there is also an own-entity of them (*rang gi ngo bo, svarūpasya*).[136]

The *Great Exposition of the Stages of the Path* — commenting upon this passage in Candrakīrti's *Commentary on (Āryadeva's) "Four Hundred"* — explains its import:

> As long as you do not realize this differentiation by the glorious Candrakīrti between the four — inherent existence and existence and lack of inherent existence and non-existence, you will unquestionably fall to the two extremes, whereby you will not realize the meaning of the middle free from the extremes. For, when a phenomenon comes to be utterly without establishment by way of its own entity, it will come to be utterly non-existent. In that case, since there is utterly no way to posit cause and effect within the emptiness that is an emptiness of inherent existence, you fall to an extreme of annihilation. Also, once a phenomenon is asserted as exist-

---

[136] *byang chub sems dpa'i rnal 'byor spyod pa gzhi brgya pa'i rgya cher 'grel pa, bodhisattvayogācāracatuḥśatakaṭīkā,* P5266. Translated in *DAE,* 199; quoted in *LRC,* 799.3:

> *dngos po yod par smra ba'i ltar na ji srid du dngos po de'i yod pa nyid yin pa de srid du rang gi ngo bo yang yin pa nyid //*

Sanskrit text from Haraprasād Shāstri, 492.13-15, given in *DAE,* 766:

> *vastusatpadārthavādino hi yāvattasya vastuno 'stitvaṃ tāvat tathāsvarūpasyaiva //*

> ing, it must be asserted as established by way of its own entity. In that case, since there comes to be no way to take cause and effect as illusory-like, appearing to exist inherently whereas they do not, you fall to an extreme of permanence.[137]

Four differentiated states are set forth in the *Great Exposition of the Stages of the Path:*

(1) inherent existence,
(2) existence,
(3) lack of inherent existence, and
(4) non-existence.

The first, inherent existence, does not exist but is conceived to exist by a mistaken awareness. The second, existence, is used in this context to mean conventional existence, the only sort of existence asserted by Dzong-ka-ba. The third state, lack of inherent existence, is the ultimate truth as asserted in the *Great Exposition of the Stages of the Path.* Finally, non-existence is not being a phenomenon. Non-existents, such as the horns of a rabbit, are utterly without an entity. Dzong-ka-ba's point is that one can go wrong with respect to the Middle Way view by conflating inherent existence with existence in general, and mistaking the lack of inherent

---

[137] Translation from *DAE,* 199-200. Tibetan text in *LRC,* 799.5-800.1:

> *rang bzhin yod med dang yod med gzhi po 'di dpel ldan zla ba grags pas phye ba 'di ma rtogs phyin chad gdon mi zad par mtha' gnyis su ltung pas mtha' bral dbu ma'i don mi rtogs pa yin te 'di ltar rang gi ngo bos grub pa ye med du nam song ba na chos de ye med du 'grol de lta na rang bzhin gyis stong pa'i stong pa la rgyu 'bras bzhags gtan med pas chad pa'i mthar ltung la yang chos de yod par 'dod //phyin chad rang gi ngo bos grub par khas blang dgos par 'gyur la de lta na rgyu 'bras rang bzhin med bzhin du der snang ba'i sgyu ma lta bur byas mi 'ong bas rtags pa'i mthar ltung ba yin no //*

existence for non-existence. Differentiating well between these four is a way to avoid falling to the two extremes.

How is it that inherent existence — the object-to-be-negated — is non-existent? Dreyfus explains that it is the putative object grasped by our own minds — it is not the actual mode of subsistence of things:

> The Geluk-ba's point is that Nāgārjuna's attack against the view that things exist is in fact directed at what the Geluk thinkers refer to as the object-to-be-negated (*dgag bya*), ultimate existence (*don dam par yod pa*), real existence (*bden par grub pa*), or intrinsic existence (*rang bzhin gyis grub pa*). According to this interpretation, Nāgārjuna is negating the putative real existence of things, not their conventional existence. Things do not truly exist, but they do exist nevertheless because they have a conventional validity that can be ascertained. Since they are observed by valid cognition, things exist.[138]

As Dreyfus remarks, positing nominal existence allows Consequentialists to interpret Nāgārjuna's statements that things do not exist as a statement that things do not *inherently* exist but that they do *conventionally* exist.[139] Dreyfus emphasizes the importance of this distinction between inherent existence and nominal existence for the tradition when he says:

> Therefore, positing the meaning of nominal existence as being different from real existence and as fulfilling the meaning of existence is a crucial move in Geluk philosophy. It allows this tradition to reconcile the antisubstantialist character of Buddhist philosophy with common-sense.[140]

---

[138] Georges Dreyfus, *Recognizing Reality* (Albany: SUNY Press, 1997), 457.

[139] Dreyfus, 457.

[140] Dreyfus, 458.

Geluks posit the meaning of nominal existence as:

(1) different from inherent existence and
(2) fulfilling the meaning of "existence" (*dngos po, bhāva*) in the works of Nāgārjuna and Candrakīrti.

For Dreyfus, this differentiation between inherent existence and nominal existence reconciles the antisubstantialist character of Buddhist philosophy with common-sense. This is because nominally existent phenomena do not need to withstand analysis, as do inherently existent phenomena, and yet they fulfill the meaning of existence since they are observed by certifying valid consciousnesses.

Ḏzong-ka-ḇa makes the related point that it is necessary for those seeking liberation to identify the object-to-be-negated. The general existence of a phenomenon is not refuted, but the *inherent* existence of a phenomenon is to be identified and refuted. It is crucial that the object-to-be-negated nature be identified precisely. The *Great Exposition of the Stages of the Path* begins its discussion of this identification when it states:

> Just as, for example, in order to ascertain that a certain person is not here, you must know the person who is not here, so in order to ascertain the meaning of "selflessness" and "lack of [inherent] nature" (*rang bzhin med*) you must also identify well that self and nature that do not exist. This is because, if the [meaning] generality of that which is to be negated does not appear well, then also the negative of that [object-to-be-negated] will not unmistakenly be ascertained.[141]

---

141 *LRC*, 780.6-781.2:

dper na gang zag 'di mi 'dug snyam du nges pa la med rgyu'i gang zag de shes dgos pa ltar bdag med pa dang rang bzhin med pa zhes pa'i don nge pa la'ang med rgyu'i bdag dang rang bzhin de legs par ngos zin dgos te dgag par bya ba'i spyi legs par ma shar na de

Here Ḏzong-ka-ḇa is saying that realization of emptiness must be preceded by an identification of the nature that does not exist. Failure to identify this putative object means that its negative — emptiness — will not clearly be seen either. In discussing the importance of the correct identification of the object-to-be-negated, Ḏzong-ka-ḇa cites Śāntideva's[142] (8th century C.E.) *Entering the Deeds of Bodhisattvas*[143] (IX.140ab) as his *locus classicus:*

> Without contacting the entity which is imputed,
> One will not apprehend the lack of that entity.[144]

This quotation from *Entering the Deeds of Bodhisattvas* — which occurs in the context of refuting the Sāṃkhya assertion of self-production — is employed by Ḏzong-ka-ḇa to affirm the importance of identifying the object-to-be-negated. Although this statement does not explicitly use the term "object-to-be-negated," it serves to point out the importance of the correct identification of the object-to-be-negated.

In the *Great Exposition,* Ḏzong-ka-ḇa discusses an object-to-be-negated that is insufficient or too narrow (literally, "underpervaded"). This section together with its compliment — the previous section of the *Great Exposition,* which describes the refutation

---

bkag pa'ang phyin ci ma log par mi nges pa'i phyir //

See *DAE,* 176.

142 *zhi ba lha.*

143 *byang chub sems dpa'i spyod pa la 'jug pa, bodhisattvacaryāvatāra,* P5272. Tibetan text, Dharamsala edition, no publication data.

144 *Entering the Deeds of Bodhisattvas,* IX.139, 36a.6:

brtags pa'i dngos la ma reg par //
de yi dngos med 'dzin ma yin //

of an object-to-be-negated that is too broad[145] — completes the identifications of overly-broad and insufficient negations that are intended to assist Proponents of the Middle School in the avoidance of extreme views. It points to an understanding of the actual object-to-be-negated asserted by Dzong-ka-ba: that things are established by way of their own entities.[146]

Dzong-ka-ba addresses the topic of essential nature in his commentaries on Nāgārjuna's *Treatise* (XV), found in the *Ocean of Reasonings* and in the *Great Exposition.* The *Ocean of Reasonings* (see Part Two, page 159) addresses the text in the traditional commentarial manner, following the logical flow of Chapter XV. This means that Dzong-ka-ba's commentary on Chapter XV in the *Ocean of Reasonings* mainly addresses the philosophical import of refuting the two-cornered "tetralemmas" of (1) self-entities/other-entities and (2) being/non-being.

Interestingly, Dzong-ka-ba's discussion of Chapter XV in the *Great Exposition* (see Part Two, page 179) has very different aims. First, Dzong-ka-ba uses his discussion of essential nature in Chapter XV to refute the assertion by "some Tibetans" that the Consequentialist object-to-be-negated is that imaginary nature that possesses the three attributes of being non-fabricated, immutable, and independent (see page 40). Then, Dzong-ka-ba reaffirms Candrakīrti's claim that Nāgārjuna refers to a reality nature that possesses the three attributes (see page 147). Finally, he refutes the assertion by Döl-bo Shay-rap-gyel-tsen (1292-1361) that reality is positive and independent (see page 104).

It is interesting that Dzong-ka-ba presents his detailed identification of an object-to-be-negated as though it were normal for

---

145 See *DAE,* 152-215, for a translation of the section on refuting too broad an object-to-be-negated.

146 *rang gi ngo bos grub pa.* See page 91.

Buddhists to do so; for although Śāntideva and others[147] may mention the concept of the object-to-be-negated, they do not clearly and explicitly employ the term "object-to-be-negated" in this context of identifying the putative object of innate ignorance. D̄zong-ka-b̄a does not offer other citations from Indian sources discussing the identification of an object-to-be-negated, and I have been unable to find any Indian Buddhist texts that speak of the object-to-be-negated in an explicit manner.

Perhaps the closest Candrakīrti comes to presenting an explicit discussion of the object-to-be-negated is in the *Clear Words* (XV), where he employs the term "object of negation."[148] The usage appears when explaining that someone cognizing emptiness might say, "That does not exist," due to realizing that the object-to-be-negated does not exist. The *Clear Words* says:

> But, someone who, like those without opthomalia with respect to the falling hairs observed by those with opthomalia, does not observe anything at all says, "That does not exist," and thus propounds non-existence due to the non-existence of the object of negation.[149]

---

[147] Napper reports that Nāgārjuna uses the term "object of negation" in the *Refutation of Objections* [14-16], but not in this context of identifying the referent object of innate ignorance. *DAE*, 81.

[148] *dgag bya med pa, pratiṣedhyābhāvāt.*

[149] *PP*, 273.13-274.1:

> *tasya pūrvopalabbhasvabhāvāpavādātsyātabhāvadarśanaṃ yastu taimirikopalabbhakeśeṣviva vitaimiriko na kiṃ cidupalabhate sa nāstīti brūvan kiṃ cinnāstīti brūyātpratiṣedhyābhāvāt //*

TSHIG, 44.4.3-44.4.4; *D-TSHIG*, 236.8-11:

> *gang zhig rab rib can gyis dmigs pa'i sgra shad dag la rab rib med pa ltar gyur zhing ci yang ma dmigs pa des med do zhes ci zhig smras pas med par smras par 'gyur te dgag bya med pa'i phyir //*

Here Candrakīrti refers to a Superior who has cognized emptiness and is able to pronounce authoritatively upon the non-existence of just that which is seen by the ignorant — inherent existence. Such a person is like one without opthomalia, who is able to certify that there are no falling hairs. D̄zong-ka-b̄a's commentary upon this passage adds more information regarding the observable nature of the negative of the object-to-be-negated, emptiness. His *Ocean of Reasonings* remarks:

> These [things] that are observed by the power of the opthomalia of ignorance, if they existed as [their own] suchness, would have to be observed by a Superior's non-contaminated exalted wisdom of meditative equipoise; but instead, in the manner of not seeing those at all, their suchness is the object of that exalted wisdom. This is because that exalted wisdom realizes the suchness of things, and because just the non-establishment of things as nature is the suchness of those things and because, whereas if the object-to-be-negated existed, it would be observable, just due to not observing it, one is posited as having realized the negative of the object-to-be-negated.[150]

D̄zong-ka-b̄a makes the point that things themselves are not suchness, else they would be observed by the meditative stabilization of Superiors, which is a non-contaminated wisdom that observes suchness. Such a wisdom does not observe things; rather,

---

150 *RGT*, 733.11-17:

> *ma rigs pa'i rab rib kyi mthus dmigs pa 'di rnams de kho na nyid du yod na 'phags pa'i mnyam gzhag zag pa med pa'i ye shes kyis dmigs dgos pa las de rnams ci yang ma gzigs pa'i tshul gyis de dag gi de kho na nyid de ye shes de'i yul du 'gyur te ye shes de nyid dngos po rnams kyi de kho na nyid rtogs pa'i phyir dang dngos po rnams de kho na nyid du ma grub pa de nyid de dag gi de kho na nyid yin pa'i phyir dang dgag bya yod na dmigs su rung ba las ma dmigs pa nyid kyis dgag bya bkag pa rtogs par 'jog pa'i phyir ro //*

this exalted wisdom observes the suchness that is the non-establishment of things as nature, i.e., their emptiness. He describes the observation of this suchness as occurring in "the manner of not seeing these at all."[151] In Dzong-ka-ba's system, prior to Buddhahood, things other than ultimates do not appear at all to consciousnesses that directly cognize the ultimate.

TWOFOLD DIVISION OF THE OBJECT-TO-BE-NEGATED

In the *Great Exposition of the Stages of the Path,* Dzong-ka-ba describes both subjective and objective aspects of the object-to-be-negated:

> In general, there are two objects of negation: a path object-to-be-negated and an object to be negated by reasoning. The first consists of the two, the afflictive obstructions and the obstructions to omniscience, as described in [Maitreya's] *Discrimination of the Middle and the Extremes,*[152] which states:
>
> > It is asserted that one is liberated having exhausted all the obstructions — those which are indicated as the afflictive obstructions and as the obstructions to omniscience.
>
> These are the objects of negation that exist among objects of knowledge because if these did not exist, all beings would be liberated without striving.
>
> Regarding the object to be negated by reasoning, Nāgārjuna's *Refutation of Objections* states, "Or, some person thinks an emanated woman is a woman. Refuting that wrong conception by means of an emanation is like [refuting] that [object to be negated by reasoning]." Nāgārjuna's *Auto-Commentary to the Refutation of Objections* states:

---

151 *de rnams ci yang ma gzigs pa'i tshul gyis.*

152 *dbus dang mtha' rnam par 'byed pa, madhyāntavibhaṅga,* P5522.

> With respect to an emanated woman who is empty by way of nature (*rang bzhin gyis stong pa*), a certain person has a wrong conception thinking that the woman exists ultimately. Therefore, due to that wrong conception, desire is generated. A Tathāgata or his Hearer emanates an emanation, overcoming that wrong conception. Similarly, my words, which are empty like an emanation, overcome the conception of inherent existence with respect to all things which are without inherent existence and empty, like an emanated woman.

Accordingly, there are two [objects of negation]: (1) wrongly conceiving consciousnesses that are called "the object-to-be-negated" and (2) inherent existence that is apprehended by them that is called "the object-to-be-negated." However, the main of these is the latter [i.e., the object to be negated by reasoning] because in order to overturn the incorrect consciousness, one must initially refute the object apprehended by that.[153]

---

[153] *LRC,* 870.2-871.3:

> *spyir dgag bya la lam gyi dgag bya dang rigs pa'i dgag bya gnyis yod do // de la dang po ni dbus mtha' las nyon mongs pa yi sgrib pa dang shes bya'i sgrib pa gnyid du bstan der ni sgrib pa thams cad de de zad nas ni grol bar 'dod ces gsungs pa ltar nyon mongs pa dang shes bya'i sgrib pa gnyis so // 'di ni shes bya la yod pa'i dgag bya yin te 'di med na lus can thams cad 'bad med du grol bar 'gyur ba'i phyir ro // rigs pa'i dgag bya ni rtsod zlog las yang na kha cig sprul pa'i bud med la ni bud med snyam log 'dzin 'byung ba sprul pa'i 'gog byed 'di ni de lta yin zhes pa'i rang 'grel las yang na skyes bu gcig sprul pa'i bud med rang bzhin gyis stong pa yin la don dam par bud med do snyam du log par 'dzin par 'gyur ro // de'i phyir de log par 'dzin pa des 'dod chags bskyed pa la de bzhin gshegs pa'am de bzhin gshegs pa'i nyan thos kyis sprul pa zhig sprul la des de'i log par 'dzin pa de zlog par byed do // de bzhin du nga'i tshig stong pa sprul pa lta bus dngos po thams cad*

In this passage, Dzong-ka-ba divides the object-to-be-negated topic into subjective and objective spheres. The subjective object-to-be-negated, i.e., the path object-to-be-negated,[154] consists of the two obstructions, the afflictive obstructions[155] and the obstructions to omniscience.[156] These obstructions are both wrongly conceiving consciousnesses.[157] They exist in the continua of ordinary sentient beings but may be gradually eradicated through meditation. The objective object-to-be-negated, i.e., the object to be negated by reasoning,[158] is the imagined inherent existence. This is the nature misapprehended to exist. In Dzong-ka-ba's system, the object-to-be-negated nature is a status of objects — establishment from its own side[159] or establishment by way of its own entity[160] — that does not exist and that is merely imagined to exist.

---

la rang bzhin med pa stong pa sprul pa'i bud med dang 'dra ba dag pa rang bzhin yod par 'dzin pa gang yin pa de zlog par byed do zhes gsungs pa ltar phyin ci log gi 'dzin pa la dgag byar gsungs pa dang des bzung pa'i rang bzhin yod pa la dgag byar mdzad pa gnyis yod do // 'on kyang dgag bya'i gtso bo ni phyi ma yin te yul can phyin ci log ldog pa la des bzung pa'i yul thog mar dgag dgos pas so //

154 *lam gyi dgag bya.*

155 *nyon mongs pa'i sgribs pa, kleśāvaraṇa.*

156 *shes bya'i sgribs pa, jñeyāvaraṇa.*

157 *log par 'dzin pa.*

158 *rigs pa'i dgag bya.*

159 *rang ngos nas grub pa.*

160 *rang gi ngo bos grub pa.*

REFUTING A FABRICATED NATURE

Nāgārjuna's *Treatise on the Middle* (XV), "The Analysis of Nature," investigates and refutes a nature that is fabricated. In the eleven stanzas comprising his analysis of nature, he seeks to discredit the possibility that a nature of things is caused. The *Treatise on the Middle* states:

> The arising of nature due to causes and conditions (*rgyu dang rkyen, hetupratyaya*) is not reasonable.[161]

Candrakīrti's commentary restructures Nāgārjuna's declarative statement so that it becomes a reply to an unnamed proponent's objection. The *Clear Words* states:

> *Objection:* A nature of things just exists because of the causal contributors (*nye bar len pa, upādāna*) — the causes and conditions that produce them (*de dag skyed par byed pa, tanniṣpādaka*).[162]

Here, the objector is arguing for the existence of a nature arisen from a causal process. D̄zong-ka-b̄a's commentary further identi-

---

[161] *MMK,* XV.1ab, 19:

na saṃbhavaḥ svabhāvasya yuktaḥ pratyayahetubhiḥ //

DBU, 6.3.1:

rang bzhin rgyu dang rkyen las ni //
'byung bar rigs pa ma yin no //

[162] *PP,* 259.1:

atrāha vidhyata eva bhāvānāṃ svabhāvastanniṣpādakahetupratyayopādānāt //

TSHIG, 42.1.8-42.2.1; *D-TSHIG,* 223.1-2:

'dir smras pa dngos po rnams kyi rang bzhin ni yod pa nyid de de dag skyed par byed pa'i rgyu dang rkyen nye bar len pa'i phyir ro //

fies that the opponent views nature as a fabricated nature. His *Ocean of Reasonings* states:

> *Objection:* Things exist by way of their nature because [their] causal contributors exist — the causes and conditions, i.e., seeds, ignorance, and so forth, that produce sprouts, compositional factors, and so forth.[163]

D̄zong-ka-b̄a identifies the nature being discussed here as a nature that arises with the effect of a causal process. A caused nature is unacceptable to Candrakīrti and later Consequentialists, who agree with Nāgārjuna's statement in the *Treatise on the Middle:*

> The arising of nature due to causes and conditions is not reasonable.[164]

Nāgārjuna argues that the nature of a thing must be just that which is non-fabricated about that thing. The *Treatise on the Middle* (XV.2cd) states:

> Nature is non-fabricated...[165]

Not only does Nāgārjuna reject a fabricated nature that is pro-

---

[163] *RGT,* 728.2-4:

> *'dir smras pa dngos po rnams ni rang bzhin gyis yod de myu gu dang 'du byed la sogs pa rnams skyed par byed pa'i rgyu dang rkyen sa bon dang ma rig pa la sogs pa nye bar len pa yod pa'i phyir //*

[164] *MMK,* XV.1ab, 19:

> *na saṃbhavaḥ svabhāvasya yuktaḥ pratyayahetubhiḥ //*

DBU, 6.3.1:

> *rang bzhin rgyu dang rkyen las ni //*
> *'byung bar rigs pa ma yin no //*

[165] *MMK,* XV.2cd:

> *akṛtrimaḥ svabhāvo //*

duced by causes and conditions, but he also maintains that a nature must be endowed with the three attributes of being non-fabricated, immutable, and independent. Two of these attributes, independence and non-fabrication, are mentioned in the *Treatise on the Middle* (XV.2cd), which says:

> Nature is non-fabricated and does not depend on another.[166]

The third attribute of a nature is its unchanging state, or immutability, which is mentioned in the *Treatise* (XV.8cd):

> Change of a nature is never feasible.[167]

In these stanzas, Nāgārjuna refutes a nature arisen from causes and conditions through asserting that the existence of a causally arisen nature of things is contradictory with the necessity that a nature be non-fabricated, immutable, and independent. If a nature exists, it must not be a product, created by causes and conditions. According to the *Great Exposition of the Stages of the Path*, "Being fabricated means not existing earlier and being created as a new

---

[166] *MMK,* XV.2cd, 19:

> *akṛtrimaḥ svabhāvo hi nirapekṣaḥ paratra ca //*

DBU, 6.3.2:

> *rang bzhin de ni bcos min dang //*
> *gzhan la bltos pa med pa yin //*

[167] *MMK,* XV.8cd, 19:

> *prakṛter anyathābhāvo na hi jātūpapadyate //*

DBU, 6.3.6-7:

> *rang bzhin gzhan du 'gyur ba ni //*
> *nam yang 'thad par mi 'gyur ro //*

arising."[168] Thus, nature cannot be fabricated since a nature by definition is not a new arising.

In the *Clear Words,* Candrakīrti replies to the above-quoted opponent's assertion that caused things have a nature by flinging the opposite consequence that if things have nature, their production by causes and conditions would be unnecessary:

> *Response:* If things — compositional factors, sprouts, and so forth — have nature, then what need have those existing things for causes and conditions?[169]

Candrakīrti's point is that a thing with its own essential nature has no need for causation since such a nature does not require production. This reasoning is based on the consideration that nature must be unproduced in the sense of being non-fabricated. D̄zong-ka-b̄a agrees in the *Great Exposition of the Stages of the Path,* where he states:

> ...if something is ultimately established, really established, and truly established, then it must not be produced by causes and conditions.[170]

---

168 *LRC,* 866.3:

> *bcos ma na sngar med gsar du 'byung ba'i byas pa //*

169 *PP,* 259.5:

> *yadi bhāvānāṃ saṃskārāṅkurādīnāṃ svabhāvo 'sti kimidānaṃ vidhyamānānāṃ hetupratyayaiḥ prayojanaṃ //*

TSHIG, 42.2.3; *D-TSHIG,* 223.4:

> *gal te dngos po 'du byed dang myu gu la sogs pa dag la rang bzhin yod na ni de'i tshe yod par gyur pa rnams la rgyu dang rkyen dag gis dgos pa ci zhig yod //*

170 *LRC,* 861.5:

> *gzhan yang don dam par dang yang dag par grub pa dang bden par grub na'ang rgyu rkyen gyis ma bskyed pa sogs su 'gyur dgos //*

Nāgārjuna, Candrakīrti, and D̄zong-ka-b̄a are in agreement that a nature must be non-fabricated. An ultimate nature of things can in part be identified by its feature of non-fabricatedness.

HEAT IS NOT THE NATURE OF FIRE

Candrakīrti continues to press his attack on a fabricated nature by arguing against the notion that heat is the nature of fire. The *Clear Words* (XV) argues against the worldly understanding that heat is the nature of fire and attempts to demonstrate that heat is not the nature of fire, even conventionally. His discussion that heat is not the nature of fire exemplifies Nāgārjuna's refutation of a fabricated nature in the *Treatise on the Middle* (XV). Candrakīrti bases his argument on the Consequentialist position that a nature must be non-fabricated. The *Clear Words* says:

> This [heat] is not suitable to be the nature [of fire] because of lacking a defining character of nature.[171]

Heat is not the nature of fire, and lacks a "defining character of nature,"[172] because of being fabricated. As we saw, fabricated means not existing earlier and being newly created. Although Nāgārjuna does not mention the commonly held opinion that heat is the nature of fire, he does state that nature is non-fabricated and does not depend on another. Heat is fabricated by causes and conditions — fuel and friction, for instance. Moreo-

---

[171] *PP*, 260.15:

> *etattu vayaṃ brūmo nāyaṃ svabhāvo bhavitumarhati svabhāvalakṣaṇaviyuktatvāt //*

TSHIG, 42.3.7-42.3.8; *D-TSHIG*, 225.7:

> *'di ni rang bzhin yin par mi 'ongs te rang bzhin gyi mtshan nyid dang bral ba'i phyir ro //*

[172] *rang bzhin gyi mtshan nyid, svabhāvalakṣaṇa.*

ver, heat is dependent and mutable — the opposite of their corresponding attributes of a nature, independence and immutability.

Candrakīrti expands upon this description of a nature by asserting that a nature is that which is the innermost entity of a thing, the entity that is the "mine" of something.[173] The *Clear Words* states:

> Here, since "own-nature" (*rang gi dngos po, svo bhāvaḥ*) is nature (*rang bzhin, svabhāva*), that which is the entity that is the "mine" of whatsoever thing is said to be its nature. What is the "mine" of something? That which is non-fabricated.[174]

Candrakīrti includes in his description of nature that the non-fabricated aspect of a nature is also "the entity that is the 'mine.'" What is this innermost entity? Candrakīrti describes it in greater detail in this citation from the *Clear Words:*

> That which, even in all three times, is the non-fabricated fundamental entity non-mistaken in fire, that which is not the subsequent arising of something that did not arise previously, and that which does not have reliance on causes and conditions, as do the heat of water or near and far, or long and short, is said to be the nature [of fire].[175]

---

173 *bdag gi ba'i ngo 'o yin pa, ātmīyaṃ rūpaṃ.*

174 *PP*, 262.12:

> *iha svo bhāvaḥ svabhāva iti yasya padārthasya yadātmīyaṃ rūpaṃ tattasya svabhāva iti vyapadiśyate // kiṃ ca kasyātmīyaṃ yadhyasyākṛtrimaṃ //*

TSHIG, 42.5.2-42.4.3; *D-TSHIG*, 226.13:

> *'di ni rang gi dngos po ni rang bzhin no zhes bya bas gang zhig dngos po gang gi bdag gi ba'i ngo 'o yin pa de ni rang bzhin yin no zhes brjod do // gang zhig gang gi bdag gi ba yin zhe na gang gis gang ma bcos pa'o //*

175 For Sanskrit and Tibetan, see note 123.

Heat is not qualified to be the nature of fire because it is (1) fabricated in the sense of not existing before and being newly arisen and also (2) produced by causes and conditions. A produced thing cannot be a non-fabricated entity and thus cannot be the nature of fire. For Candrakīrti, the "mine" of something must be non-fabricated.

Ḏzong-ka-ḇa gives a more detailed description of the "innermost entity," i.e., that which is the "mine" of something. The *Ocean of Reasonings* states:

> What — and of what — is the "mine"? That which is a non-fabricated quality of whatsoever substratum is [the "mine"] of that [substratum]. Whatever is fabricated is not the "mine" of that [substratum], like, for example, the heat of water. Whatever does not depend on something else is the "mine" of that [substratum], like for instance, one's servant and one's wealth [which do not depend on someone else, but on oneself]. Whatever does depend on something [or someone] else, is not the "mine" of that [substratum], like for instance, a temporarily loaned thing not under one's control.[176]

To exemplify the independence of the "mine," Ḏzong-ka-ḇa gives the rather curious examples of "one's servant"[177] and "one's wealth."[178] It is curious for Ḏzong-ka-ḇa to label one's servants

---

[176] *RGT,* 731.15-732.1:

> *gang zhig gang gi bdag gi ba yin zhe na chos can gang gi chos gang ma bcos pa de ni de'i 'o // gang zhig bcos ma yin pa de ni de'i bdag gi ba ma yin te dper na chu'i tsha ba lta bu'o // gang zhig gzhan la rag ma las pa de yang de'i bdag gi ba yin te dper na rang gi khol po dang rang gi nor dag bzhin no // gang zhig gzhan la rag las pa de ni de'i bdag gi ba ma yin te dper na re zhig brnyan po rang dbang med pa lta bu'o //*

[177] *rang gi khol po.*

[178] *rang gi nor.*

and one's wealth "independent" because, of course, those two things are dependent-arisings. Nevertheless, there is a sense in which they are independent: they are independent of other people's influences, even though this is only because both our servants and our wealth are dependent on *our* influences.

However, Ḏzong-ka-ḇa is not using these examples to illustrate the Consequentialist meanings of dependence. His more relative intentions come clear when he gives "a temporarily loaned thing not under one's control"[179] as an example for what is *not* the "mine" of something. Just as a temporarily loaned thing not under one's control *is* dependent on others, so it can be said in relation to that, that one's servant or wealth is *not* dependent on others. One's servant and wealth do not depend on others in the sense that others do not control one's servant or wealth since one oneself controls them. Thus, a common usage of dependent is given here as an analogy for a more technical usage.

Ḏzong-ka-ḇa employs examples expressing a qualified type of dependence here, because he employs a narrow usage of dependence discussing the "mine" — dependence on comparisons, such as long and short. This type of qualification is perhaps inevitable on the occasion of explaining how a feature of emptiness (a dependent-arising) can be non-dependence on another.

Noteworthy is the fact that later Geluk exegetes adapt an unusual meaning of dependence so that non-dependence can be a feature of something that is the "mine." In this situation, the reformulating of the meaning of dependence insures that there is nothing contradictory in the assertion that the innermost entity of a thing is independent and yet remains a dependent-arising.

---

179 *re zhig brnyan po rang dbang med pa.*

CATEGORIZATION OF THE THREE ATTRIBUTES INTO ENTITY, STATE, AND CERTIFICATION

Following Nāgārjuna's description of the triply-qualified reality nature in the *Treatise on the Middle* (XV), later Consequentialists devised a scheme placing each attribute in its own category of entity, certification, and state. D̄zong-ka-b̄a uses this scheme in his discussion of nature in the *Great Exposition of the Stages of the Path:*

> (1) the entity attribute is not fabricated by causes and conditions (*ngo bo rgyu rkyen gyis bcos ma min pa*),
> (2) the conventional certification attribute does not depend on another (*tha snyad rnam 'jog chos gzhan la ltos pa med pa*), and
> (3) the state attribute is immutable (*gzhan du mi 'gyur pa*).

This scheme provides a frame for the presentation of the three attributes by speaking of the individual attributes from three generic points of view.

The origin of this categorization of the three attributes is uncertain. It does not appear in Nāgārjuna or Candrakīrti, nor does it originate with D̄zong-ka-b̄a. N̄ya-cha-wa Ts̄ön-drü-s̄eng-gay — who studied the commentaries of Candrakīrti with B̄a-tsap Nyi-ma-drak — in his 12th-century *Ornament of Logical Correctness* (a commentary on the *Treatise on the Middle*) presents an earlier version of the threefold categorization.[180] The *Ornament of Logical Correctness* presents its commentary on the *Treatise on the Middle* (XV) in this way:

---

[180] The *Ornament of Logical Correctness* refers to the "suchness nature" (*de kho na'i rang bzhin*), instead of the "reality nature."

> The defining character of objects of uncontaminated exalted wisdom consciousnesses — the natures that are the suchness of phenomena — is that which is endowed with the three qualities of:
>
> (1) its entity is not fabricated by causes and conditions (*ngo bo rgyu rkyen gyis bcos ma min pa*),
> (2) its conventional certification does not depend on another (*tha snyad rnam 'jog chos gzhan la ltos pa med pa*), and
> (3) [its state is] immutable (*gzhan du mi 'gyur pa*).[181]

N̄ya-cha-wa Tsön-drü-s̄eng-gay omits mention of the category of a state attribute, immutability, but this omission is probably without significance. Further research may determine that the categorization of the three attributes into entity, certification, and state originated with B̄a-tsap.

CONFUSING A NATURE OF THINGS HAVING THE THREE ATTRIBUTES WITH THAT WHICH IS TO BE NEGATED

In the *Great Exposition of the Stages of the Path,* D̄zong-ka-b̄a treats the topic of nature at length in the section entitled "The Refutation of an Identification of the Object-to-be-negated That Is Too Narrow."[182] In this section, D̄zong-ka-b̄a denounces the position of certain unnamed Tibetans who assert that the *Treatise on the Middle* (XV) expresses the Consequence School's object-to-be-negated in a manner that is insufficient or partial from the point

---

181 *Ornament of Logical Correctness,* 177.4-5:

> *zag pa med pa'i ye shes kyi yul chos rnams kyi de kho na'i rang bzhin dag gi mtshan nyid ni ngo bo rgyu rkyen gyis bcos ma min pa dang tha snyad rnam 'jog chos gzhan la ltos pa med pa dang gzhan du mi 'gyur pa ste chos gsum dang ldan pa //*

182 See Document 4, page 179.

of view of being too narrow, or of too small scope.[183]

The word "narrow" can have many meanings, but here Je Dzong-ka-ba is specifically referring to the identification of an object-to-be-negated nature merely being a nature endowed with the three attributes[184] of being non-fabricated, immutable, and independent. Dzong-ka-ba ascribes these three attributes as features of emptiness, but he does not consider them to be the uncommon object-to-be-negated of the Consequence School.

The *Great Exposition of the Stages of the Path* makes the following statement (with bracketed commentary by Dra-di Ge-shay writing in the *Four Interwoven Annotations*):

> In general, if it were asserted that external and internal things such as sprouts and so forth are established as such natures having the three attributes, then Proponents of the Middle also would have to refute such [but the refutation of such a nature is not sufficient].[185]

It is clear that the Geluk system does not at all agree that refuting a nature endowed with these three attributes constitutes a refutation of the nature that represents the "self" in selflessness. Briefly, the negated nature is said to be "wider" than a nature endowed with the three attributes in the sense that it is the object conceived by an innate ignorance.[186] The nature having the three attributes,

---

[183] *khyab chung ba.*

[184] *rang bzhin khyad par gsum dang ldan pa.*

[185] *LRC,* 860.5-861.2; bracketed commentary in *MCHAN,* 388.4-5:

> *spyir myu gu la sogs pa'i phyi nang gi dngos po rnams rang bzhin de 'dra ba zhig tu grub par 'dod na dbu ma pas dgag par bya dgos mod kyang [de 'dra'i rang bzhin de tsam bkag pas mi chog] //*

[186] *ma rig pa lhan skyes, *sahajāvidyā.*

on the other hand, is said to be "narrower" in that it is an object conceived of by a learned ignorance.[187]

These confused Tibetans (perhaps the abbots of Sang-pu — see page 40) mistakenly believed that the presentation in Chapter XV of a nature endowed with three attributes is descriptive of the Consequentialist's uncommon object-to-be-negated. D̄zong-ka-b̄a disagrees with their identification of the three attributes as the object-to-be-negated. His reaction to their opinion that he finds confused is twofold: (1) the three attributes are posited as features of emptiness and (2) the three attributes are not subtle enough to be identified as the Consequence School object-to-be-negated. Writing in the *Four Interwoven Annotations,* Jam-ȳang-shay-b̄a makes these two points:

> Since these [three attributes] are a feature of emptiness, how could the nature [mentioned in the *Treatise*] be suitable as the object-to-be-negated! One who propounds such, [i.e., that the object-to-be-negated nature possesses the three attributes] has not identified the object-to-be-negated well.[188]

The first of these reactions — that the three attributes are posited as features of emptiness — is dictated by Candrakīrti's insistence that Nāgārjuna's discussion of a triply-qualified nature concerns the reality nature. To indicate this, the *Clear Words* states:

> What is this nature? It is emptiness.[189]

---

187 *kun brtags pa'i ma rigs pa, *parikalpitāvidyā.*

188 *MCHAN*, 387.6; 388.3:

> *'di stong nyid kyi khyad par yin pas dgag byar ga la rung...de skad smra ba des ni dgag bya legs par ngos ma zin //*

189 *PP*, 264.13:

> *kā ceyaṃ prakṛtiḥ // yeyaṃ śūnyatā //*

TSHIG, 43.1.4; *D-TSHIG*, 228.1:

D̄zong-ka-b̄a is following the tradition of Candrakīrti when he holds that the triply-qualified nature refers to the attributes of emptiness. The second of D̄zong-ka-b̄a's reactions to the identification of the three attributes as the object-to-be-negated — that the three attributes are not subtle enough to be identified as the Consequence School object-to-be-negated — is more innovative.

D̄ZONG-KA-B̄A'S IDENTIFICATION OF THE OBJECT-TO-BE-NEGATED

D̄zong-ka-b̄a denies that negation of just these three attributes is sufficient to be the actual object-to-be-negated in the Consequence School. To underscore this point, D̄zong-ka-b̄a's annotators draw a parallel between identifying the object-to-be-negated as the nature having the three attributes and citing "thing" in order to identify a pot. Writing in the *Four Interwoven Annotations,* Dra-d̄i Ge-shay states:

> For, like the example of showing the entity of thing (*dngos po, bhāva*) when identifying pot, identifying the uncommon object-to-be-negated of the view [of emptiness] as this nature that possesses the three attributes [is incorrect because] such a nature is wider than that.[190]

It is incorrect to identify the object-to-be-negated as this nature that possesses the three attributes because the three attributes are wider than the object-to-be-negated. Why are they being said here to be wider when they have already been identified as too narrow? The *Four Interwoven Annotations* do not elaborate, but the three

---

rang bzhin 'di yang gang yin // stong pa nyid do //

190 *MCHAN*, 388.3:

> *dper na bum pa ngos zin pa la dngos po'i ngo bo ston pa ltar lta ba'i thun mong min pa'i dgag bya ngo 'dzin pa la de'i khyab byed rang bzhin khyad par gsum ldan ngos bzung ba'i phyir ro //*

attributes are probably being called "wide" here because they are not just limited to discussions of the object-to-be-negated since they are features of a reality nature, and thus can be applied to a discussion of emptiness also. As the example demonstrates, citing "thing" does not identify pot — "thing" is too wide. Citing the three attributes does not identify the object-to-be-negated because these three actually identify the reality nature.

From D̄zong-ka-b̄a's point of view, the actual object-to-be-negated of the Consequence School is more subtle than the three attributes: it is a thing's establishment by way of its own entity[191] or from its own side.[192] The *Great Exposition of the Stages of the Path* states:

> There does not exist in phenomena even a particle of the nature that is establishment by way of a thing's own entity.[193]

D̄zong-ka-b̄a reveals more of his understanding of the object-to-be-negated being "establishment by way of a thing's own entity" or "establishment from a thing's own side" in the *Great Exposition of the Stages of the Path:*

> Compounded phenomena such as eyes, and so forth, are not established as a nature in the sense of establishment by way of own entity or nature... Hence, [compounded phenomena such as eyes, and so forth] are not established as any nature. Although the ultimate truth is established [as the nature in the sense of] positing reality as nature, [an ultimate truth] is posited by way of its two positors, non-fabrication and non-dependence on another, and hence [the ultimate] does not at

---

191 *rang gi ngo bos grub pa.*

192 *rang ngos nas grub pa.*

193 *LRC*, 864.5:

chos rnams la rang gi ngo bos grub pa'i rang bzhin ni rdul tsam yang med do //

> all come to be established by way of its own entity. Therefore [the ultimate] is only established conventionally.[194]

D̄zong-ka-b̄a makes it clear that phenomena do not possess the object-to-be-negated nature, and that includes emptiness itself. Nothing at all is established by way of its own nature, and refutation of such a status eliminates the most subtle ignorance regarding the self of persons and phenomena.

Although Candrakīrti in the *Clear Words* does not elaborate upon Nāgārjuna's discussion of the three attributes — except to explain them as the attributes of the reality nature — his *Commentary on (Āryadeva's) "Four Hundred"* is reminiscent of the *Treatise on the Middle* (XV.2) in its description of the object-to-be-negated nature as independent:

> Here "self" is a nature of phenomena, that is, non-dependence on another. The non-existence of this is selflessness.[195]

Candrakīrti appears to be taking a position that D̄zong-ka-b̄a asserts to be confused and insufficient — that the triply-qualified

---

[194] *LRC*, 866.1:

> *de ltar na mig la sogs pa'i 'dus byas 'di dag ni rang gi ngo bos grub pa'i rang bzhin du'ang ma grub la chos nyid la rang bzhin du bzhag pa der yang ma grub pas rang bzhin gang du'ang ma grub pa dang don dam pa'i bden pa ni chos nyid la rang bzhin du bzhag pa der grub kyang rang bzhin der 'jog byed bcos ma min pa dang gzhan la mi ltos pa ni rang gi ngo bos grub pas rang bzhin der cung zad kyang med pas tha snyad du grub pa tsam mo //*

[195] From Candrakīrti's *Commentary on (Āryadeva's) "Four Hundred,"* P5266, Vol. 98, 256.1.7, Chapter XII:

> *de la bdag ces bya ba ni gang zhig dngos po rnams kyi gzhan la rag ma las pa'i ngo bo rang bzhin te de med pa ni bdag med pa'o //*

nature is the object-to-be-negated. His *Clear Words* also describes an entity of suchness[196] that possesses the three attributes:

> What is this suchness? It is that entity of suchness that does not change and always abides. For, that which is not produced in any way, because of not being fabricated and because of not relying on another, is called the nature of fire and so forth.[197]

Later Geluk exegetes such as Nga-w̄ang-b̄el-den place an interpretive spin on Candrakīrti's description (in the previous citation) of the object-to-be-negated, in order to make his statement accord with that of D̄zong-ka-b̄a. Nga-w̄ang-b̄el-den's *Annotations* states:

> ...non-dependence on another in this [statement by Candrakīrti] is to be taken as establishment in the object from the point of view of its own entity and not being posited through the force of another, i.e., a conventional consciousness. That is called "self" or "nature."[198]

---

[196] *de bzhin nyid kyi ngo bo, tathābhāva.*

[197] *PP*, 265.1-265.2:

> *keyam tathatā tathābhāvo 'vikāritvam sadaiva svāyitā // sarvadānutpāda eva hi agnyādīnām paranirapekṣatvād akṛtrimatvātsvabhāva //*

TSHIG, 43.1.5-43.1.6; *D-TSHIG*, 228.3-7:

> *de bzhin nyid 'di yang gang zhig ce na de bzhin nyid kyi ngo bo 'gyur ba med pa nyid dang rtag tu gnas pa nyid de rnam pa thams cad du skye ba med pa nyid ni bcos ma ma yin pa'i phyir dang gzhan la bltos pa med pa'i phyir me la sogs pa rnams kyi rang bzhin yin no //*

This passage shows Candrakīrti's usage of *svabhāva* and *prakṛti* as synonyms and their corresponding translations into Tibetan as *rang bzhin.*

[198] *Annotations,* section *dbu,* note *da,* 136.8-137.1:

> *'di'i gzhan la rag ma las zhes pa yang sngar bshad pa ltar gzhan*

Nga-w̄ang-b̄el-den interprets Candrakīrti's use of "independent" in two ways: (1) "independent" means establishment in the object from the point of view of its own entity (which D̄zong-ka-b̄a considers to be more subtle than independence in the triad of qualities) and (2) "independent" means not being posited through the force of a conventional consciousness.

INNATE VERSUS ARTIFICIAL IGNORANCE: REFUTING THAT THE THREE ATTRIBUTES ARE THE OBJECT-TO-BE-NEGATED NATURE

Je D̄zong-ka-b̄a — in denying that the three attributes are the object-to-be-negated nature — makes the point that the ignorance that binds creatures in cyclic existence must be innate[199] rather than artificial.[200] The *Great Exposition of the Stages of the Path* states:

> When the view is delineated, one is to consider the refutation of the conceived object of innate ignorance to be the main point, and refute the conceived object of artificial ignorance as a branch of that.[201]

D̄zong-ka-b̄a's point is that the conception of the three attributes is not innate, but rather is artificial or learned. Since conceiving of the three attributes is not an innate ignorance but an artificial

---

> *tha snyad pa'i shes pa'i dbang gis bzhag pa min par rang gi ngo bo'i sgo nas yul gyi steng du grub pa la byed pa dang de la bdag gam rang bzhin zhes zer ba yin //*

199 *lhan skyes, sahaja.*

200 *kun brtags, parikalpita.*

201 *LRC,* 862.3-4:

> *lta bas gtan la 'bebs pa'i dus su lhan skyes kyi ma rig pas ji ltar bzung ba'i don med par gtan la 'bebs pa gtso bor bzung nas de'i yan lag tu kun brtags kyi 'dzin pa'i yul rnams sun 'byin pa... //*

one, realizing the lack of the three attributes in impermanent phenomena is missing the main point.

Ḏzong-ka-ḇa's brief discussion does not attempt to provide reasonings proving that the conception of the three attributes is learned. However, to better illustrate his point, Ḻo-sang-dor-jay[202] (20th century), in his *Ship for Entering into the Ocean of Textual Systems, Decisive Analysis of (Ḏzong-ka-ḇa's) "Stages of the Path to Enlightenment,"*[203] offers the example of an ant to demonstrate that the conception of the three attributes is learned:

> ...that which possesses the three such attributes is not the final object to be negated by a correct sign analyzing the ultimate because a valid cognition that realizes a sprout as empty of possessing the three features does not realize the opposite of the referent object of the conception of true existence which conceives a sprout to truly exist. That the reason is so follows because (1) the conception of true existence exists in the continua of ants and so forth whose minds have not been affected by tenets and (2) they do not conceive phenomena as possessing the three attributes.[204]

---

[202] *blo bzang rdo rje.*

[203] *byang chub lam gyi rim pa'i mtha' dpyod gzhung lugs rgya mtshor 'jug pa'i gru gzings zhes bya ba la lhag mthong gi mtha' dpyod* (New Delhi: Mongolian Lama Gurudeva, 1980).

[204] *Ship,* 79 (Hopkins' translation from unpublished manuscript), 597.5-598.1:

> *de lta bu'i khyad chos gsum ldan de don dam la dpyod pa'i rtags yang dag gi dgag bya mthar thug ma yin par thal myu gu khyad chos gsum ldan gyis stong par rtogs pa'i tshad ma des myu gu bden par 'dzin pa'i bden 'dzin gyi zhen yul gyi bzlog phyogs ma rtogs pa'i phyir // der thal grub mthas blo ma bgyur ba'i grog sbur sogs gyi rgyud la bden 'dzin yod pa gang zhig de la khyad chos gsum ldan gyi 'dzin tshul de med pa'i phyir //*

Since the conception of inherent existence is an innate ignorance, it exists even in the minds of insects. Therefore, that conception cannot be that a thing has a nature endowed with the three attributes. For, conceiving of a nature having the three attributes in a thing is a misconception learned from wrong scriptures and/or reasoning. Insects do not have this sort of misconception, or any other misconceptions derived from wrong tenets. Thus, this cannot be the root innate conception of self because not all creatures share it.

An artificially conceived status of objects is an ignorance that is learned in this life through incorrect scriptures and/or reasoning. However, this artificially conceived status is not the putative object of innate ignorance, and refuting a coarser artificial conception is not an antidote to the innate conception and thus will not bring about liberation.

In laying the ground for the argument that refuting the three attributes only identifies artificial ignorance, the *Great Exposition of the Stages of the Path* draws a parallel between two other insufficient refutations and that of the three attributes:

> If, not knowing that the main thing is to use the artificial as a branch of that, one forsook refuting the mode of apprehension of an innately ignorant consciousness and at the time of refuting a self of persons refuted a permanent, unitary, independent self and at the time of refuting a self of phenomena refuted (1) apprehended objects that are partless particles and (2) apprehending consciousnesses that are partless moments and (3) the nature possessing the three attributes, and so forth — that are imputed only by proponents of tenets — then such refutations are unsuitable in all ways.[205]

---

205 *LRC*, 862.3-5:

de'i yan lag tu kun brtags kyi 'dzin pa'i yul rnams sun 'byin pa ma shes par lhan skyes kyi ma rig pa'i 'dzin ltangs sun 'phyin pa

Dzong-ka-ba is saying that these three insufficient refutations are not the modes of apprehension of an innately ignorant consciousness but instead are modes of apprehension of artificial ignorant consciousnesses. Although he does not mention textual sources for this threefold enumeration of the modes of apprehension of artificial ignorant consciousness, the first two modes are discussed in Geluk texts on tenets, where (1) the conception of a permanent, unitary, independent self is a coarse afflictive obstruction for all Buddhist schools of tenets below the Consequence School, and (2) partless particles and moments are asserted to be ultimate truths in the Great Exposition School.[206] According to this same scheme of tenets, the Consequence School asserts that the conception of a self-sufficient person is a coarse afflictive obstruction, and also asserts non-establishment by way of a thing's own nature as the principal object of meditation.

Dzong-ka-ba's argument in the *Great Exposition of the Stages of the Path* makes another point: the three attributes are not subtle enough to be the object-to-be-negated nature because they are refuted even in the Great Exposition and Sūtra Schools. Since these schools are "lower" than the Consequence School, it follows they must have as their object-to-be-negated a coarser object than that propounded by the Consequence School. Dra-di Ge-shay — contributing in the *Four Interwoven Annotations* to Dzong-ka-ba's twofold reason why the triply-qualified nature is not the object-

---

dor nas gang zag gi bdag 'gog pa na rtags gcig rang dbang can gyi bdag dang chos kyi bdag 'gog pa na gzung rdul phran cha med dang 'dzin pa skad cig cha med dang rang bzhin khyad par gsum ldan la sogs pa grub mtha' smra ba kho nas btags pa rnams 'gog pa ni rnam pa thams chad du mi rung //

[206] *bye brag smra ba, vaibhāṣika.* Source for this tenet scheme is *MED,* 200, 338.

to-be-negated — provides a succinct statement of Geluk reasoning on this point:

> For, our own schools such as the Great Exposition and Sūtra Schools, and so forth, have already established that products, compounded phenomena, are created by causes and conditions and that they change state by way of disintegrating each moment. Therefore if the object-to-be-negated [is as you say it is, then] there would be the faults that (1) it would not be necessary to prove the lack of existence by nature to those schools — the Great Exposition and Sūtra Schools, and so forth — and (2) those Proponents of the Great Exposition, Proponents of Sūtra, and so forth, even would absurdly cognize the lack of existence by nature of things. Hence, how could your identification be getting at the final uncommon object-to-be-negated for the view realizing emptiness![207]

The quotation makes the two points that if the three attributes were the object-to-be-negated then (1) it would not be necessary to prove the lack of inherent existence to Hearers because they would already assert it themselves, since they have refutations of the three attributes. Also, (2) those Great Exposition and Sūtra School proponents would absurdly cognize the lack of inherent existence of things since the lack of inherent existence would be realized through the refutation of the three attributes.

---

[207] *MCHAN* 389.1-3:

> *'dus byas rnams rgyu rkyen gyis bskyed pa'i byas pa dang skad cig gis 'jig pa'i sgo nas gnas skabs gzhan du 'gyur ba ni bye mdo sogs rang gi sde pa rnams kyis kyang grub zin pa yin pas bye mdo sogs sde pa de dag la rang bzhin gyis med pa bsgrub mi dgos par 'gyur pa dang bye mdo sogs de dag gyis kyang dngos po rnams rang bzhin gyis med par rtogs par 'gyur ba sogs kyi skyon yod pas na khyed gyi ngos 'dzin des stong nyid rtogs pa'i lta ba'i skabs kyi thun mong ma yin pa'i dgag bya mthar thug pa de ga la yin //*

MODERN SCHOLARS ON NĀGĀRJUNA'S TRIPLY-QUALIFIED NATURE

Some modern non-Tibetan scholars hold — in common with Ḏzong-ka-ḇa's unnamed Tibetan disputants — that the *Treatise on the Middle* (XV.2) speaks of a non-existent object-to-be-negated nature. Richard Robinson holds that Nāgārjuna speaks of a non-existent independent nature in Chapter XV. Richard Hayes concurs with Robinson's statement that "It is absurd to maintain that a *svabhāva* exists."[208] Robinson states:

> If it [i.e., the *svabhāva* spoken of by Nāgārjuna] exists, it must belong to an existent entity, that is, it must be conditioned, dependent on other entities, and possessed of causes. But by definition it is free from conditions, nondependent on others, and not caused. Therefore, it is absurd to maintain that a *svabhāva* exists.[209]

D. S. Ruegg is also confident that Nāgārjuna is discussing a non-existent nature in XV.2. When Ruegg discusses the definition of *svabhāva,* he states that it must be "independent of any other thing causing or conditioning it,"[210] and he also claims that following the tetralemmic refutations of the *Treatise*, "No entity possessing a *svabhāva* of any kind is to be postulated."[211]

Giving a brief synopsis of the subject-matter of Chapter XV, Ruegg states:

---

[208] Richard P. Hayes, "Nāgārjuna's Appeal," *Journal of Indian Philosophy*, Vol. 22 (1994), 324, quoting Richard Robinson, "Did Nāgārjuna Really Refute All Philosophical Views," *Philosophy East and West*, Vol. 22 No. 3 (1972), 326.

[209] Robinson, 326.

[210] Ruegg, *Literature,* 14.

[211] Ruegg, *Literature,* 41.

> (XV) Own being (*svabhāva*, 'aseity', which would be entailed by the causality of *hetu-pratyayas*). This notion is subjected to a critique showing that it is not compatible with the idea of production by causes and conditions because by definition *svabhāva* should be independent of any other thing causing or conditioning it; it is therefore not produced.[212]

Ruegg understands the non-fabricated *svabhāva* to be a non-existent. He states that it is subjected to a critique by Nāgārjuna since it is not compatible with the idea of production by causes and conditions. This description of Chapter XV runs counter to the assertions by Candrakīrti and D̄zong-ka-b̄a that it is a fabricated nature that is being subjected to critique, not an independent nature of aseity. According to them, the independent nature, emptiness, is not subjected to critique in Chapter XV, but is simply described as possessing the three features of non-fabrication, independence, and immutability.

Jay Garfield feels that Nāgārjuna's purpose in writing Chapter XV is to "reject the coherence of the concept of essence."[213] He believes that the only "essence" (Garfield's translation of *svabhāva*) spoken of by Nāgārjuna is non-existent. Garfield states:

> Essence by definition is eternal and independent. So it can't arise dependently. Chapter XV: 1, 2 develop this point directly. But since all entities arise dependently, it follows that none of them have essence.[214]

For Garfield, Nāgārjuna is describing an essence of which phenomena are empty. He states:

---

[212] Ruegg, *Literature,* 14.

[213] Jay L. Garfield, *The Fundamental Wisdom of the Middle Way,* (London: Oxford University Press, 1995), 220.

[214] Garfield, 220.

> In these first two verses, Nāgārjuna indicates the three cardinal characteristics of an essence: An essence (or an entity that exists in virtue of possessing an essence) is uncaused, independent of other phenomena, and not fabricated from other things. It is important to bear this in mind in any Madhyamika analysis of emptiness. For when Nāgārjuna argues that phenomena are all empty, it is of essence in this sense that they are empty.[215]

Garfield asserts that phenomena are empty of the putative nature having the three attributes and also feels this is taught in the first two stanzas. He identifies the meaning intended by the term *svabhāva* to be the non-existent nature possessing the three attributes of non-fabrication, independence, and immutability.

William Ames' discussion of *svabhāva* is in some ways closer to that of Candrakīrti and D̄zong-ka-b̄a than those of the scholars cited above. Ames concurs with D̄zong-ka-b̄a that Candrakīrti describes two different kinds of *svabhāva.* He sees that there is a *svabhāva* that is an intrinsic establishment that things do not have and that does not exist, and also realizes that "Candrakīrti asserts that Nāgārjuna does, indeed, accept that a *svabhāva* of the sort which he defines in *MMK* 15-2cd exists."[216]

Ames recognizes that Candrakīrti asserts Nāgārjuna to be speaking of emptiness in XV.2, yet he is puzzled about the existential status of this *svabhāva.* He states:

> Candrakīrti apparently equates this genuine *svabhāva* with ultimate reality (*paramārtha*). Thus although *svabhāva* exists, it, like *paramārtha,* is neither an entity nor a non-entity.[217]

---

[215] Garfield, 221.

[216] William Ames, "The Notion of *Svabhāva* in the Thought of Candrakīrti," *Journal of Indian Philosophy*, Vol. 10 (1982), 164.

[217] Ames, 165.

In Dzong-ka-ba's presentation, emptiness is an existent entity. Although the reality nature exists, the object-to-be-negated nature does not exist at all as a real object.

THE INDEPENDENT AND POSITIVE NATURE

Döl-bo Shay-rap-gyel-tsen, one of the most influential religious thinkers of Tibet's 14th century, developed an innovative doctrinal synthesis composed of themes borrowed from sūtra and tantra. He called his synthesis the Great Middle Way.[218] One of the central Great Middle Way teachings was that the ultimate is an uncontaminated primordial wisdom, empty of all contaminated phenomena while being a positive, independent *tathāgatagarbha.*

Praised by some and excoriated by others, Shay-rap-gyel-tsen's doctrines took hold in the latter half of the 14th and early 15th centuries, and his school — the Jo-nang-ba — became widespread in a religious climate that seemed to favor creative synthesis.

Dzong-ka-ba came of age in a disputatious tradition. His own Sa-gya lama, the scholar Ren-da-wa, disputed the Jo-nang assertion of a positive Buddha nature and even cast aspersions on the Jo-nang-ba's tantric lineage, the Kālachakra. In turn, later Jo-nangs called Ren-da-wa "an evil demon who would spread the nihilist view."[219]

Dzong-ka-ba himself did not target the Kālachakra, but he did subject almost every other aspect of Döl-bo's synthesis to scathing rebuttal, not only in the *Great Exposition of the Stages of the Path,* but also — and principally — in his later *The Essence of Elo-*

---

[218] *dbu ma chen po, *mahāmadhyamika.*

[219] Cyrus R. Stearns, "The Buddha From Dol po and His Fourth Council of the Buddhist Doctrine," University of Washington (unpublished dissertation), 88.

quence. In these works Dzong-ka-ba tries to reverse the syncretism introduced by Döl-bo that contained the view of a permanent, stable *tathāgatagarbha.* In *The Essence of Eloquence,* Dzong-ka-ba expends considerable energy refuting the Jo-nang notion that passages of the *Sūtra Unravelling the Thought* — usually held to be Mind Only — present the views of Döl-bo's Great Middle Way. In the *Great Exposition of the Stages of the Path,* he devotes a section of the chapter on refuting a too narrow object-to-be-negated to the refutation of the Jo-nang-ba concept of a positive, independent nature.

DÖL-BO'S SYNTHESIS

The presence in the Perfection of Wisdom Sūtras of discussions of the three natures was held to be significant by the syncretic Döl-bo Shay-rap-gyel-tsen. For Shay-rap-gyel-tsen, the presence of three-nature discussions in the Perfection of Wisdom Sūtras was evidence that the three natures are not just Mind Only doctrines but are also part of an overarching Great Middle Way. Stearns describes this situation:

> Although the *trisvabhāva* theory is an integral part of the *Yogācāra* system, as Dol po pa pointed out it is also found in some of the *Prajñāpāramitāsūtras.* In Tibet this fact had important hermeneutical implications for the understanding of the development of Indian Buddhist doctrine. In particular, what might be called the "orthodox" Tibetan view of the Three Turnings of the *Dharmacakra* was challenged by the presence of this theory in the *Prajñāpāramitāsūtra.*[220]

The presence of the three-nature doctrines in the Perfection of Wisdom Sūtras was evidence, for Döl-bo Shay-rap-gyel-tsen, of a system hinted at by Indian authors of an ontologically substantial

[220] Stearns, 136.

ultimate — an "other-emptiness"[221] — that transcends the so-called "self-emptiness"[222] usually associated with the Middle Way School. According to Stearns, this innovative hermeneutic by Döl-b̄o S̄hay-rap-gyel-tsen draws from discussions of the three natures expounded in the *Bṛhaṭṭīkā*[223] commentary on the Perfection of Wisdom Sūtras.

Döl-b̄o S̄hay-rap-gyel-tsen drew not only on the Perfection of Wisdom Sūtras, but also on treatise literature. For instance, his *Ocean of Definitive Meaning*[224] quotes Maitreya's *Treatise on the Later Scriptures of the Mahāyāna*[225] to the effect that the afflictions preventing Buddhahood do not exist as their own reality and thus the basic constituent (the *tathāgatagarbha*) has a pure nature of good qualities:

> Because of being fabricated [by conditions] and being adventitious,
> The faults [i.e., the afflictive emotions and so forth] of sentient beings do not [exist as their] own reality.
> In reality these faults are selfless

221 *gzhan stong.*

222 *rang stong.*

223 *'phags pa shes rab kyi pha rol tu phyin pa 'bum pa dang nyi khri lnga stong pa dang khri brgyad stong pa'i rgya cher bshad pa, ārya śatasāhasrikā pañcaviṃśatisāhasrikāṣṭādaśasāhasrikā prajñāpāramitā bṛhaṭṭīkā* (often attributed to Vasubhandu and called, *yum gsum gnod 'joms*), Tibetan Tripitika, Vol. 93: 202.1.1-339.3.6.

224 *ri chos nges don rgya mtso zhes bya ba'i bstan bcos dang bsdus don* (Bir: D. Tsondu Senghe, 1984).

225 Maitreya[nātha] (*byams mgon*), *theg pa chen po rgyud bla ma'i bstan bcos, mahāyānottaratantraśāstra*, P5525, with bracketed commentary by Mi-pam.

> [And thus the basic constituent has from the start] a pure
> nature of beneficent qualities.[226]

Döl-b̄o S̄hay-rap-gyel-tsen's understanding of the nature in the phrase, "a pure nature of beneficent qualities," is that it is the ultimate reality.

In D̄zong-ka-b̄a's system, the ultimate is a negative phenomena — the substrata that is the lack of the object-to-be-negated nature. It exists as one entity with its conventional truth. For Döl-b̄o S̄hay-rap-gyel-tsen, the nature is the Great Middle Way "other-emptiness;" an ultimate truth that is a substantially ontic *tathāgatagarbha*[227] present in all beings. On the conventional level, phenomena are empty of self nature;[228] they are actually non-existent. On the ultimate level exists the *tathāgatagarbha*, itself empty of other phenomena.[229] Stearns explains the situation succinctly:

> Dol po used the term *gzhan stong*, "empty of other," to describe absolute reality as empty of other relative phenomena. This view is Dol po's primary legacy...In Dol po's view the absolute and the relative are both empty, as Buddhism has always proclaimed, but they *must* be empty in different ways. Phenomena at the relative level (*saṃvṛti, kun dzob*) are empty

---

[226] *ri chos nges don rgya mtso zhes bya ba'i bstan bcos dang bsdus don*, 63.1. Commenting upon Maitreya's *theg pa chen po rgyud bla ma'i bstan bcos:*

> *bcos ma glo bur pa nyid phyir // sems can skyon de yang dag min // yang nyes de bdag med pa // yon tan rang bzhin dag pa yin //*

[227] The *Blue Annals* reports that the term "Natural Buddha" (*rang bzhin sangs rgyas*) is found in Döl-b̄o's *Fourth Council* (*Blue Annals*, 777).

[228] *rang stong, svabhāvaśūnya.*

[229] *gzhan stong, *parabhāvaśūnya.*

> of self-nature (*svabhāvaśūnya, rang stong*), and are no more real than the fictitious horn of a rabbit, or the child of a barren woman. In contrast, the reality of absolute truth (*paramārtha, don dam bden pa*) is empty only of other (**parabhāvaśūnya, gzhan stong*) relative phenomena, and not itself empty.[230]

Döl-b̄o identified the ultimate of this school with a substantially existent *tathāgatagarbha* inherent in everyone's continuum, having all the major and minor marks of a fully enlightened Buddha. This other-emptiness is a positive, independent, and enlightened nature within each individual's continuum.

Unlike the ultimate found in D̄zong-ka-b̄a's Consequentialist system, which is a negative — a mere lack of inherent existence — the Jo-nang ultimate is positive and independent. Although it is not a conventional consciousness, this other-emptiness is still gnosis. Stearns reports that Döl-b̄o describes this *tathāgatagarbha* to be "naturally luminous clear light, which is synonymous with the *dharmakāya*, and a primordial, indestructible, and eternal state of great bliss inherently present in all its glory within every living being."[231] Although this *tathāgatagarbha* which is *dharmakāya* is a gnosis, it is not impermanent, since it is the essential nature. Döl-b̄o's *Fourth Council* states:

> Therefore the Victors have stated, "Gnosis transcending the momentary is the ultimate essential nature of all *dharmas*."[232]

Stearns remarks that this quote from Döl-b̄o paraphrases the Kālachakra commentary, *Great Commentary on the "Kālachakra*

230 Stearns, 4.

231 Stearns, 125.

232 Stearns, quoting the autocommentary (*bka' bsdu bzhi pa'i rang 'grel*) 13a.

Tantra," *the Stainless Light*, [233] which states that, "Gnosis free from single and multiple moments is the essential nature of the Victors."[234] Stearns reports, moreover, that Döl-b̄o thinks of this gnosis in terms of its being a "wisdom basis of all":

> The *tathāgatagarbha* is the gnosis which is the ground or substratum (*kun gzhi ye shes, *ālayajñāna*) for every phenomenon experienced in *saṃsāra* and *nirvāṇa*.[235]

Thus, the nature asserted by the Jo-nang-b̄as is revealed here to be positive in that it is a consciousness. It is independent in the sense that it is absolute. Empty of all conventional phenomena, this nature is self-arisen, not a dependent-arising.

Döl-b̄o S̄hay-rap-gyel-tsen agrees with Nāgārjuna that nature must be non-fabricated. In his commentary on the *Treatise on the Middle* (XV.2) — in the *Ocean of Definitive Meaning* — Döl-b̄o places an interesting spin on Nāgārjuna's statement that "Nature is non-fabricated and does not depend on another." He states:[236]

> Nature is the Nature Body. This is because the statements [in the *Treatise on the Middle*] that "Nature is non-fabricated and does not depend on another," and "Change of a nature is never feasible" refer to the Sugatagarbha.[237]

---

[233] Kalkī Puṇḍarīka (*rigs ldan pad ma dkar po*), *Great Commentary on the "Kālachakra Tantra," the Stainless Light* (*bsdus pa'i rgyud kyi rgyal po dus kyi 'khor lo'i 'grel bshad rtsa ba'i rgyud kyi rjes su 'jug pa stong phrag bcu gnyis pa dri ma med pa'i 'od ces bya ba, vimālaprabhānāmamūlatantrānusāriṇīdvādaśasāhasrikālaghukālacakratantrarājaṭīkā*), P2064.

[234] Stearns, 178.

[235] Stearns, 125.

[236] *ri chos nges don rgya mtso zhes bya ba'i bstan bcos dang bsdus don* (Bir: D. Tsondu Senghe, 1984).

[237] *Ocean of Definitive Meanings*, 163.5:

Döl-b̄o S̄hay-rap-gyel-tsen's interpretation of these stanzas differs radically from that of D̄zong-ka-b̄a. Not subscribing to an ultimate beyond that of the Middle Way School emptiness, D̄zong-ka-b̄a asserts that the emptiness spoken of by Nāgārjuna is a negative phenomenon, one entity with its corresponding subject or base. Döl-b̄o S̄hay-rap-gyel-tsen thinks of the other-emptiness ultimate as an omniscient Buddha nature that is not any conventional phenomenon.

REFUTING THE INDEPENDENT AND POSITIVE NATURE

D̄zong-ka-b̄a devotes a section of the *Great Exposition of the Stages of the Path* to the refutation of an assertion by Döl-b̄o to the effect that nature is positive and independent:

> Some [i.e., the Jo-nang-b̄as following Döl-b̄o Shay-rap-gyel-tsen] did not posit the ultimate truth as a mere elimination of the elaborations of the two selves, the object-to-be-negated, and so forth. They asserted that when one realizes the ultimate mode of being, [that entity] appears — as the object of a non-erroneous mind — in the way that blue, yellow, and so forth appear in the manner of being established independently. They also asserted that the ascertainment of its existing in this way is the view realizing the profound meaning.
>
> Also, they assert that the realization of these external and internal phenomena — which are the bases that sentient beings misapprehend as the two selves — as not existent [by][238]

---

rang bzhin ni rang bzhin gyi sku ste rang bzhin dag ni bcos min dang gzhan la ltos pa med pa yin // rang bzhin gzhan du 'gyur pa ni nam yang 'thad pa ma yin no zhes pa bde gsheg snying po'o //

238 The particle *gyis* is inserted in the *MCHAN,* 405.6.

> nature, is a place for going astray with respect to the correct view (*lta ba'i gol sa*).[239]

Đzong-ka-ƀa himself holds that the ultimate truth is a mere negative of the elaboration of the two selves of persons and phenomena. It is the Geluk view that all Mind Only and Middle Way systems assert that negative phenomena must be imputedly existent. Jam-ȳang-shay-ƀa, writing in the *Four Interwoven Annotations,* states:

> In any Mind Only or Middle Way system a negative phenomenon must be imputedly existent;[240] therefore the assertion that reality is a positive independent phenomenon that does not depend upon the elimination of an object-to-be-negated is wrong.[241]

Therefore, the assertion that reality is positive and independent and does not depend upon the elimination of an object-to-be-negated goes against a basic Geluk tenet. Writing in the *Four In-*

---

239 *LRC,* 868.5-869.1:

> *gang dag don dam pa'i bden pa dgag bya bdag gnyis la sogs pa'i spros pa rnams par bcad pa tsam la mi 'jog par sngo ser la sogs pa ltar yin lugs rtogs pa'i blo ma 'khrul ba'i yul du rang dbang du grub pa'i tshul gyis 'char ba dang de ltar yod par nges pa ni zab mo'i don rtogs pa'i lta ba yin par 'dod cing sems can rnams kyis gang la bdag gnyis su zhen pa'i gzhi phyi nang gi chos 'di rnams rang bzhin med par rtogs pa ni yang dag pa'i lta ba'i gol sar 'dod pa //*

240 Jam-ȳang-shay-ƀa may be forgetting that in the Mind Only system, emptiness — a negative — is truly existent.

241 *MCHAN,* 405.1:

> *dbu sems su'i lugs la dgag pa la btags yod dgos pas dgag bya bcad pa la ma ltos pa'i rang bdang ba'i sgrub par 'dod pa mi 'thad //*

terwoven Annotations, Jam-ȳang-shay-b̄a provides further information:

> The Jo-nang-b̄as, who pretended[242] to take as their source the Kālacakra and Maitreya's *Treatise on the Later Scriptures of the Great Vehicle,*[243] or some Tibetans who profess to be wise,[244] did not posit the ultimate truth as a mere elimination of the elaborations of the two selves of persons and phenomena, the object-to-be-negated, and so forth. They asserted that even when one realizes the ultimate mode of being, that entity appears — as the object of a non-erroneous mind — in the way that blue, yellow, and so forth appear to the mind as unmixed diverse substances in the manner of its entity being established independently (*rang dbang du*), unmixed with any other, from its own side, and not dependent on another. They also asserted that what appears in this way exists in accordance with its appearance and that the ascertainment of its existing in this way is the final view realizing the profound meaning in the Kālacakra system and Asaṅga's system.

---

[242] The verb Jam-ȳang-shay-b̄a uses is *khul.* [405.1]. Chandra Das provides a paradigm sentence: "If you do not know, act the manner of knowing [i.e., pretend to know]" (*yang ma shes na shes khul byas*). Das, *Tibetan-English Dictionary* (New Delhi: Gaurav Publishing House, 1985), 149.

[243] Maitreya[nātha] (*byams mgon*), *theg pa chen po rgyud bla ma'i bstan bcos, mahāyānottaratantraśāstra,* P5525.

[244] These two identifications are by different annotators:

(1) Jam-ȳang-shay-b̄a's note says, "The Jo-nang-b̄as, who pretended to take as their source the Kālacakra and Maitreya's *Treatise on the Later Scriptures of the Great Vehicle*" (*jo nang pas dus 'khor dang rgyud bla ma'i khung byed khul gyi*) [405.1]

(2) Nga-w̄ang-rap-d̄en's note says, "some Tibetans who

> Also, they assert that the realization by Nāgārjuna, Haribhadra, and so forth, of these external and internal phenomena — which are the bases that sentient beings misapprehend as the two selves of persons and phenomena — as not existent by nature (*rang bzhin gyis med pa*), is a view of annihilation and a place for going astray with respect to the correct view (*lta ba'i gol sa*).[245]

The annotators add their opinion that the Jo-nang-b̄a view is the result of a mistaken syncretistic mixture of the Kālacakra Tantra and Maitreya's *Treatise on the Later Scriptures of the Mahāyāna.*

---

profess to be wise" (*bod kyi mkhas par khas 'che ba*) [405.1-2].

[245] *MCHAN*, 405.1-405.5:

> *jo nang pas dus 'khor dang rgyud bla ma'i khungs byed khul gyi pod kyi mkhas par khas 'ches ba gang dag don dam pa'i bden pa dgag bya chos dang gang zag gi bdag gnyis la sogs pa'i spros pa rnams par bcad pa tsam zhig la mi 'jog par sngo ser la sogs pa rdzas so so ma 'dres pa blo la shar ba ltar don dam par yin gnas lugs rtogs pa'i tshe na'ang blo ma 'khrul ba'i yul du kho rang gi ngo bo gzhan dang ma 'dres par yul steng nas gzhan la ltos med du rang dbang du grub pa'i tshul gyis 'char bar 'dod pa dang gang shar ba de ltar du yod pa yin la de ltar yod par nges pa ni dus 'khor dang thogs med kyi lugs kyi zab mo'i don rtogs pa'i lta ba mthar thug yin par 'dod cing klu sgrub dang seng bzang sogs kyis sems can rnams kyis gang la gang zag dang chos kyi bdag gnyis su zhen pa'i gzhir gyur pa'i phyi nang gi chos 'di rnams rang bzhin gyis med par rtogs pa ni chad lta dang yang dag pa'i lta ba'i gol sa* [...] *r 'dod pa //*

I have omitted from the quotation a gloss on the phrase "place for going astray with respect to the correct view" (*lta ba'i gol sa*). In brief, according to the *MCHAN,* the phrase "place for going astray with respect to the correct view" comes to mean "direction opposite to the correct view" (*yang dag pa'i lta ba'i log phyogs*). For the full citation see page 217.

The Jo-nang-b̄a position as stated here in the *Four Interwoven Annotations* is that the ultimate entity, when perceived by a non-erroneous mind (i.e., a Superior's uncontaminated meditative equipoise), appears in the way that diverse substances appear to the mind as if (1) unmixed, like blue and yellow, (2) on the side of the object, (3) independent, and (4) established under its own power.[246]

D̄zong-ka-b̄a finds these doctrines so heterodox as to be non-Buddhist. The *Great Exposition of the Stages of the Path* states:

> Such assertions are outside the sphere of all the scriptures of the Greater and Lesser Vehicles because (1) those [Jo-nang-b̄as] assert that it is necessary to overcome the conception of self that is the root binding persons in cyclic existence, and (2) the bases that are apprehended by this [conception] as self are these [phenomena] realized as not existent by nature. Hence, without overcoming that, they assert that the conception of self is overcome through realizing some other phenomenon unrelated with that [conception of self] as true.[247]

D̄zong-ka-b̄a makes the point that the Jo-nang-b̄as themselves assert that individuals must overcome the conception of inherent

---

[246] Further research is required to determine whether this is a correct assessment of Döl-b̄o Shay-rap-gyel-tsen's thought. Our focus here is on the Geluk response to an assertion about nature which they perceived as being heterodox.

[247] *LRC*, 869.1-3:

> *theg pa che chung gi gsung rab thams cad las phyi rol tu gyur pa yin te sems can thams cad 'khor bar ching ba'i rtsa ba bdag du 'dzin pa sdog dgos par ni 'dod la des bdag tu bzung ba'i gzhi de rang bzhin med par rtogs pas de mi ldog par de dang 'brel med kyi chos gzhan zhig bden par song bar rtogs pas bdag tu 'dzin pa ldog par 'dod pa'i phyir ro //*

existence to free themselves from cyclic existence. Although they assert this, they attempt to reverse the conception of self *not through realizing the lack of the object-to-be-negated nature* but instead through realizing some other, unrelated phenomenon.

Although Dzong-ka-ba and the annotators of the *Four Interwoven Annotations* do not establish either of these points with a quotation from Döl-bo Shay-rap-gyel-tsen, Dzong-ka-ba does present an analogy that aptly describes the situation as he sees it:

> Regarding this, for instance, it is no different than if [some person] conceives there is a snake to the east and becomes distressed, and if [someone else] thinking the distress cannot be overcome by thinking there is no snake to the east — instead says, "Think on the fact that to the west there is a tree. Through this, you will get rid of your conception of a snake in the room and will overcome your distress."[248]

In this analogy the snake in the east is the object-to-be-negated nature, the cause of fear and distress. For Dzong-ka-ba, putting forth the other-emptiness of Döl-bo Shay-rap-gyel-tsen is akin to speaking of a tree in the west to dispell the conception of the snake in the east — it is completely beside the point. This analogy helps Dzong-ka-ba clarify his primary point: the positive, independent nature spoken of by Döl-bo Shay-rap-gyel-tsen is not a Mahāyāna assertion because Mahāyāna ultimates are negative phenomena.

---

[248] *LRC,* 869.3-6:

> *dper na shar phyogs na sbrul med bzhin du yod par bzung nas skrag ste sdug bsngal bar gyur ba'i sdug bsngal ldog pa la shar phyogs su sbrul cung zad kyang ma grub po snyam du bzung bas sbrul 'dzin de mi ldog gi nub phyogs na shings dong yod do snyam du zungs shig dang dras sbrul 'dzin dang sdug bsngal de sdog par 'gyur ro zhes zer ba dang khyad par ci yang mi snang ngo //*

Döl-b̄o Shay-rap-gyel-tsen's positive, independent ultimate violates these criteria. Moreover, D̄zong-ka-b̄a believes that realization of it does not address the main issue of Buddhist soteriology: abandoning the conception of inherent existence that underlies all afflictive emotions. Instead, D̄zong-ka-b̄a says, Döl-b̄o Shay-rap-gyel-tsen's ultimate involves an unrelated topic, as unrelated to the realization of emptiness as thinking about a tree in the west is unrelated to a snake in the east.

5 NĀGĀRJUNA AND HIS DETRACTORS

Monks, do not lament after I am gone, for all karmically constituted things are subject to disintegration.

— *Mahāparinirvāṇasūtra*

TRIVIALIZING NĀGĀRJUNA

Robinson and Hayes are two of the greatest modern scholars of Mādhyamika. Nevertheless, they share a hostile presentation of Nāgārjuna, accusing him of being a philosophical charlatan who employed fallacious and misleading methods. How can their conclusions regarding this philosopher be so different from those of millions of Buddhists who have revered Nāgārjuna for centuries? The answer is that their conclusions are based on six assumptions about Nāgārjuna's methodology not shared by D̄zong-ka-b̄a. Robinson and Hayes believe the following:

(1) Nāgārjuna is primarily concerned with refuting opponents' views.
(2) Nāgārjuna defines his opponents' views in a self-contradictory axiomatic way.
(3) Nāgārjuna's axioms are at variance with common sense.
(4) Nāgārjuna's axioms need to be accepted in their entirety by other philosophies but are not.
(5) Nāgārjuna uses the term *svabhāva* in ways that none of his opponents do.
(6) Nāgārjuna uses the term *svabhāva* in several different senses at key points in his argument.

To adopt for a moment Je D̄zong-ka-b̄a's point of view, these six assumptions about Nāgārjuna can be refuted under three topic headings:

(1) Nāgārjuna is not primarily concerned with refuting opponents' views, but instead with refuting innate ignorant misconceptions. This argument shows that Nāgārjuna does not define his opponents' views in a self-contradictory axiomatic way.

(2) Nāgārjuna does not employ axioms that are at variance with common sense because he employs the putative consequences of inherent existence as evidence of *svabhāva*. This argument shows that Nāgārjuna's "axioms" need not be accepted by other philosophical schools.

(3) Nāgārjuna does not use the term *svabhāva* in several different senses at key points in his argument because in the *Treatise on the Middle* Chapter XV.1-2, Nāgārjuna consistently uses the term *svabhāva* to refer to the reality nature. This argument shows why Robinson and Hayes are wrong in criticizing Nāgārjuna for using the term *svabhāva* in ways that none of his opponents do.

Let us look into each of these topics in order to see Dzong-ka-ba's opposing viewpoints regarding Nāgārjuna's aims and methods.

NĀGĀRJUNA IS NOT PRIMARILY CONCERNED WITH REFUTING OPPONENTS' VIEWS

A number of Richard Robinson's conclusions in his article "Did Nāgārjuna Really Refute All Philosophical Views" are based on the assumption that Nāgārjuna's dialectic is mainly concerned with refuting the views of other Indian Buddhist or non-Buddhist philosophical schools. Robinson states:

> The validity of Nāgārjuna's refutations hinges upon whether his opponents really upheld the existence of a *svabhāva* or *svabhāva* as he defines the term.[249]

---

[249] Robinson, 326.

Although Robinson is convinced that Nāgārjuna's dialectic is mainly focused upon refuting the systems of other philosophical schools, Je D̄zong-ka-b̄a and his followers do not mainly discuss Nāgārjuna's dialectic in the context of its refuting other schools' views. Instead, they feel his dialectic is designed logically to undermine the conceived object of innate ignorance — the conception that things are inherently existent.

In evidence of that, the *Great Exposition* praises Nāgārjuna's texts in terms of their commenting on the profound meaning, emptiness, and not in terms of refuting other schools. The *Great Exposition* states:

> Since the Superior Nāgārjuna, renowned in the three levels, was very clearly prophesied by Buddha, the Supramundane Victor himself, in many sūtras and tantras as commenting on the profound meaning free from all extremes of existence and non-existence, the essence of the teaching, you should seek the view realizing emptiness based on his texts.[250]

For D̄zong-ka-b̄a, Nāgārjuna's texts demonstrate a view that is capable of dispelling the innate ignorance that binds beings to cyclic existence. The *Great Exposition* says:

> When the view is delineated, one is to consider the refutation of the conceived object of innate ignorance to be the main point.[251]

Thus, in D̄zong-ka-b̄a's opinion, Nāgārjuna is refuting the conceived object of innate ignorance, not the learned or artificial tenets of some erroneous school of thought. This is an important aspect of Buddhist soteriology, and thus Nāgārjuna's analyses are an important aspect of the Buddhist path.

---

[250] *DAE,* 159. *LRC,* 766.3.

[251] *LRC,* 391.1.

Further discussion showing that Nāgārjuna is refuting innate ignorance and not primarily refuting philosophical schools is presented in D̄zong-ka-b̄a's *Essence of Eloquence.* In his commentary on that, the *Interwoven Annotations on the Difficult Points of the Essence of Eloquence,*[252] D̄a-ḍin-rap-d̄en[253] (1920-1986) states:

> All the ultimate analysis of the Middle Way School is said to be solely for the purpose of uprooting the mode of apprehension of the ignorance which is the root of cyclic existence. Having identified how this ignorance exists in one's own continuum, make effort for the sake of refuting just that [ignorance]. Do not admire those scholars who are mere sophists and propounders of tenets.[254]

The question of whether — here in his discussion of nature — Nāgārjuna is primarily refuting philosophical schools or not is an important one. If Nāgārjuna *is* primarily refuting philosophical schools, then, as Robinson remarks, "The validity of Nāgārjuna's refutations hinges upon whether his opponents really upheld the existence of a *svabhāva* or *svabhāva* as he defines the term."[255] However, if D̄zong-ka-b̄a is correct in assuming that Nāgārjuna is refuting the innate ignorance misconceiving a self, then there is no necessity that Nāgārjuna's points be accepted by other philosophical schools.

---

[252] *drang nges rnam 'byed legs bshad snying po dka' gnad rnams mchan bur bkod pa gzur gnas blo gsal dga' ston* (Delhi: Lhun-grub-chos-grags, 1978).

[253] *rta mgrin rab brtan.*

[254] *Interwoven Annotations on the Difficult Points of the Essence of Eloquence,* 363.2.

[255] Robinson, 326.

NĀGĀRJUNA DOES NOT EMPLOY AXIOMS BUT RATHER THE PUTATIVE CONSEQUENCES OF INHERENT EXISTENCE

Je Dzong-ka-ba's *Great Exposition* implies that Nāgārjuna's texts are capable of dispelling the innate ignorance that binds beings to cyclic existence. From his perspective, Nāgārjuna's texts do this, in part, by positing the consequences of inherent existence, and then searching for these putative qualities in things. Putative consequences such as simultaneity and so forth are not themselves inherent existence, but rather serve as evidence of the presence of inherent existence.[256]

The identification and use of these putative consequences of inherent existence can perhaps best be demonstrated by referring to their employment in the refutation of true production known as the diamond chips[257] — sometimes referred to as "refuting production by the four extreme [types]."[258] The diamond chips presents a tetralemmic refutation of the mode of subsistence of production, and is derived from Chapter I of Nāgārjuna's *Treatise on the Middle*, called "Analysis of Conditionality."[259] The investigation into production is useful not only for its insights into the nature of production, but also for the study of Nāgārjuna's use of putative consequences of inherent existence. This is because the diamond chips clearly and vividly demonstrates the process of ul-

---

[256] As for inherent existence itself, Dzong-ka-ba describes that as a "thing's establishment by way of its own entity" (*rang gi ngo bos grub pa*). See page 91.

[257] *rdo rje gzegs ma.*

[258] *mtha' bzhi skye 'gog.*

[259] *rkyen brtag pa, pratyaya-parīkṣā.* Stanzas from Chapter XX, "Investigation of Collections" (*tshogs brtag pa, sāmagrī-parikṣā*), are also important in later Middle Way treatises on production.

timate analysis through conducting an exhaustive search for the putative consequences of inherently existent production.

The diamond chips refutes inherent existence by refuting that things have inherent production from (1) causes that are either the same as their effects, or (2) other than their effects, or (3) both, or (4) production without causes. Ruegg identifies this type of four-cornered reasoning as a tetralemma (*catuṣkoṭi*) in which:

> ...the nature of a postulated entity and its relation to a predicate is investigated in such a way that all conceptually imaginable positions are exhausted; for an entity and its predicate can be conceptually related only in terms of these four limiting positions.[260]

In the case of the refutation of production by the four extreme types, the "nature of a postulated entity" is inherently existent things and its relation to a predicate is that these must be produced from self, other, both, or causelessly. The thesis, that things are not inherently produced, has the meaning of the emptiness discoursed upon by the Buddha in the Perfection of Wisdom Sūtras. Geshe Gendun Lodrö and Kensur Lekden both state that the four extreme types are individually theses which are non-affirming negatives:

> They do not imply anything positive in their place, such as the existence of no production from self. Still, they do imply another non-affirming negative — that things are not inherently produced.[261]

Thus, according to Geluk scholars, the diamond chips reasoning establishes a non-affirming negative phenomenon, which is the

---

[260] D. S. Ruegg, "The Uses of the Four Positions of the Catuṣkoṭi and the Problem of the Description of Reality in Mahāyāna Buddhism," *Journal of Indian Philosophy*, Vol. 5 no. 1 (1977), 1.

[261] *MED*, 133.

absence of true production of a thing from self, other, both, and causelessly. It does not establish any positive phenomenon, such as imputed production of a thing, but it does establish a concomitant negative, that things are not inherently produced.

The diamond chips offers many examples of the analytical process that identifies the putative consequences of inherent existence and searches for these as evidence of inherent existence. To give one example of such a clear Geluk usage of putative consequences, in the *Annotations*, Nga-w̄ang-b̄el-den refutes inherently existent production from other in part with the reasoning that cause and effect would have to be simultaneous. The *Annotations* states:

> The two, seed and sprout, are not inherently established others because a sprout is not simultaneous with the seed. There is entailment because, if something exists inherently, its time is never abolished, and hence, the sprout would have to exist even at the time of the seed.[262]

Here it is explicitly noted that the presence or absence of simultaneity — a putative quality of inherently existent production — is taken as evidence for the presence or absence of inherent existence itself. The analysis concludes that since inherent things must always exist, there would be simultaneity of seed and sprout. Because such simultaneity is not seen, the analysis concludes that seed and sprout are not inherently existent others. This example, using the putative consequence of the simultaneity of seed and sprout, is similar to the way other putative consequences — im-

---

[262] The *Annotations, dbu,* Note *tsha,* 143.5-6:

> *sa myug gnyis rang bzhin gyis grub pa'i gzhan min te myu gu sa bon dang dus mnyam du med pa'i phyir // khyab ste rang bzhin gyis grub pa yin na dus nam yang ldog pa med pas myu gu de sa bon gyi dus su'ang yod dgos pa'i phyir //*

mutability, visible entities of otherness, endless production, darkness arising from a flame, and so forth — are used to refute true production.

The four refutations of true production from self, other, both, and causelessly are able to prove that things are not inherently produced because these four represent all possibilities of true production. This is what Ruegg means when he states, "The predicate is investigated in such a way that all conceptually imaginable positions are exhausted; for an entity and its predicate can be conceptually related only in terms of these four limiting positions."[263]

According to typical Geluk exegesis, although the tetralemma exhausts possibilities of extreme types of production for causes and effects that are inherently existent, it is not exhaustive regarding possibilities for production in general. This is because the tetralemma does not include within its analytical scope the search for conventionally existent production from other. Conventionally existent production of effects from causes that are merely conventionally other is not refuted by the diamond chips because the diamond chips is an ultimate analytical reasoning. From Geluk perspectives, the presence or absence of the putative consequences of inherent existence — which are the objects searched for by the diamond chips — are not evidence of the presence or absence of imputed production that exists only conventionally. Imputed production from other is the only type of production that Geluks assert.

Does such unsubstantial production as imputed production really count as production? Radhakrishnan recognizes that Proponents of the Middle do not just posit a dichotomy of inherent existence and non-existence but assert a middle way of depen-

---

[263] Ruegg, "Uses of the Four Positions," 1.

dently-arisen existence. He states the position of Proponents of the Middle this way:

> There is no real production (*samutpāda*), but only conditioned (*pratītya*), relative, apparent production.[264]

Radhakrishnan's "relative, apparent production" is similar to conventional or nominal production as presented in Geluk texts, for this is the sort of production that Geluk Consequentialists assert is not negated by the four-cornered reasoning. For Geluk Consequentialists, an utter refutation of production would be an extreme of annihilation, since it would be a deprecation of something that exists conventionally.

According to the followers of D̄zong-ka-b̄a's system, Nāgārjuna does not define self-contradictory views for opponents as Robinson suggests, because the axioms Robinson observes Nāgārjuna using are not axioms at all, but rather the putative consequences of inherent existence.

For instance, Robinson identifies three putative consequences of inherent existence from Nāgārjuna's text but identifies them as philosophical "axioms." Robinson notes that according to these axioms, phenomena possessing *svabhāva* must be:

(1) indivisible,
(2) manifest, and
(3) existent in isolation from all others.[265]

Robinson scorns these three points as philosophical "axioms" and accuses Nāgārjuna of employing them dishonestly.

---

[264] Radhakrishnan, *Indian Philosophy* (London: George Allen and Unwin, 1923), Vol. I, 698.

[265] This list is taken from Robinson's list of six axioms in "Did Nāgārjuna Really Refute All Philosophical Views," 327.

Geluks do not share this opinion, since they take these "axioms" to be putative consequences of inherent existence, to be searched for as evidence of inherent existence. Because Robinson has taken these putative consequences to be philosophical "axioms," he misses the point of the Geluk view that Nāgārjuna is identifying the hypothetical outflows of inherent existence.

NĀGĀRJUNA DOES NOT USE THE TERM SVABHĀVA *IN SEVERAL DIFFERENT SENSES*

Richard Robinson accuses Nāgārjuna of faulty argumentation: specifically, of using the fallacy of equivocation in Chapter XV of the *Treatise on the Middle.* Hayes elaborates by accusing Nāgārjuna of intellectual dishonesty:

> To the various fallacies and tricks brought to light by Robinson in his articles, we can now add the informal fallacy of equivocation as outlined above. That is, not only did Nāgārjuna use the term "svabhāva" in ways that none of his opponents did, but he himself used it in several different senses at key points in his argument.[266]

Hayes' first point is that none of Nāgārjuna's opponents define the word *svabhāva* in just the ways Hayes feels Nāgārjuna defines it: as (1) a thing's own, distinct "nature that no other simple property has," i.e., its identity[267] and as (2) the causally independent nature:

> ...the word "svabhāva" can be interpreted in two different ways. It can be rendered either as *identity* (which I shall call $svabhāva_1$) or as *causal independence* ($svabhāva_2$).[268]

Although Hayes does not explicitly say so, it appears that he feels

---

[266] Hayes, 325.

[267] Hayes, 311.

[268] Hayes, 312.

that when Nāgārjuna speaks of the "causally independent" *svabhāva* in Chapter XV.2, he is referring to a non-existent nature. Regarding this nature, Hayes says:

> Nāgārjuna observed that a being that has identity (*prakṛti, svabhāva*) cannot undergo change. Add this to the ābhidharma conclusion that the change of complex beings is a derivative idea rather than a primitive fact of the world, and one arrives at Theorem 2: nothing can undergo the process of change.[269]

Hayes feels that Nāgārjuna's statement that a nature must be immutable implies that there are no phenomena that are mutable. Thus, Nāgārjuna speaks of a nature to be negated by the dialectic. Further evidence that Hayes believes Nāgārjuna speaks of a non-existent nature is that he concurs with Robinson's statement that "It is absurd to maintain that a *svabhāva* [mentioned by Nāgārjuna in XV.2] exists."[270]

From D̄zong-ka-b̄a's point of view, Hayes is misidentifying Nāgārjuna's intended meaning of *svabhāva.* In contradistinction to Hayes' belief that Nāgārjuna speaks equivocably of an identity nature and a causally independent, non-existent nature, D̄zong-ka-b̄a feels that in Chapter XV.1-2 Nāgārjuna uses the term *svabhāva* to refer to an existent emptiness nature. The *Great Exposition* states:

> [*Objection:*] When the Master Nāgārjuna set forth non-fabrication and non-dependence on another as the characteristics of the entity of nature, did he speak hypothetically or does such a nature exist in fact?
>
> *Response:* The reality which is mentioned [in the Perfection of Wisdom Sūtras] in the phrase "whether the Tathāga-

---

269 Hayes, 307.

270 Hayes, 324, quoting Robinson, 326.

> tas appear or not the reality of phenomena [just abides]"[271] is posited as the nature. This is non-fabricated and does not depend on another. That nature does exist.[272]

Candrakīrti shares this view that Nāgārjuna is speaking of emptiness as being non-fabricated, independent, and immutable. However, the existent reality nature to which Candrakīrti and Dzong-ka-ba feel Nāgārjuna is referring is not one of the two meanings of *svabhāva* that Hayes puts forth as Nāgārjuna's intent. Since Candrakīrti and Dzong-ka-ba see Nāgārjuna as consistently referring to emptiness with the word *svabhāva*, they do not see him to be guilty of the fault of equivocation.

CONCLUSIONS

As the above sections have shown, Robinson's and Hayes' three crucial assumptions about Nāgārjuna are not shared by Je Dzong-ka-ba. From the Geluk perspective, Nāgārjuna is seeking to demonstrate how phenomena exist for a soteriological purpose. To ignore Dzong-ka-ba's explanation of the soteriological implications of Nāgārjuna's dialectic is to trivialize Nāgārjuna.

We have also seen that Dzong-ka-ba presents his discussion of nature as if it were just Candrakīrti's. Nevertheless, it cannot be denied that Dzong-ka-ba is an innovative thinker whose assertions about reality go beyond Candrakīrti. The question remains: which of Dzong-ka-ba's assertions about nature originate with Candrakīrti and which are innovations originating in Tibet with Dzong-ka-ba himself?

---

271 Alex Wayman places this scriptural source in the *Sūtra on the Ten Grounds* (*mdo sde sa bcu pa, daśabhūmikasūtra,* P761.31). He cites the Rahder edition, sixth *bhūmi*, 65.

272 *LRC,* 863.2-6.

In the course of his discussion of the meaning of Nāgārjuna's verses on nature, D̄zong-ka-b̄a makes the following points:

(1) The triply-qualified nature mentioned in the *Treatise on the Middle* (XV) refers to a reality nature, emptiness.

(2) The reality nature is a mere lack of the object-to-be-negated and therefore a negative phenomenon (*dgag pa, pratiṣedha*).

(3) That the triply-qualified nature refers to the object-to-be-negated is a misrepresentation of the Consequence School's uncommon object-to-be-negated (*mthun mongs ma yin pa'i dgag bya*).

(4) The triply-qualified nature is not the Consequence School's uncommon object-to-be-negated because (1) the Hearer schools refute such and (2) the apprehension of such is merely a learned or artificial conception of self (*bdag 'dzin kun btags*) and not the innate conception of self.

(5) The Consequence School's uncommon object-to-be-negated is a thing's "establishment by way of its own nature" (*rang gi ngo bos grub pa*).

Only the first and the last of these points are explicitly made by Candrakīrti: (1) The triply-qualified nature mentioned in the *Treatise on the Middle* (XV) refers to a reality nature, emptiness. The *Clear Words* (see page 147) states that the triply-qualified nature refers to emptiness:

> What is this nature? It is emptiness. What is this emptiness? It is the lack of nature. What is this lack of nature? It is suchness. What is this suchness? It is that entity of suchness that does not change and always abides. For, that which is not produced in any way, because of not being fabricated and because of not relying on another, is called the nature of fire and so forth.

And (5) the Consequence School's uncommon object-to-be-negated is a thing's "establishment by way of its own nature." In his *Commentary on (Āryadeva's) "Four Hundred,"* in the context of a discussion of desire, Candrakīrti states that desire is empty because it is "not established by way of its own entity."[273]

Except for these two points, Dzong-ka-ba's presentation of nature differs considerably from that of Candrakīrti. Among these differences is that (1) Dzong-ka-ba explicitly describes emptiness as an existent negative, (2) he identifies the object-to-be-negated in terms of avoiding views that are too broad or narrow, (3) he denounces unnamed opponents for mistaking Nāgārjuna's triply-qualified nature as the object of innate ignorance, and (4) he rejects the idea of a positive, independent nature.

Our investigation must conclude that portions of the Geluk exegetical enterprise commenting upon the topic of nature go beyond what is explicitly stated in the *Treatise on the Middle.* Nevertheless, other interpretations of the text seem to be justifiably obvious extensions of Nāgārjuna's meaning. Dzong-ka-ba makes a strong case for his doctrines and also for their conformity to the underlying meaning of the *Treatise on the Middle,* but we must not forget that along with his philosophical need to avoid identifying an object-to-be-negated that negates too little, he also has a partisan agenda: he must identify for the Consequentialists an object-to-be-negated that is more subtle than that identified in other schools. He must do so even if it means adjusting the subtlety of an object-to-be-negated which, after all, is not clearly identified in Candrakīrti's text.

---

[273] See the *Four Hundred,* 229.4.8. *'dod pa rang gi ngo bos ma grup pa'i phyir stong pa yin.* Further research will probably unearth other instances.

Ḏzong-ka-ḇa's precise identification of the object-to-be-negated is as central to his philosophical method as is his search for the putative consequences of inherent existence with ultimate analysis. Candrakīrti does not perform such an identification, although he does search for the putative consequences of inherent existence.

Ḏzong-ka-ḇa is both an innovator and a fairly strict follower of Candrakīrti's Middle Way thought. Whether one is pleased with Ḏzong-ka-ḇa's innovations or feels them to be distortions of Nāgārjuna's original thought, one can still admire Ḏzong-ka-ḇa's and Candrakīrti's brilliant theoretical extensions of Nāgārjuna's *svabhāva* theory.

PART TWO: TRANSLATIONS OF THE TEXTS

In order to provide textual support for D̄zong-ka-b̄a's discussion of *svabhāva*, Part Two of this book provides translations of portions of five texts important to his lineage:

(1) Nāgārjuna's *Treatise on the Middle,* Chapter XV: "The Analysis of Nature" (page 134). In the *Treatise*, Nāgārjuna scrutinizes a variety of phenomena — motion, production, cause and effect, and so forth — to demonstrate that phenomena cannot be found under analysis. Phenomena that cannot be found under analysis must be empty of inherent existence, or own-being (*svabhāva*). In Chapter XV, Nāgārjuna discusses own-being itself and also rejects the notion that a nature can be fabricated.

(2) Candrakīrti's commentary on XV in the *Clear Words* (page 141). In this influential commentary, Candrakīrti demonstrates that the nature of fire is not heat, and also identifies the non-fabricated nature as emptiness (*dharmatā*).

(3) D̄zong-ka-b̄a's *Ocean of Reasonings*[274] Chapter XV (page 159), explains the text of Nāgārjuna's

[274] Composed in 1407. Dates are taken from *DAE,* 6-7 and Leonard W. J. van der Kuijp, "Apropos of a Recent Contribution to the History of Central Way Philosophy in Tibet: *Tsong Khapa's Speech of Gold* in *Berliner Indologische Studien* (Reinbek: Verlag für Orientalistische

Chapter XV in terms of emptiness being a negative, yet existent, phenomena that is the absence of establishment by way of a thing's own entity. Dzong-ka-ba gives the defining character of nature when he says, "It is the entity of phenomena, and entity is nature; nature is emptiness; and emptiness is the lack of nature; that [lack of nature] is suchness; and that [suchness] immutably and always abides as the entity of suchness.

(4) Dzong-ka-ba's *Great Exposition of the Stages of the Path* is not a commentary on Nāgārjuna's *Treatise*, but rather a meditation manual. Nevertheless, Chapter XV is treated during identification of the object-to-be-negated. There, Dzong-ka-ba criticizes those Tibetans who do not follow Candrikīrti's explanation of nature as emptiness. He refutes their contention that nature is the illusion that things are non-fabricated, independent, and immutable in his section entitled "The Refutation of an Identification of the Object-to-be-negated That Is Too Narrow"[275] (page 179).

(5) An interwoven commentary — entitled *Four Interwoven Annotations* — on Dzong-ka-ba's *Great Exposition of the Stages of the Path,* "The Refutation of an Identification of the Object-to-be-

---

Fachpublikationen, 1985), 68, n. 2. Kay-drup's biography sets the date at 1418 (120.9-120.20). See *DAE,* 648.

[275] *dgag bya ngos 'dzin khyab chungs ba dgag pa* [860.4-870.1]. According to A-gya-yong-dzin, the *Great Exposition* was composed in 1402. A-gya-yong-dzin (*dbyangs can dga' ba'i blo gros, a kya yongs 'dzin,* 18th century), *A Brief Explanation of Terminology Occuring in* (*Dzong-ka-ba's*) *"Great Exposition of the Stages of the Path"* (*byang chub lam gyi rim pa chen mo las byungs ba'i brda bkrol nyer mkho bsdus pa*), 82.3. Tibetan dates converted to the Julian calendar in *DAE,* 644.

negated That Is Too Narrow"[276] (page 193). This useful commentary is a composite by four later Geluk authors, Jam-ȳang-shay-b̄a (1648-1721),[277] Ba-so Chö-gyi-gyel-tsen (1402-1473),[278] De-druk-ken-chen Nga-w̄ang-rap-den (17th century),[279] and Dra-di Ge-shay Rin-chen-dön-drup (17th century).[280] Although these authors do not depart significantly from D̄zong-ka-b̄a's interpretation of Candrakīrti, they do provide a wealth of grammatical elaboration and scholarly referencing that is always useful and sometimes necessary for understanding D̄zong-ka-b̄a's text.

---

276 *dgag bya ngos 'dzin khyab chungs ba dgag pa* [386.6-408.1].

277 *'jam dbyangs bzhad pa.*

278 *ba so chos kyi rgyal mtshan.*

279 *sde drug mkhan chen ngag dbang rab rten.*

280 *bra sti dge bshes rin chen don grub.*

DOCUMENT ONE:
NĀGĀRJUNA'S TREATISE ON THE MIDDLE
CHAPTER XV: "THE ANALYSIS OF NATURE"

The following English translation of Chapter XV is extracted from the translation of the *Clear Words* commentary presented below as Document Two. The Sanskrit text is taken from J.W. de Jong, ed., *Nāgārjuna, Mūlamadyamakakārikāḥ* (Adyar: Adyar Library and Research Centre, 1977), pp. 19-20. The Tibetan text is from the Peking edition, P5224, Vol. 95, 6.3.1-6.4.1.

ENGLISH TEXT

I

The arising of nature due to causes and conditions is
not reasonable.
A nature produced by causes and conditions would have
a nature of fabrication.

II

How could nature be said to be fabricated?
Nature is non-fabricated and does not depend on
another.

III

When there is no own-being, how could there be other-
being?
For an own-being of other-being is said to be an
[other-]being.

IV

Where again is being apart from own-being and other-
being?
And if there is own-being or other-being, being would
be established.

V

If there is no establishment of being, non-being also is not established.
People call non-being the change of being.

VI

Those who see own-being, other-being, being, and non-being
Do not see the suchness in the Buddha's teaching.

VII

The Blessed One, knowing being and non-being,
Refuted in the *Advice to Kātyāyana* both existence and non-existence.

VIII

If there were existence by way of nature, there would not be a non-existence of it.
Change of a nature is never feasible.

IX

If there is no nature, of what would there be change?
If nature did exist, how could change be suitable?

X

Saying "exists" is a conception of permanence; saying "does not exist" is a view of annihilation.
Therefore, the wise do not abide in existence or non-existence.

XI

Whatever exists by way of its nature is permanent since it does not become non-existent.
If you say that what arose formerly [by way of its nature] is now non-existent, through that [an extreme] of annihilation is entailed.

SANSKRIT TEXT

I

na saṃbhavaḥ svabhāvasya yuktaḥ pratyayahetubhiḥ //
hetupratyayasaṃbhūtaḥ svabhāvaḥ kṛtako bhavet //

II

svabhāvaḥ kṛtako nāma bhaviṣyati punaḥ katham //
akṛtrimaḥ svabhāvo hi nirapekṣaḥ paratra ca //

III

kutaḥ svabhāvasyābhāve parabhāvo bhaviṣyati //
svabhāvaḥ parabhāvasva parabhāvo hi kathyate //

IV

svabhāvaparabhāvābhyām ṛte bhāvaḥ kutaḥ punaḥ //
svabhāve parabhāve ca sati bhāvo hi sidhyati //

V

bhāvasya ced aprasiddhir abhāvo naiva sidhyati //
bhāvasya hy anyathābhāvam abhāvaṃ bruvate janāḥ //

VI

svabhāvaṃ parabhāvaṃ ca bhāvaṃ cābhāvam eva ca //
ye paśyanti na paśyanti te tattvaṃ buddhaśāsane //

VII

kātyāyanāvavāde cāstīti nāstīti cobhayam //
pratiṣiddhaṃ bhagavatā bhāvabhāvavibhāvinā //

VIII

yady astitvaṃ prakṛtyā syān na bhaved asya nāstitā //
prakṛter anyathābhāvo na hi jātūpapadyate //

IX

prakṛtau kasva vāsatyām anyathātvaṃ bhaviṣyati //
prakṛtau kasva vā satyām anyathātvaṃ bhaviṣyati //

X

astīti śāśvatagrāho nāstity ucchedadarśanam //
tasmād astitvanāstitve nāśrīyeta vicakṣaṇaḥ //

XI

asti yad dhi svabhāvena na tan nāstīti śāśvatam //
nāstīdānīm abhūt pūrvam ity ucchedaḥ prasajyate //

TIBETAN TEXT

I

rang bzhin rgyu dang rkyen las ni //
'byung bar rigs pa ma yin no //
rgyu dang rkyen las byung ba yi //
rang bzhin byas pa can du 'gyur //

II

rang bzhin byas pa can zhes byar //
ji ltar bur na rung bar 'gyur //
rang bzhin dag ni bcos min dang //
gzhan la bltos pa med pa yin //

III

rang bzhin yod pa ma yin na //
gzhan gyi dngos po ga la yod //
gzhan gyi dngos po'i rang bzhin ni //
gzhan gyi dngos po yin zhes brjod //

IV

rang bzhin dang ni gzhan dngos dag //
ma gtogs dngos po ga la yod //
rang bzhin dang ni gzhan dngos dag //
yod na dngos po 'grub par 'gyur //

V

gal te dngos po ma grub na //
dngos med 'grub par mi 'gyur ro //
dngos po gzhan du gyur pa ni //
dngos med yin par skye bo smra //

VI

gang dag rang bzhin gzhan dngos dang //
dngos dang dngos med nyid lta ba //
de dag sangs rgyas bstan pa la //
de nyid mthong ba ma yin no //

VII

bcom ldan dngos dang dngos med pa //
mkhyen pas kā tā ya na yi //
gdams ngag las ni yod pa dang //
med pa gnyi ka dgag par gsungs //

VIII

gal te rang bzhin gyis yod na //
de ni med nyid mi 'gyur ro //
rang bzhin gzhan du 'gyur ba ni //
nam yang 'thad par mi 'gyur ro //

IX

rang bzhin yod pa ma yin na //
gzhan du 'gyur ba gang gi yin //
rang bzhin yod pa ma yin yang //
gzhan du 'gyur ba ji ltar rung //

X

yod ces bya ba rtag par 'dzin //
med ces bya ba chad par lta //
de phyir yod dang med pa la //
mkhas pas gnas par mi bya'o //

XI

gang zhig rang bzhin gyis yod pa //
de ni med pa min pas brtag //
sngon byung da ltar med ces pa //
des na chad par thal bar 'gyur //

DOCUMENT TWO:
CANDRAKĪRTI'S CLEAR WORDS
CHAPTER XV: "THE ANALYSIS OF NATURE"

The *Clear Words* is Candrakīrti's commentary to the *Treatise on the Middle.* Unlike Candrakīrti's *Introduction* (written before the *Clear Words*) — which is not available in Sanskrit — the Sanskirt and Tibetan for the *Clear Words* are both extant. The Sanskrit text of the following translation of Chapter XV is Louis de la Vallée Poussin's *Mūlamadhyamikakakārikā de Nāgārjuna avec la Prasannapadā Commentaire de Candrakīrti,* pp. 259-279. The Tibetan text is Peking 5260, Vol. 98, 42.1.8-45.2.1. This translation of Chapter XV was originally prepared at the University of Virginia in 1987 under the Sanskrit tutelage of Karen Lang.

CHAPTER XV: "THE ANALYSIS OF NATURE"

Objection: A nature of things just exists because of the causal contributors (*nye bar len pa, upādāna*) — the causes and conditions that produce them (*de dag skyed par byed pa, tanniṣpādaka*). Here, that which does not exist does not have causation by causes and conditions producing [it], like, for example, a flower of the sky. The seeds, ignorance and so forth, that are the causes and conditions producing sprouts, compositional factors, and so forth are causal contributors, and, therefore, a nature of things just exists.

Response: If things — compositional factors, sprouts, and so forth — have nature, then what need have those existing things for causes and conditions? Just as ignorance, seeds, and so forth do not act as causal contributors for the sake of producing again presently existing things such as compositional factors, sprouts, and so forth, so also at other [times], there would not be causation for the sake of producing them because their nature would [already] exist. In order to indicate this, [Nāgārjuna] said:

> The arising of nature due to causes and conditions is not reasonable.

Objection: Due to something's existing [already] production would be senseless; [hence] there is no nature of anything prior to its production. Then what is the case? Only a nature that does not exist prior to [a thing's] production arises later [i.e., after production] in dependence on causes and conditions.

Even if such is asserted, [Nāgārjuna says]:

> A nature produced by causes and conditions would have a nature of fabrication.

Objection: We just assert that due to arising from causes and conditions nature is produced. Therefore, because we assert that nature is indeed produced, the [unwanted] consequence [that nature is] produced does not harm us.

[*Response:*] This, too, is not reasonable. [Nāgārjuna] says:

> How could nature be said to be fabricated?

Since they are mutually contradictory, to say something is a product and is also nature is a meaningless statement. For, here, because the etymology of "nature"[281] is "own-entity" (*rang gi ngo bo, svaḥ bhāvaḥ*), that which is a produced thing is not called nature in the world. This is like, for example, produced things such as the heat of water, and the [artificial] rubies and so forth [that are produced] through the exertions of one skilled in transforming quartz, and so forth.

Whatever is nature is not produced; this is like, for instance, the heat of fire, or entities of rubies etc., which are of the actual type of rubies. These, because of not being produced through contact with some other thing are [incorrectly] called the nature of those.

---

281 *rang bzhin, svabhāva.*

Therefore, in this way it abides in the conventions of the world that nature is not produced. And, now, we propound that it should be apprehended that even heat, because of being produced, is not the nature of fire. Here, fire, which arises from the meeting of a crystal, fuel, and the sun, or from the rubbing of sticks, is observed as relying on causes and conditions. And, because just heat apart from fire does not exist, heat also is produced by causes and conditions. Therefore, it is produced, and because of being a product, it is clearly ascertained that, like the heat of water, [heat] is not the nature [of fire].

Objection: Is not it renowned to beings, shepherds, women, and above, that just heat is the nature of fire?

[*Response:*] Did we say it was not renowned? [But] we propound that this is not suitable to be the nature [of fire] because of lacking a defining character of nature. Because of following the error of ignorance, the world conceives aspects of things that do not have nature as having nature. Just as those having opthomalia, due to the condition of opthomalia, adhere to that which lacks a nature of falling hairs and so forth as [such] a nature, so childish beings, due to the degeneration of the eye of intelligence by the opthomalia of ignorance, adhere to aspects of things that lack nature as having nature.

In accordance with their conception, they speak of "own-character," saying, "Due to being uncommon because of not being observed separately [from fire], the nature, that is to say, own-character, of fire is heat." For, "its own character"[282] is "own-character."[283]

By way of just what is renowned to them, the Supramundane Victor, in the *abhidharma,* made a presentation of a conventional

---

[282] *bdag nyid kyi mtshan nyid.*

[283] *rang gi mishan nyid.*

own-entity[284] of those and explained that that which is shared, impermanence and so forth, is their general character.

When [considered] in terms of the perception of those having the eye of stainless wisdom free from the opthomalia of ignorance, at that time, just as those free from opthomalia do not see the falling hairs observed by those having opthomalia, so Superiors do not perceive the nature that is imputed by the minds of childish beings, whereby they say clearly, "This is not the nature of things." In this way the *Descent into Laṅkā Sūtra* says:

> Just as those having opthomalia wrongly apprehend falling hairs,
> So this imputation as thing[285] is a wrong imputation by childish beings.
>
> There is no nature, no consciousness, no basis-of-all, and no things,[286]
> But children, bad logicians, and those like corpses impute them.

Similarly, it is set forth extensively, "Great Intelligent One, thinking of the non-production of a nature, I said, 'All phenomena are not produced.'"

Objection: If you propound that just the heat and so forth of fire and so forth, because of being produced due to arising from causes and conditions are not the nature [of fire and so forth], then you should say what a defining character of the nature of those is and what that nature is.

---

284 *rang gi ngo bo kun rdzob pa.*

285 *dngos por brtag pa, bhāvavikalpa.*

286 *dngos med, na svabhāva.*

Response:

> Nature is that which is non-fabricated
> And does not depend on another.

Here, since "own-nature"[287] is nature, that which is the entity that is the "mine" of whatsoever thing is said to be its nature. What is the "mine" of something? That which is non-fabricated. That which is fabricated is not its "mine," like for example, the heat of water. Also, that which does not depend on something else is the "mine" of something, like, for example, one's servant and one's wealth. Whatever is controlled by another of something is not its "mine," like for example a temporarily loaned thing not under one's control.

Because we do not assert that that which is fabricated and depends on another in this way is a nature, therefore it is unreasonable to say that just heat is the nature of fire because it depends upon causes and conditions and because it is a later arising of something that did not arise previously, whereby it is produced.

Because it is thus, therefore, that which, even in all three times, is the non-fabricated fundamental entity non-mistaken in fire, that which is not the subsequent arising of something that did not arise previously, and that which does not have reliance on causes and conditions, as do the heat of water, or near and far, or long and short, is said to be the nature [of fire].[288]

---

287 *rang gi dngos po, svo bhāvaḥ.*

288 *PP*, 263.5-264.2:

> *yadevāgneḥ kālatraye apyavyabhāri nijaṃ rūpamakṛtrimaṃ pūrvām abhūtvā paścādhyanna bhavati yacca hetupratyayasāpejñaṃ na bhavatyapāmauṣṇyavatpārāvāravadṛīrdhahrasvavavā tatsvabhāva iti vyapadiśyate //*

TSHIG, 42.5.6-42.5.8; *D-TSHIG*, 227.5-9:

Objection: Does there exist such a non-fabricated and non-relative entity of fire?

Response: Such a nature is not existent by way of its own entity[289] and is not [utterly] non-existent either. Though it is so, in order to get rid of the fear of the listeners, when this is taught, it is said upon making a superimposition that it exists conventionally.[290]

It is like the statement by the Supramundane Victor in this vein [in the *King of Meditative Stabilizations Sūtra*]:

> What hearing, what teaching is there
> Of the inexpressible doctrine?
> The inexpressible is heard and taught
> Upon superimposition.

This same text [i.e., Chapter XXII of the *Treatise on the Middle*] will explain:

---

de'i phyir dus gsum du yang me la mi 'khrul ba gnyug ma'i ngo bo ma bcos pa gang zhig sngar ma byung bas phyis 'byung ba ma yin pa gang zhig chu'i tsha ba 'am tshur rol dang pha rol lam ring po dang thung ngu ltar rgyu dang rkyen la bltos pa dang bcas par ma gyur pa gang yin pa de rang bzhin yin pa brjod do //

289 *rang gi ngo bo, svarūpaṃ.*

290 *PP,* 264.2-4 [brackets added by Poussin from the Tibetan]:

kiṃ khalu [agneḥ] taditthaṃ svarūpamasti // na tadasti na cāpi nāsti svarūpataḥ // yadhyapyevaṃ tathāpi śrotṛṇāmuttrāsaparivarjñanārthaṃ saṃvṛtyā samāropya tadastīti brūmaḥ //

TSHIG, 42.5.8-43.1.1; *D-TSHIG,* 227.9-12:

ci me'i rang gi ngo bo de lta bur gyur pa yod dam zhe na // de ni rang gi ngo bos yod pa ma yin pa med pa yang ma yin no // de lta yin mod kyi 'on kyang nyan pa po rnams kyi skrag pa sbang bar bya ba'i phyir sgro btags nas kun rdzob tu de yod do zhes bya bar smra'o //

We do not say "empty"
Nor should one say "not empty."
Nor both nor neither.[291]
[These] are expressed for the sake of imputation.

Objection: In that it is said that [nature] exists upon superimposition, what is it like? [264.11]

[*Response:*] That which is the own-entity of those, called the reality of phenomena is that [nature]. In that case, what is this reality of phenomena? It is the entity of phenomena. What is this entity? It is nature.[292] What is this nature? It is emptiness. What is this emptiness? It is the lack of nature. What is this lack of nature? It is suchness. What is this suchness? It is that entity of suchness that does not change and always abides. For, that which is not produced in any way, because of not being fabricated and because of not relying on another, is called the nature of fire and so forth.

This is what was said: That entityness which by its nature becomes the object of those Superiors free from the opthomalia of ignorance, in the manner of non-perception of the aspects of things that are observed through the force of the opthomalia of ignorance, is posited as the nature of those [things].[293]

Nature is non-fabricated and does not depend on another.

You should know that this statement by the master [Nāgārjuna] presents a defining character of this [nature]. [265.7]

You should [also] know that just this lack of [true] production, which is the nature of things, is just a non-thing due to not being

---

[291] *D-TSHIG,* 227.16. Text corrected from *gnyis mon* to *gnyis min* in accordance with *TSHIG,* 43.1.2.

[292] *rang bzhin, prakṛti.*

[293] See the commentary in *MCHAN,* page 215.

anything at all, whereby because [its] entity [i.e., that of a lack of true production] does not exist, it is not the nature of things.

In this vein the Supramundane Victor says:

> Whoever knows things as non-things
> Is never attached to all things.
> Whoever is never attached to all things
> Contacts the meditative stabilization without signs.

Objection: Even if things have no own-being, nonetheless, they have other-being because that has not been refuted.

[*Response*:] If they had an other-being, they would also have own-being because, without own-being, other-being is not established. Hence [Nāgārjuna says:]

> When there is no own-being, how could there be other-being?
> A own-being of other-being is called [other-]being.

Objection: Here, in the world, only some natures are called other-being in terms of another nature.

[*Response*:] If heat were the nature of fire, then it would be called other-being in terms of water, which has a nature of wetness. But, when upon analyzing, [it is seen] that own-being itself does not exist anywhere, then how could otherness exist? Since otherness does not exist, it is established that own-being also does not exist.

Objection: Even if own-being and other-being do not exist, nonetheless being, for one, exists because of not having been refuted.

[*Response*:] If being existed, then it would have to be either own-being or other-being, and therefore, own-being and other-being also would exist. [Nāgārjuna] says:

> How could there be being
> Apart from own-being and other-being?

> If own-being and other-being existed
> Being would be established.

If one investigates being in this way, it must be either own-being or other-being. But those do not exist in the manner that has been previously explained. Therefore, one should ascertain that since those two do not exist, being also does not exist.

Objection: Even if you have refuted being, nonetheless non-being just exists because of not having been refuted. [270] Therefore, because the opposite class exists, being also would exist, just like non-being.

Response: [Nāgārjuna,] saying, "If non-being alone existed, then being also would exist, but it does not exist," says:

> If being is not established
> Non-being also would not be established.
> Persons propound as non-being
> The change of being.

That is, if some "being" existed, due to its change, there would be non-being. For pots and so forth degenerate from their present state, attain another [state], and are, in the world, expressed with the term, "non-being." When these pots and so forth are not established as an entityness of being, then how could there be change of these whose nature is non-existent? Therefore, non-being also does not exist.

Therefore, with respect to this non-existence in all ways of nature, other-being, being, and non-being, [regarding] those who, due to the degeneration of the eye of intelligence by the dimness of ignorance erroneously [view nature, it is said]:

> Those who view nature, other-being,
> Being, and non-being
> Do not see the suchness
> In the Buddha's teaching.

Whoever, through claiming to be explaining non-erroneously the scriptures of the One Gone Thus, propounds a nature of things, (such as, the nature of earth is hardness), [or] of feeling, [or] experience, [or that] the nature of consciousness is individual knowledge of objects, and propounds other-being, such as "form is other, consciousness is also other and feeling too is just other;" and propounds the present state of consciousness and so forth, as being and the past state of consciousness and so forth as non-being, those persons do not propound the suchness that is supremely profound dependent-arising. [271.5]

The existence of nature, other-being, and so forth is contradictory with the reasonings already explained, and the One Gone Thus did not speak of a nature of things that is contradictory with reasoning because he himself has realized non-erroneously the reality of all things. Therefore, scholars call "authoritative" the speech of only the Buddha, the Supramundane Victor, because it is non-deceptive due to having reasonings.

Therefore, because of coming from one who has abandoned all faults and is believable, or, because of causing thorough understanding — that is, causing thorough understanding of suchness — or, because of going in the direction of it — that is, because in dependence upon it — the world goes to nirvāṇa, just the speech of the fully enlightened one is presented as "scripture" (*lung, āgama*), and textual systems which are other than that, due to lacking reasoning, are presented as not authoritative and not "scripture."

Because these views of nature, other-being, being, and non-being — because of lacking reasonings — are not suchness, for beings who are trainees wishing liberation:

> The Supramundane Victor, due to knowing
> Being and non-being,

In the *Advice to Kātyāyana* refuted
Both existence and non-existence.

The Supramundane Victor, in the *Sūtra of Advice to Kātyāyana,* said extensively:

> Kātyāyana, because worldly beings mostly adhere to existence and non-existence, therefore they are not released from birth, aging, sickness and death, from sorrow and lamentation, suffering, mental unease, and disturbance; they are not released from the suffering of the torment of death.

And, this sūtra is recited by all the [Buddhist] schools.

Therefore, because of this scripture and the reasonings that have been explained, it is unsuitable for the wise to assert a view of nature, other-being, being, and non-being, this being very contradictory with the words of the One Gone Thus. For, the Supramundane Victor refuted [such].

What distinguishes the Supramundane Victor? Knowledge of being and non-being, for, since he has an inner mode of knowing being and non-being he knows being and non-being. Because of knowing thoroughly and non-mistakenly just as it is the nature of being and non-being, just the Supramundane Victor is called "knower of being and non-being." Because the Supramundane Victor, the knower of being and non-being, refuted both existence and non-existence, it is not reasonable to assert that the view of being and non-being is suchness.

Similarly [Buddha said in the *Heap of Jewels Sūtra*]:

> Kāśyapa, "existence" is one extreme; "non-existence" is another extreme. That which is the middle between those two — without analysis, without indication, not dependent, without appearance, unperceived, without abiding — that, Kāśyapa, is the path of the Middle Way, called individual analysis of phenomena.

Similarly [Buddha said in the *King of Meditative Stabilizations Sūtra*]:

> Both existence and non-existence are extremes;
> Purity and impurity are also extremes.
> Therefore, having thoroughly abandoned both extremes
> Scholars do not make a standpoint even in the middle.
>
> Existence and non-existence is a dispute;
> Purity and impurity is also a dispute.
> Through dispute, suffering is not pacified;[294]
> When there is no dispute suffering is stopped.

Objection: Even if there were existence by way of their nature of fire and so forth, what fault would there be?

[*Response*:] The fault has already been set forth:

> A nature arisen from causes and conditions would be fabricated.

And so forth. Furthermore, in order to indicate that if just this nature of these, fire and so forth, did exist, that which existed would not change, [Nāgārjuna] said:

> If there were existence by way of nature, there would not be a non-existence of it.

That is, if there were a nature, i.e., an own-entity, of these things, fire and so forth, then that nature which existed by way of its nature would not later change. Why?

> Change of a nature is never feasible.

If there were nature of these, fire and so forth, then because that nature is just immutable, it is not feasible that it would ever change. Just as the non-obstructiveness of space never changes, so also fire and so forth, those things that exist by way of their nature, also would not later change. But even you observe their destruction, whose definition is change, the cessation of continuity.

---

[294] *TSHIG*, 44.1.4; *D-TSHIG*, 233.9. Although both texts read *rtsod par gyur pa'i*, I have translated the line as if it reads *rtsod par gyur pas*.

Therefore, you should know that, because of having the quality of change, like the heat of water, there is no nature of these.

Objection: Even if it is said that, because that which exists by way of its nature does not change and because change is observed, these things do not have nature, nonetheless:

> If there is no nature, of what would there be change?

Because this — like a sky-flower — does not exist by way of its nature, that is, its entity, of what would there be change? Therefore, because change is not observed among what does not have nature, and because change is seen, nature exists.

Response: If it is being propounded by your system that, because there is no change among what does not exist by way of its nature, that is, its [own] entity, and because change is seen, nature exists, then [Nāgārjuna responds]:

> If nature did exist, how could change be suitable?

Because of existing now, at present, by way of its nature, that is, its [own] entity, of what would there be change? Therefore, because there is no change among what exists by way of its nature, change would in all ways not occur. Therefore, it should be known that things do not have nature.

Also, the explanation, "Because change is seen, there is no nature," is said in the context of a seeing of change that is renowned to others. We do not assert ever anywhere that change exists.

Therefore, in this way, nature does not exist at all, and all phenomena are that of which nature does not exist, and also change of those does not exist. But, now, some conceive that things just exist and just do not exist; for those who conceive such, it definitely only follows that:

> Saying "exists" is a conception of permanence;
> Saying "does not exist" is a view of annihilation.

Since these views of permanence and annihilation are obstacles to the paths [leading] to high status [in cyclic existence] and liberation, they are a great impropriety.

> Therefore, the wise do not abide
> In existence or non-existence.

Objection: Why is it that when there are views of being and non-being, it follows that there are views of permanence and annihilation?

Response: As follows:

> Whatever exists by way of its nature is permanent
> Since it does not become non-existent.
> If one says that what arose formerly [as existent
> By way of its nature] is now non-existent,
> Through that [an extreme of] annihilation is entailed.

That which is said to exist by way of its nature is never non-existent since nature is not overcome. In that case, through asserting [something] as just existent by way of its nature, one comes to have a view of permanence.

And, having asserted a nature of things when formerly they were abiding, through asserting that now, later, they are destroyed whereby they do not exist, it follows that one has a view of annihilation.

For that person for whom a nature of things is not feasible, views of permanence and annihilation are not entailed due to the non-observation of a nature of things.

Objection: One who asserts, "Things do not exist by way of their nature," due to not having a view of being, indeed does not have a view of permanence. But is it not the case that there definitely is the entailment of [that person's having] a view of annihilation?

Response: There is no such view of non-existence. For, whoever, having formerly asserted a nature of things, later relies upon a reversal of those, would have a view of non-existence due to deprecating that nature of things observed formerly. But, someone who, like those without opthomalia with respect to the falling hairs observed by those with opthomalia, does not observe anything at all says, "That does not exist," and thus propounds non-existence due to the non-existence of the object-to-be-negated. In order to overcome the wrong conceptions of those who are in error, we, like those without dimness of sight, propound, "All things do not exist." But, when we propound such, there is no entailment that we have a view of annihilation. [274.2]

In this vein, sūtra says extensively:

> Supramundane Victor, that one who having formerly asserted desire, hatred, and bewilderment as things, later propounds that these things of desire, hatred, and ignorance do not exist, is a Nihilist.

Some, having asserted just the things that are other-powered phenomena — minds and mental factors — [say that] since an imputed entityness does not exist in them, the view of existence is dispelled, and, since other-powered things exist merely as the causes of the thoroughly afflicted and the very pure, the view of non-existence is dispelled.

In that case, because the thoroughly imputed does not exist and because other-powered phenomena do exist, there would be both views of existence and non-existence, whereby how could the two extremes have been abandoned? Because it has already been shown that the things that are produced by causes and conditions having nature is not reasonable, their explanations are just not reasonable.

Therefore, one should know in this way, that only the view of the Middle Way School is without the entailment of views of existence and non-existence, and that those of others — the views of those who propound consciousness and so forth — are not. Because of that, Nāgārjuna's *Precious Garland* (LXI) says:

> Ask the Worldlings, the Sāṃkhyas,
> Owl-Followers, and Nirgranthas,
> The proponents of a person and aggregates,
> If they propound what passes beyond "is" and "is not."
>
> Thereby know that the ambrosia
> Of the Buddha's teaching is called profound,
> An uncommon doctrine passing
> Far beyond existence and non-existence.

One should know that, like the propounding of a [substantially existent] person of the Saṃmitīyas, the propounding of [mere] consciousness is a teaching of interpretable meaning, taught by the Supramundane Victor, due to the other-power of compassion, for the conceptuality of such trainees, for the sake of serving as a method for seeing the ultimate. It is not of definitive meaning. In this vein the *King of Meditative Stabilizations Sūtra* says:

> One knows as instances of sūtras of definitive meaning [those which teach]
> In accordance with the emptiness explained by the Sugata.
> One knows as of interpretable meaning all those [verbal] doctrines
> In which "sentient being," "person," and "creature" are taught.

This should be known in detail from the *Teachings of Akṣhayamati Sūtra* and so forth.

Therefore, those who desire the excellent liberation, having realized that as long as there exists opportunity for controversy regarding the two views of being and non-being there is cyclic existence, clear away those two views.[295] They should meditate in accordance with the Middle Path.

The Supramundane Victor said:

> Since all is inconceivable and unarisen,
> Apprehension of things and non-things should be destroyed.
> Those children who are under the control of thought
> Suffer in hundreds of ten millions of cyclic existences.

And:

> I remember a former past time.
> An inconceivable number of aeons ago, a chief of men,
> A great sage, was born for the sake of the world.
> He was named "Arisen from Non-being."
>
> Just after he was born, remaining in the sky
> He taught all phenomena as without being.
> At that time given a name concordant with that,
> He was renowned by that name in all the world.
>
> All the gods proclaimed
> This one called "Non-being" will be a Conqueror.
> As soon as he was born, taking seven steps
> This Conqueror explained phenomena as without being.
>
> Whenever a subduer, a Buddha who teaches
> All phenomena, a king of doctrine, arises,
> The sound "All phenomena lack being" comes forth
> From grass, trees, bushes, medicinal plants, rocks, and mountains.
>
> As far as sound extends in the world,
> "All lacks being, there is nothing at all,"
> For so far does there very much arise
> The roar of sound of the leader of the world.

---

[295] *TSHIG*, 45.1.1; *D-TSHIG*, 238.4. Boths texts read *gsal* although *bsal* seems more correct.

Because a nature of things is not correct, [the sūtra] says, "Phenomena lack nature." Thus, one should understand the meaning of the sūtra in this way. And, because [the sūtra] says, "As far as sound extends in the world, 'All lacks being, there is nothing at all,'" because of a wish to express a non-affirming negative, "lacking being" means a lack of nature.[296]

This is the commentary on the fifteenth chapter [of Nāgārjuna's *Treatise on the Middle*] "The Analysis of Nature" from the *Clear Words* by the master Candrakīrti.

---

[296] *PP*, 279.3:

> *abhāvapratiṣedhavivakṣatatvāt bhāvābhāvārtha eva svabhāvābhāvārthaḥ* //

TSHIG, 45.1.8; *D-TSHIG*, 239.3-5:

> *med par dgag pa brjod par 'dod pa'i phyir dngos po med pa'i don ni rang bzhin med pa'i don yin no* //

In conversation, Geshe B̄el-den Ḍak-b̄a of L̄o-sel-l̄ing Monastic College took this as a clear source for Candrakīrti saying that emptiness must be a non-affirming negative.

DOCUMENT THREE:
D̄ZONG-KA-B̄A'S OCEAN OF REASONINGS
CHAPTER XV: "THE ANALYSIS OF NATURE"

The composition of the *Ocean of Reasonings, Explanation of (Nāgārjuna's) "Treatise on the Middle"* began in 1407, when D̄zong-ka-b̄a was fifty years old.[297] D̄zong-ka-b̄a had already written the *Great Exposition* in 1402. Although he began the text at Chö-ding (*chos sdings*) Hermitage on the northern outskirts of Hla-s̄a, and continued work on it at "Goat-Face Crag" (*rva kha brag*), D̄zong-ka-b̄a discontinued work on the *Ocean of Reasonings* in order to compose his *The Essence of Eloquence.* After completing *The Essence of Eloquence* in 1408, D̄zong-ka-b̄a returned to work on the *Ocean of Reasonings.* In 1415, he went on to write the *Medium Exposition of the Stages of the Path,*[298] and finally, at age sixty-one, one year before his death, he wrote a commentary on Candrakīrti's *Introduction to (Nāgārjuna's) "Treatise on the Middle,"* the *Illumination of the Thought.*

This translation was first prepared in a third-year Sanskrit course taught in 1987 at the University of Virginia by Karen Lang. It has since been revised by me under the direction of Jeffrey Hopkins. The edition used here is Varanasi: Pleasure of Elegant Sayings Printing Press, 1975, pages 727.19-742.2.

---

[297] Dates are taken from *DAE,* 6-7 and Leonard W. J. van der Kuijp, "Apropos of a Recent Contribution to the History of Central Way Philosophy in Tibet: *Tsong Khapa's Speech of Gold*" in *Berliner Indologische Studien* (Reinbek: Verlag für Orientalistische Fachpublikationen, 1985), 68, n. 2. Kay-drup's biography sets the date at 1418 (120.9-120.20). See *DAE,* 648.

[298] *skyes bu gsum gyi nyams su blang ba'i byang chub lam gyi rim pa;* P 6002, Vol. 152-153.

CHAPTER XV: "THE ANALYSIS OF NATURE"

Refuting that those which are causal contributors, i.e., causes and conditions, exist by way of [their] nature has three parts: [728] (I) explaining the text of the chapter; (II) conjoining this with scriptures of definitive meaning; and (III) condensing the meaning and indicating the title.

I. EXPLAINING THE TEXT OF THE CHAPTER

Objection: Things exist by way of their nature because [their] causal contributors exist — the causes and conditions, i.e., seeds, ignorance, and so forth, that produce sprouts, compositional factors, and so forth.

This is how Candrakīrti makes the transition [to this chapter] in the *Clear Words*. In the *Buddhapālita Commentary on [Nāgārjuna's] "Treatise on the Middle,"* it is said:

> [*Objection:*] You [Proponents of the Middle] assert that things are dependent-arisings and you also propound them as without entityness; if that is so, [i.e., in that case] how is it that things could both arise and be without entityness? If the entityness of things does not arise from causes and conditions, then what other thing would arise from those? If just the entityness of wool does not arise from threads, its causes, does just an entityness of the causes, thread, arise, or does nothing arise? In that case, why is "arise" said?
>
> [*Response:*] Are you like someone who while riding on a horse does not see that horse? Even you propound that things are dependent-arisings, yet you do not see that there is just no entityness of them.

Thus [Buddhapālita] makes the transition to the explanation by this [statement in] Chapter [XV of Nāgārjuna's *Treatise on the Middle*] that the two — (1) an entityness of things that are established by way of their own entities not being suitable in the least, and (2) asserting that nonetheless things arise in dependence upon causes and conditions — which [the Proponents of Truly Existent Things] conceive to be contradictory, are not contradictory.

This differentiation mixing these two [i.e., no entityness and production in dependence on causes and conditions] is the most important essential to these reasonings.

With regard to refuting in this way the propounding of establishment by way of nature, there are two parts: refuting that things exist by way of their nature and indicating that if one propounds existence by way of nature, one does not pass beyond holding an extreme.

REFUTING THAT THINGS EXIST BY WAY OF THEIR NATURE

This has two parts, refuting the proofs of existence by way of nature and indicating damage to existence by way of nature.

REFUTING THE PROOFS OF EXISTENCE BY WAY OF NATURE

This has three parts: the actual meaning, indicating that this refutes the other three extremes, [729] and criticizing the views [of those who hold such] for the sake of refuting them.

THE ACTUAL MEANING

This has two parts: indicating that nature does not need causes and conditions and that [to have them] would be contradictory, and indicating the defining character of nature in our own system.

INDICATING THAT NATURE DOES NOT NEED CAUSES AND CONDITIONS AND THAT [TO HAVE THEM] WOULD BE CONTRADICTORY

If compositional factors, sprouts, and so forth had nature, then it would be unreasonable for them to arise from causes and conditions such as ignorance, seeds, and so forth. For, that which has nature does not need to be produced.

Objection: Although if [that nature] existed prior to [something's] production, production would be senseless, only a nature that does not exist prior [to production] arises in dependence on causes and conditions.

[*Response:*] In that case, that nature, which is an effect because of arising from causes and conditions, would be fabricated.

Objection: I just assert that its being a product is entailed.

[*Response:*] How could it be suitable to propound that something is both a product and nature? That is to say, it is not, for [those two] are mutually exclusive. With respect to that, the two, fabricated and non-fabricated, are a dichotomy, whereby if one eliminates one in terms of a particular base, the other must be positively included. Products are necessarily fabricated, and nature, that is, an essence (*gshis*), is necessarily non-fabricated, whereby the two, that which is a product and that which is an essence, are unsuitable to be included in one basis.

This is like the way in which, in the world, the heat of water and the transformation of quartz and so forth into fabricated rubies and so forth by one skilled in transforming jewels are not called the nature of those [rubies and so forth].

You might wonder, since, in the world, the heat of fire and entities of the actual type [that is, the actual non-fabricated type] of rubies and so forth are called the nature of those [fire and rubies], how is it reasonable that whatever is a product is not an essence?

[*Response:*] That in the world the verbal convention "nature" or "essence" is not used for the fabricated, here [in the Consequence system] is also asserted, but we propound that, in that case, even though the heat of fire is indeed renowned in the world as the nature, or essence, of fire, [730] it is not the essence of fire for it lacks the defining character of essence. Fire is observed in reliance on its causes and conditions, a fire crystal, and so forth, and heat also is similar. Hence, because of being a product, it is clearly ascertained that, like the heat of water, [the heat of fire] is not [fire's] nature.

Here, it is indeed renowned in the world that although the two, the heat of water and the heat of fire, are similar in being produced by causes and conditions, they are not similar in being fabricated or not being fabricated, whereby they are not similar in being or not being the nature of [water and fire, respectively]. However, Proponents of True Existence do not assert, with regard to water's being produced as hot and fire's being produced as hot, a difference of one's being produced by way of its nature and one's not, whereby they do not assert this worldly mode of not using the verbal convention "nature" if something is posited as fabricated, but, in our own system, such is asserted.

When childish beings, believing that things that do not exist by way of their nature do exist by way of their nature, see [something] in just this phenomenon and do not see it in other phenomena, they propound [it] as its defining character, just as they believe that fire's own character is heat. For, they take own-defining character (*bdag nyid kyi mtshan nyid*) to be own self-character (*rang gi mtshan nyid*). [730.13]

By way of what is renowned to them, the Teacher presented in the *abhidharma* a conventional "own-entity" (*rang gi ngo bo*) of those and explained that impermanence and so forth, which are shared with other phenomena, are "general characters" (*spyi'i mtshan*).

With respect to that, even though it is not the case even conventionally that heat is the essence of fire and impermanence is the essence of compounded phenomenon, from among common and uncommon characteristics, it is our own system that, in accordance with the statement in the *abhidharma,* they do exist conventionally as the specific [or self-character] and general characters of those.

Therefore, there is a very great difference between the two, [something's] existing by way of its own character or by way of its own-entity and [something's having] its own unshared characteristics (*thun mong ma yin pa'i rang gi mtshan nyid*). The statement in the *Commentary*[299] that specific and general characters are explained in the *abhidharma* by way of just their being renowned to those [worldly beings] refers to the fact that since childish beings apprehend this and that defining character of this and that phenomenon as being their essence (*gshis*), Buddha — without refuting that [link between defining character and essence, even though he did not accept it] — explains [in the *abhidharma*] two characters [specific and general] with respect to those [phenomena]. It is not saying that just as [childish beings] apprehend the heat of fire and so forth as being the essence [of fire and so forth], so also in the *abhidharma* the two characters are posited with respect to the essences of those because:

> (1) Candrakīrti's *Introduction* says those [two characters] were refuted equally by the Buddha in the sūtras on the mode of the Perfections and were set forth equally in the teachings on manifest knowledge [that is, in the *abhidharma*].

And, in the *Auto-Commentary on the "Introduction to (Nāgārjuna's) 'Treatise on the Middle'"* it is said that since in the *abhidharma* all five aggregates are equally indicated by way of differentiations such as their specific and general characters and in the Mother Sūtras [the Perfection of Wisdom Sūtras] all five are said to be just empty of nature (*rang bzhin gyis stong pa nyid*), they are

---

[299] Candrakirti's *Clear Words.* See page 144.

equal in not existing ultimately and existing conventionally.

> (2) ...and we do not assert even conventionally that the heat of fire is the essence of fire.

Therefore, something like the heat of fire is not said to be renowned to others because we do not assert it ourselves; rather it is posited as being merely being renowned to others because just that apprehension of the two — the heat of fire and the nature of fire — as one, without differentiating them individually, is not established for us.

INDICATING THE DEFINING CHARACTER OF NATURE IN OUR OWN SYSTEM

Objection: If you propound that due to being a product [something] is not a nature, then what is the definition of nature and what is that nature?

Response: Since in this [text], the verbal convention "own-entity" (*rang gi ngo bo*) is used for nature (*rang bzhin*), whatever is the "mine" (*bdag gi ba*) of whatsoever thing is said to be its nature. What — and of what — is the "mine"? That which is a non-fabricated quality of whatsoever substratum is [the "mine"] of that [substratum]. Whatever is fabricated is not the "mine" of that [substratum], like, for example, the heat of water. Whatever does not depend on something else is the "mine" of that [substratum], like for instance, one's servant and one's wealth [which do not depend on someone else, but on oneself]. Whatever does depend on something [or someone] else, [732] is not the "mine" of that [substratum], like for instance, a temporarily loaned thing not under one's control.

Since such is said, this does not indicate that all things that are fabricated and depend on something else are not the "mine" of those phenomena, but rather indicates that the "mine" which is posited as the nature or essence of some phenomenon must be non-fabricated in terms of it and must be something that is not like a borrowed thing that depends on someone other than oneself. [The *Clear Words* states:]

> Because it is thus, therefore, that which, even in all three times, is the non-fabricated fundamental entity non-mistaken in fire, that which is not the subsequent arising of something that did not arise previously, and that which does not have reliance on causes and conditions, as do the heat of water, or near and far, or long and short, is said to be the nature [of fire].[300]

Does such a nature of fire exist? [Candrakīrti's] statement, "It does not exist by way of its own entity and it also does not not exist by way of its own entity," means that it does indeed exist[301] but it does not exist by way of its own entity. This is as was said in Candrakīrti's *Auto-Commentary:*

> With respect to this, the ultimate is the "its own entity" (*bdag gi rang gi ngo bo*) found due to being just the special object of the exalted wisdom (*ye shes kyi khyad par gyi yul*) of those who see reality; it is not established by way of its own selfness (*rang gi bdag nyid kyis ma grub pa*).

Although indeed such does not exist by way of its own entity, in order to dispell the fear of the listeners, we propound, upon superimposition, "It exists conventionally." It is unreasonable, for the sake of that purpose, to propound that since the ultimate truth is said to exist here [in Candrakīrti's *Clear Words*], it is not an object of knowledge. For, the *Compendium of Perfect Teachings Sūtra* (*chos yang dag par sdud pa*) says:

> In order to thoroughly dispel the source of fear of the world, it is said through the force of verbal conventions, "There is production; there is cessation."

---

[300] For Tibetan and Sanskrit, see note 123.

[301] *RGT*, 732.10. Text corrected from *yod med kyi* to *yod mod gyi.*

Production and cessation also would not be objects of knowledge.

Also propounding that since [Candrakīrti] says "upon superimposition," the ultimate truth is not an object of knowledge, is not reasonable. For, as a source for the statement that it exists upon superimposition, [Candrakīrti] cites a stanza from the *King of Meditative Stabilizations Sūtra,* which states: [733.2]

> What hearing, what teaching is there
> Of the inexpressible doctrine?
> The inexpressible is heard and taught
> Upon superimposition.

In this, the hearers, explainers, and doctrines to be explained are all said to be done upon superimposition, whereby these too would come not to be objects of knowledge.

Therefore, since even with regard to teachings upon imputation by the mind, it is often said, "upon superimposition," this need not be something like the superimposition of the two selves.

Objection: [In that] it is said that that [nature] exists upon superimpostion, what is it like?

[*Response:*] [Candrakīrti's] statement, "That which is the own-entity (*rang gi ngo bo, svarūpam*) of those, which is called the reality (*chos nyid, dharmatā*) of phenomena,"[302] and so forth, is the answer to the previous second question [above — what is the defining character of that final nature and what is that final nature?]. It is the entity of phenomena, and entity is nature; nature is emptiness; and emptiness is the lack of nature; that [lack of nature] is suchness; and that [suchness] immutably and always abides as the entity of suchness. [733.11]

These [things] that are observed by the power of the opthomalia of ignorance, if they existed as [their own] suchness, would have to be observed by a Superior's non-contaminated exalted

---

302 See page 147.

wisdom of meditative equipoise; but instead, in the manner of not seeing those at all, their suchness is the object of that exalted wisdom. This is because that exalted wisdom realizes the suchness of things, and because just the non-establishment of things as nature is the suchness of those things, and because, whereas, if the object-to-be-negated existed, it would be observable, but it is not observed, due to which one is posited as having realized the negative of the object-to-be-negated.

Moreover, with regard to the meaning of the statement [in sūtra], "Non-seeing is the highest seeing," not seeing anything is not ascertained as seeing. Rather, as explained earlier, not seeing the elaborations [of inherent existence] is posited as seeing what is free from elaborations, whereby seeing and not seeing do not refer to one basis. Similarly, the *Condensed Perfection of Wisdom Sūtra* says:[303] [734]

> The Tathāgata teaches that one who does not see forms,
> Does not see feelings, does not see discriminations,
> Does not see intentions, does not see consciousness,
> Mind, or intellect sees reality (*chos, dharma*).
>
> "Space is seen," sentient beings express with words.
> Investigate the meaning of how space is "seen."[304]
> The Tathāgatha teaches that seeing reality is like that.
> The seeing cannot be explained by another example.

Hence this says that what is not seen are the five aggregates and what is seen is reality (*chos*). And, that means suchness; this is like the statement "The one who sees dependent-arising sees reality."

---

303 *shes rab kyi pha rol tu phyin pa sdud pa, sañcayagathaprajñāpāramitā*, P735, XII.8. See the Obermiller edition, 50.

304 *RGT*, 734.4-5, text corrected from *nam mkha' ji ltar mthong ste des 'di brtag par gyis* to *nam mkha' ji ltar mthong zhes don 'di brtag par gyis* in accordance with the Obermiller edition of the sūtra, 51.

Furthermore, to give an example: Space is the mere elimination of obstructive contact. Seeing, or realizing [it], refers to not seeing the object-to-be-negated, obstructive hindrance, which, if it existed, would be observable. Here also, what is seen is space and what is not seen is an obstructive hindrance.

The last two lines [of the above sūtra passage] refute that one sees suchness while seeing blue; this is not a "seeing" in accordance with the example.

The statement that the five aggregates are not seen indicates that subjects are not seen by a non-contaminated meditative equipoise. In that case, seeing suchness is not — without being real — a mere imputation, but the ultimate is also not established by way of its own entity. Although all subjects (*chos can*) are not established as such a nature, reality (*chos nyid*) is established; but, no phenomenon (*chos*) is established as a nature which is established by way of its own entity.

SECOND, INDICATING THAT THIS REFUTES THE OTHER THREE EXTREMES

Objection: Even if through refuting that things exist by way of their nature, self-entities (*rang dngos*), [i.e., own-being] have been refuted, still it has not been refuted that other-entities (*gzhan dngos*), [i.e., other-being] exist by way of their nature, whereby, if those exist, then own-being also would exist by way of its nature.

[*Response:*] If heat were established as the own-being of fire, then it would be suitable to posit as an other-being in relation to an own-being of wetness, in which case, in that, when analyzed there is no thing that exists as an own-being, then how could other-being exist by way of its nature? It could not, because the establishment by way of its own-being of a nature — that is, an entity — of other-being is called the establishment by way of its nature of other-being.

Objection: Indeed one [thing being] its own-being, or entity, and other-being, or entity, has been refuted, but being exists by way of its nature because it has not been refuted.

[*Response:*] How could there be a being that was not either own-being or other-being? There could not, whereby if something existed by way of its own entityness as either own-being or other-being, the existence of being by way of its nature would be established. But, since those two have been refuted previously, it does not exist.

Objection: Even if you have refuted being, still, non-being, since you have not refuted it, exists by way of its nature, and if that exists, since its opposite class would exist, being would also exist.

[*Response:*] If the existence by way of nature of being is not established, then the existence by way of its nature of non-being would not be established. For, in the world, persons propound the change from a present state of being of pots and so forth as the non-existence of that former being.

Here, although indeed one must refute true existence also with respect to non-being whose object-to-be-negated does not occur among objects of knowledge, due to the essential of greater or lesser force of the conception of true existence with respect to existent versus non-existent objects of negation, [Nāgārjuna's] thought is that if one establishes as without true existence the non-being of the state of destructedness of an existent being which is its object-to-be-negated, it is then easier to establish other [types of] non-being as without true existence.

THIRD, CRITICIZING THE VIEWS [OF THOSE WHO HOLD SUCH] FOR THE SAKE OF REFUTING THEM

Thus, whoever — with respect to this non-establishment by way of entityness of own-being, other-being, being, and non-being — due to claiming to explain the scriptures non-erroneously [736]

views the two, nature and other-being, by means of such statements as "the nature of fire is heat" and "the nature of feeling is the experience of objects," and so forth, and views the present of consciousness and so forth as existing by way of [its own] entityness as being and the past and so forth of those as existing by way of [their own] entityness as non-being does not see or propound the suchness which is the supreme profound dependent-arising in the teachings of the Buddha, the Supramundane Victor.

For, nature and so forth existing by way of entityness is contradictory with reasoning, and the Conquerors also do not explain a nature of things that is contradictory with reasoning because they understand non-erroneously the suchness of all things.

Therefore, the wise take the speech of only the Conqueror as authoritative because, since it has reasonings, it is non-deceptive. Through making an explanation in terms of the Sanskrit equivalent of "scripture" (*āgama*), only the words of the fully accomplished Buddha are posited as "scripture" due to (1) coming from a trustworty person who has extinguished all faults, (2) causing understanding in all ways, that is causing understanding in all ways of suchness, and (3) going in the direction — that is, in dependence on this — the world goes to nirvāṇa. And, textual systems which are other than this, since they are devoid of reasoning, are not posited as "scripture."

INDICATING DAMAGE TO EXISTENCE BY WAY OF AN OBJECT'S NATURE

This has two parts: indicating scriptural damage and indicating damage by reasoning.

INDICATING SCRIPTURAL DAMAGE

Own-being, other-being, being, and non-being, viewed as existing by way of [their own] entityness, are not suchness because of a lack of reasoning [to support such a view]. Therefore, to those beings wishing liberation who are trainees, the Supramundane Victor, in the *Advice to Kātyāyana Sūtra,* refuted both extremes, of existence and non-existence:

> Kātyāyana, because worldly beings mostly adhere to existence and non-existence, therefore they are not released from birth, aging, sickness and death, from sorrow and lamentation, suffering, mental unease, and disturbance; they are not released from the suffering of the torment of death.

Also, since this sūtra is recited by all [Buddhist] schools, because of this scripture as well as the reasonings that have been explained, we do not assert that the four, own-being, and so forth, exist by way of [their own] entityness.

By what is the Supramundane Victor distinguished? He knows unmistakenly the nature of being and non-being.

INDICATING DAMAGE BY REASONING

Furthermore, if fire and so forth exist by way of their nature, then that nature which exists by way of its nature would not become non-existent by way of later change. Why? Because change of what exists by way of its nature would never be feasible, like the way in which the non-obstructiveness of space never changes. Because of being a quality that changes, [the heat of fire], like the heat of water, is not a nature.

Objection: If it is propounded that because there is no change among that which exists by way of its nature, and because change is observed, things do not exist by way of their nature, if there is no existence by way of its nature, of what would there be change? Therefore, among that which does not exist by way of its nature, change is not feasible, and because that [i.e., change] is seen, things exist by way of their nature.

[*Response:*] If there were existence by way of its nature, that is, its entity, how would change be suitable? It would not.

In the *Buddhapālita Commentary,* the first two lines [of stanza 9] refute the existence of things that change due to the non-existence by way of their nature of things that would change; the last two lines refute that things exist by way of their nature, since change is unfeasible among what exists by way of its nature. All four are one's own system.[305]

Here in the [*Clear Words*] commentary Candrakīrti says:

> Also, the explanation, "Because change is seen, there is no nature," is said in the context of a seeing of change that is renowned to others. We do not assert ever anywhere that change exists. [235.1-5]

This is said with respect to explaining the statements made earlier, above, "Even you observe change of that which exists by way of its nature, fire and so forth," [and] since nature is seen to change, there is no existence by way of something's nature; [Candrakīrti] is not saying that he does not assert mere change.

INDICATING THAT IF ONE PROPOUNDS EXISTENCE BY WAY OF NATURE, ONE DOES NOT PASS BEYOND HOLDING AN EXTREME

For that person who, whereas there is not in the least existence by way of nature, conceives of things as existing [by way of their nature] and of the formerly [existent becoming] non-existent upon disintegration, it follows only definitely that saying "exists" is a conception of permanence and saying "does not exist" is a view of annihilation.

Further, views of permanence and annihilation are obstacles to high status and liberation, whereby they are a great impropriety.

---

[305] That is, unlike Candrakīrti's interpretation — in which the first two lines are an opponent's objection and the last two are Nāgārjuna's response — in Buddhapālita's commentary, all four lines are taken as Nāgārjuna setting forth his own position.

Therefore, the wise should not abide in the two extremes of existence and non-existence.

Objection: Why, if one has views of being and non-being, does one have views of permanence and annihilation?

Response: Whatever is expressed as existing by way of nature would never become non-existent, since nature is not overcome. Therefore, through asserting existence by way of nature there comes to be a view of permanence, whereas through asserting mere existence, there is not.

Having asserted that a thing that arose at a former time is established by way of its nature, if one asserts that now, that is, later, having been destroyed, it does not exist, [739] it follows that one has a view of annihilation whereas through asserting merely that what exists at a former time disintegrates at a later time, one does not.

We have no views of permanence and annihilation that depend upon nature because we do not assert that things exist by way of their nature.

Objection: Even if you do not have a view of permanence, still you have a view of annihilation.

Response: If, having asserted formerly an existence by way of its nature of a thing that was to be annihilated, one later asserts it as non-existent, since one is deprecating that existence by way of its nature, which must always exist, one comes to have a view of annihilation. However, if one says with respect to that which is utterly without establishment by nature, "It does not exist," since there is no deprecation with respect to that, one does not come to have a view of annihilation. In this fashion, the *Descent into Laṅkā Sūtra* says:

> Supramundane Victor, the one who, having previously asserted desire, hatred, and bewilderment, later propounds,

> "Desire, hatred, and bewilderment are not things," is a Nihilist.

If one asserts that things exist by way of their nature, even if one does not propound them as permanent, one comes to have a view of permanence. And, if one asserts that something that existed by way of its nature at a former time is destroyed at a later time, then even if one does not assert that its continuum is annihilated, one comes to have a view of annihilation. Hence, once one asserts that things are established by way of their nature, one does not pass beyond views of permanence and annihilation.

If one does not assert things to be established by way of their nature, one does not have views of both permanence and annihilation that depend upon nature. But, if one has no way to posit cause and effect, then since one comes to deprecation, one has a view of annihilation.

Here one cannot propound, "Because I do not assert things that are to be annihilated, I do not have a view of annihilation." For, this is like the way in which the worldly Materialists even though they do not, having formerly asserted things that are to be annihilated — former and later lives, the effects of actions, and so forth — later propound them as non-existent, cannot dispell [the fact] that they are those having a view of annihilation.

Followers of Yogic Practice [740] assert that they dispell the view of annihilation due to [their assertion that] other-powered phenomena — mere minds and mental factors — are established by way of their own character, and dispell the view of permanence due to [their assertion that] other-powered phenomena lack the imputed. With respect to this, due to [their] deprecation of the conventional existence of apprehended [objects] and apprehending [subjects] in terms of external [objects] and due to their superimpositions with respect to non-truly existent other-powered phenomena, they fall into the extremes of both permanence and annihilation. Therefore, only the view of the Mādhyamikas does not fall into the extremes of existence and non-existence and is free from the faults of permanence and annihilation. Others are not.

In this vein, Nāgārjuna's *Precious Garland* says:

> Ask the Worldlings, the Sāṃkhyas,
> Owl-Followers and Nirgranthas,
> The proponents of a person and aggregates,
> If they propound what passes beyond "is" and "is not."
>
> Thereby know that the ambrosia
> Of the Buddhas' teaching is called profound,
> An uncommon doctrine passing
> Far beyond existence and non-existence.

Those who propound mere persons are the Buddhist proponents of the person as substantially existent. Those who propound merely the aggregates are the Buddhists who propound the person as not substantially existent but the aggregates as substantially existent.

In brief, for as long as one does not know how to posit the effects of actions and bondage and release and so forth as existing within a lack of nature, that is to say, establishment by way of own-entity, no matter what sort of mode of dispelling views of permanence and annihilation one engages in, one does not pass beyond the two extremes. For, when one dispells the view of annihilation, one must assert an extreme of existence, and when one dispells the view of permanence, one must assert an extreme of non-existence.

Therefore, the mode of the [proponents of] mere knowledge who say that form does not exist but consciousness exists, and that imputations are not established by way of their own character but the other two natures are established by way of their own character, is [a teaching of] interpretable meaning, that, like the propounding of the person [as substantially existent] of the Saṃmitīyas, was set forth for such trainees by the compassionate Teacher for the sake of leading [them] gradually to techniques for realizing the ultimate. It is not of definitive meaning.

What sort of scriptures are to be posited as of interpretable meaning and what sort are to be posited as of definitive meaning should be known in accordance with the *King of Meditative Stabilizations Sūtra* and the *Teachings of Akṣhayamati Sūtra.* These points should be known in detail from [my] *Essence of the Good Explanations, Treatise Discriminating the Interpretable and the Definitive.*

II. CONJOINING THIS WITH SCRIPTURES OF DEFINITIVE MEANING

This which has been taught with reasoning in this way — that all things are without nature, that is to say, establishment by way of their own entities — is also established by profound scriptures. In order to indicate that all scriptures teaching such are explained by this chapter, there is a partial exemplification that associates this with scriptures of definitive meaning. The *King of Meditative Stabilizations Sūtra* says:

> Since all is inconceivable and unarisen,
> Knowledge of things and non-things should be destroyed.
> Those children who are under the control of thought
> Suffer in hundreds of ten millions of cyclic existences.

And:

> I remember a former past time.
> An inconceivable number of aeons ago, a chief of men,
> A great sage, was born for the sake of the world.
> He was named "Arisen from Non-being."

> Just after he was born, remaining in the sky
> He taught all phenomena as without being.
> At that time given a name concordant with that,
> He was renowned by that name in all the world.
>
> All the gods proclaimed
> This one called "Non-being" will be a Conqueror.
> As soon as he was born, taking seven steps
> This Conqueror explained phenomena as without being.
>
> Whenever a subduer, a Buddha who teaches
> All phenomena, a king of doctrine, arises,
> The sound "All phenomena lack being" comes forth
> From grass, trees, bushes, medicinal plants, rocks, and mountains.
>
> As far as sound extends in the world,
> "All lacks being, there is nothing at all,"
> For so far does there very much arise
> The roar of sound of the leader of the world.

Here, the meaning of "non-being" has the meaning of "lack of nature." [742.2]

III. CONDENSING THE MEANING AND INDICATING THE TITLE

One should ascertain the meaning which is taught explicitly, namely that being and non-being in general, and nature, other-being, and the nature which is the suchness of phenomena in particular, are not at all positable within existence through the force of own-entity. And, at that time, implicitly, one should induce ascertainment of dependent-arising, thinking, "All those are very correct within a mere positing [of phenomena] as existing through the force of verbal conventions."

This is the explanation of Chapter XV, called "The Analysis of Nature," having a nature of eleven verses.

DOCUMENT FOUR: FROM ḎZONG-KA-ḆA'S GREAT EXPOSITION

The *Great Exposition of the Stages of the Path* is the earliest of Ḏzong-ka-ḇa's five major works on the Middle Way School. He composed it in 1402 when he was forty-five years old. The last section of the *Great Exposition of the Stages of the Path* is on special insight (*lhag mthong, vipaśyanā*) into emptiness. From within this, the following section is called "The Refutation of an Identification of the Object-to-be-negated That Is Too Narrow."

Page numbers to the Dharamsala edition of the Tibetan text [860.4-870.1] are inserted into the translation in square brackets. Headings are according to Jam-ȳang-shay-ḇa's interlinear table of contents included within the *Four Interwoven Annotations*. See the Tibetan text for this section, pages 246-257.

THE REFUTATION OF AN IDENTIFICATION OF THE OBJECT-TO-BE-NEGATED THAT IS TOO NARROW

This section has three parts: (1) refuting the assertion that the object-to-be-negated is that which possesses the three attributes (*khyad chos gsum ldan*); (2) in our system, the nature possessing the three attributes (*khyad par gsum ldan gyi rang bzhin*) is emptiness; and (3) refuting the assertion that reality (*chos nyid, dharmatā*) is independent and positive.

FIRST, REFUTING THE ASSERTION THAT THE OBJECT-TO-BE-NEGATED IS THAT WHICH POSSESSES THE THREE ATTRIBUTES

Some [Tibetans] say:

> [On the occasion of this Consequence School,] that which is to be refuted is nature and that [Consequence School object-to-be-negated nature] possesses the three attributes of (1) an

> entity attribute, that it is not produced by causes and conditions, (2) a state attribute, that it is immutable, and (3) a certification attribute, that it does not depend on another.

These three attributes, moreover, are mentioned in the *Treatise on the Middle,* which says:

> The arising of nature due to causes and conditions is not reasonable.
> A nature produced by causes and conditions would have a nature of fabrication.
> How could nature be said to be fabricated?
> Nature is non-fabricated and does not depend on another. [861]

In general, if it were asserted that external and internal things such as sprouts and so forth are established as such natures having the three attributes, then Proponents of the Middle also would have to refute such [but the refutation of such a nature is not sufficient].

Here the identification of the object-to-be-negated is the identification of the root object-to-be-negated, through which the Middle Way view realizing the lack of nature of phenomena is generated in one's continuum when it is refuted without depending [on negating something else also].[306]

For, our own schools such as the Great Exposition and Sūtra Schools, and so forth, have already established that products, compounded phenomena, are created by causes and conditions and that they change. Therefore [if the object-to-be-negated is as you say it is] then there would be the faults that it would not be necessary to prove the lack of existence by way of nature to those schools [i.e., the Great Exposition and Sūtra Schools], and so

[306] See *MCHAN,* 388.6.

forth. Hence, how could your identification be getting at the final uncommon object-to-be-negated!

[Proponents of True Existence say that] things have a nature in the sense of establishment by way of their own entities. In response to that, [the Consequentialists] make the logical extension that "if things were established by way of their own entities, then they would not depend on causes and conditions, they would be immutable, and so forth." Although there are many such logical extensions in Middle Way texts, those are cases of expressing fallacies from the viewpoint of a pervader [something wider]. This is not an identification of the object-to-be-negated from the viewpoint of its own entity.

[Another reason is that] if something is ultimately established, really established, and truly established, then it must not be produced by causes and conditions, it must be immutable, and so forth; but even if that is so, still, not[307] being produced by causes and conditions and so forth is not the meaning of being ultimately established and so forth.

For example, although impermanence pervades pots, impermanence is not suitable as the meaning of pot; whereas that which is a bulbous thing, and so forth, is posited as the meaning of pot. Similarly, if something is ultimately established and so forth, then it would have to be a partless thing. Still, partless thing is not asserted to be the basic object-to-be-negated here. Since such partless things are just imputed by the uncommon conceptions of proponents of [false] tenets, such a conception [exists only among those whose mental continua are affected by tenets and thus] is not the root that binds the embodied in cyclic existence.

---

307 *MCHAN,* 390.3. Text amended from *rgyu rkyen gyis skyed pa* to *rgyu rkyen gyis ma skyed pa.*

Although one meditated on partless things as empty of nature upon delineating [such a view], that would not damage at all the innately ignorant conception (*ma rig pa'i 'dzin pa*)[308] that has operated since beginningless time.[309] Hence, even though one brought to completion the direct realization of that meaning [i.e., the lack of inherent existence of partless things, and so forth], this would not at all damage the innate afflictive emotions (*lhan skyes kyi nyon mongs*) as well.

When the view is delineated, one is to consider the refutation of the conceived object of innate ignorance to be the main point, and refute the conceived object of artificial ignorance as a branch of that.

If, not knowing that the main thing is to use the artificial as a branch of that, one forsook refuting the mode of apprehension of an innately ignorant consciousness and at the time of refuting a self of persons refuted a permanent, unitary, independent self, and at the time of refuting a self of phenomena refuted (1) the apprehended, objects that are partless particles, (2) apprehending consciousnesses that are partless moments, and (3) the nature possessing the three attributes, and so forth, that are imputed only by proponents of tenets, then such refutations are unsuitable in all ways. [862.5]

---

308 Dra-di Ge-shay [*MCHAN,* 390.6] glosses "conception" (*'dzin pa*) with "subject" (*yul can*). Within the dichotomy of object (*yul*) and subject (*yul can*), the "innately ignorant conception" is a subject, or consciousness.

309 Every emptiness is predicated upon an existent phenomenon of which it is the final mode of being. This means that a conventional truth and its own ultimate nature are one entity. Since "partless thing" does not exist, it cannot be a conventional truth that is one entity with its own emptiness.

If it were not unsuitable, then, since when delineating the view one delineated nothing beyond the non-existence of a permanent, unitary, and independent [self], and so forth, then at the time of meditation also one would have to meditate only on such. Why? Delineation of the view is for the sake of meditation. Therefore, even if one manifested such a selflessness upon meditation, and completed familiarization with it, that would be exhausted as only that [i.e., manifestly perceiving the non-existence of a permanent, unitary, and independent self]. [863]

If one did assert in that way that merely directly perceiving the non-existence of the two selves only as they are imputed by artificial conceptions can abandon the innate afflictions, desire, and so forth, that would be extremely absurd. Candrakīrti's *Introduction* [VI.140] states:

> [You propound] that when selflessness is realized
> One abandons the permanent self, [but] you do not assert that
> As the base of the conception of self. Hence, it is fantastic to propound
> That through knowing selflessness the view of self is eradicated.[310]

Candrakīrti's *Auto-Commentary* says:

> In order to illuminate by way of an example this senseless proposition that the innate conception of a self is abandoned through only refuting a permanent self, the root text says that:

---

[310] *Introduction,* VI.140 [264.2-5]:

> *bdag med rtogs tshe rtag pa'i bdag sbong zhing*
> *'di ni ngar 'dzin rten ruang mi 'dod pa*
> *de phyir bdag med shes pas bdag lta ba*
> *cis kyang 'byin zhes smra ba shin tu mtshar.*

> When an ignorant person sees a snake living inside the wall of the house and is frightened, another person says, "Do not be frightened by that snake. There is no elephant inside the wall." Alas, the assertion that fears of a snake could be removed by the words that there is no elephant is source of laughter by others, when they see this. [863.3]

Even though this is mentioned with respect to the selflessness of persons it also should be applied to the selflessness of phenomena:

> When [they assert that] the selflessness [of phenomena] is realized, they abandon an artificial self [of phenomena] and therefore they do not assert this [artificial self] as the basis that is ignorance. Therefore the proposition that [the innate] ignorance is removed by knowing the non-existence of [artificial] self [of phenomena] is very amazing.[311] [863.5]

---

[311] D̄zong-ka-b̄a's *Middling Exposition* suggests that when putting it together with the two selflessnesses, the stanza could be put together this way:

> [You propound] that when selflessness is realized
> One abandons the artificial self, [but] you do not assert that
> As the base of ignorance. Hence it is fantastic to propound
> That through knowing selflessness ignorance is eradicated.

See Jeffrey Hopkins, "Special Insight: From D̄zong-ka-b̄a's *Middling Exposition of the Stages of the Path to Enlightenment Practised by Persons of the Three Capacities* with supplementary headings by Trijang Rinbochay" (unpublished manuscript, 1979), 19. See also D̄zong-ka-b̄a's *GRS*, 386.12-15.

SECOND, IN OUR SYSTEM THE NATURE POSSESSING THE THREE ATTRIBUTES IS EMPTINESS

[*Objection:*] When the Master Nāgārjuna set forth non-fabrication and non-dependence on another as the characteristics of the entity of nature, did he speak hypothetically or does such a nature exist in fact?

Response: The reality that is mentioned [in the Perfection of Wisdom Sūtras] in the phrase "whether the Tathāgatas appear or not the reality of phenomena [just abides]" is posited as the nature. This is non-fabricated and does not depend on another. That nature does exist. [863.6] Candrakīrti's *Auto-Commentary* supplies a scriptural source:

> *Objection:* Does the Master Nāgārjuna assert that a nature qualified in such a way exists or not?
>
> *Response:* That reality in terms of which the Supramundane Victor says in the Perfection of Wisdom Sūtras, "Whether the Tathāgatas appear or not the reality of phenomena just abides," exists.
>
> *Objection:* What is this reality?
>
> *Response:* It is the final mode of abiding of these phenomena, eyes, and so forth.
>
> *Objection:* What is the nature that is the mode of abiding of these like?
>
> *Response:* It is their non-fabricatedness, i.e., non-falsity, their mode of subsistence which does not depend on other causes and conditions and is the entity realized by a Superior's knowledge [of meditative equipoise] free from the visual dimness of ignorance and its predispositions by way of not being polluted by those.
>
> *Objection:* Does that nature exist?
>
> *Response:* Who could say that it does not exist? If it did not exist, for what purpose would Bodhisattvas cultivate the path of the perfections? Bodhisattvas initiate hundreds of efforts for the sake of realizing such a reality.

Objection: Did you not earlier refute an establishment by nature with respect to all phenomena?

Response: Did we not say earlier many times that there does not exist in phenomena even a particle of the nature that is establishment by way of a thing's own entity (*rang gi ngo bos grub pa'i rang bzhin*) and which does not depend on internal mental imputation? Therefore what need is there to say anything about other phenomena, products and so forth, as being established as a nature in the sense of being established by way of their own entities without depending on internal imputation! Even the reality of things, the ultimate truth, is not in the least established as such a nature. Candrakīrti's *Clear Words* says:

> Because it is thus, therefore, that which, even in all three times, is the non-fabricated fundamental entity non-mistaken in fire, that which is not the subsequent arising of something that did not arise previously, and that which does not have reliance on causes and conditions, as do the heat of water, or near and far, or long and short, is said to be the nature [of fire].[312]
>
> *Objection:* Does there exist such a non-fabricated and non-relative entity of fire?
>
> *Response:* Such a nature is not existent by way of its own entity (*rang gi ngo bo, svarūpaṃ*) and is not [utterly] non-existent either. Though it is so, in order to get rid of the fear of the listeners, when this is taught, it is said upon making a superimposition that it exists conventionally.

Thus Candrakīrti refutes that a nature is established by way of its own entity and says that it exists conventionally.

Objection: Candrakīrti says that [such a non-fabricated entity of fire] is taught to be conventionally existent *upon making a su-*

---

312 For Sanskrit and Tibetan see note 123.

perimposition in order to get rid of the fear of listeners. The Master [Candrakīrti] himself does not assert that it exists.

Response: That is not reasonable. Those which [exist conventionally] upon imputation for the purpose of abandoning the fear of listeners are not just the nature but other phenomena also. If such a nature did not exist, then all other phenomena also would be senseless.[313]

Also, Candrakīrti's *Auto-Commentary* states: [865.4]

> It is not just that the master Nāgārjuna asserts this nature; also other persons can be caused to assert the meaning of this nature [in debate]. Hence, this nature is also presented as just established for both [disputants].

Otherwise [if nature were non-existent], one would have to assert that the Middle Way system asserted that release could not be attained [because the cessation that is an ultimate truth did not exist]. The attainment of nirvāṇa means the actualization of nirvāṇa, and nirvāṇa on this occasion is explained as true cessation and because [true cessation] is said to be the ultimate truth, the ultimate truth would not exist [if the nature did not exist]. Moreover, the source for this — Candrakīrti's *Commentary on (Nāgārjuna's) "Sixty Stanzas of Reasoning"* — proves with much vigor that when nirvāṇa is attained the ultimate truth of cessation must be actualized. [866]

Compounded phenomena such as eyes, and so forth, are not established as a nature in the sense of establishment by way of

---

313 *LRC,* 865.2-3:

> *rang bzhin de yang rang gi ngo bos grub pa bkag nas tha snyad du yod par gsungs so // gal te nyan pa po'i skrag pa spong pa'i phyir du sgro btags nas bstan par gsungs pas yod par mi bzhed do snyam na de ni rigs pa ma yin te dgos pa de'i phyir du btags nas gsungs pa ni chos gzhan rnams kyang yin pas de dag kyang med par 'gyur ro //*

own-entity or nature, meaning reality when reality is posited as nature. Hence, [compounded phenomena such as eyes, and so forth] are not established as any nature. Although the ultimate truth is established [as the nature in the sense of] positing reality as nature, [an ultimate truth] is posited by way of its two positors, non-fabrication and non-dependence on another, and hence [the ultimate] does not at all come to be established by way of its own entity. Therefore [the ultimate] is only established conventionally.

Here, being fabricated means not existing earlier and being created as a new arising. Depending on another means depending on causes and conditions. [866.3]

Forms and so forth are not established as either of those two types of nature. Therefore, one cultivates the path in order to see the nature that is reality. Hence, [Candrakīrti] says that its basis, pure behavior, is not senseless.

Moreover, it is explained that it is not contradictory (1) utterly not to assert a nature of phenomena in the sense of their establishment by way of their own entity and (2) to assert for each phenomena a [reality] nature that is a convention. Candrakīrti's *Auto-Commentary* states:

> *Objection:* Incredible! Amazing! You persons who assert there are no inherently existent things at all and who also contingently, i.e., conventionally, assert a nature that is non-fabricated and not dependent on others are propounding something that is mutually contradictory and senseless.
>
> *Response:* You who say such do not understand that the thought of these statements in [Nāgārjuna's] *Treatise* is that if just these entities of eyes, and so forth, which are dependent-arisings and which are apprehendable by childish ordinary beings, were the nature of those entities of eyes and so forth, then such a nature would be realized even by those who are erroneous. In that case, maintenance of purity would be senseless. Therefore, just these [entities of eyes and so forth] are not the final nature, and hence maintenance of

> purity for the sake of viewing that [final nature] is purposeful.
>
> [Regarding how it conventionally exists having the three attributes, Candrakīrti himself] says that, in terms of conventional truth, [the final nature] is not fabricated and is not dependent on other [causes and conditions].
>
> That [entity] which is not something seen by childish beings is suitable to be the [final] nature. Due to just those [positors of this as a nature], just that ultimate is not a thing (*dngos po, bhāva*) and is also not a non-thing, because that ultimate is by nature pacified [of all elaborations].

Here [in this context of the above quotation from Candrakīrti's *Auto-Commentary*], "existing as a thing" (*dngos po yod pa*) — as explained before on the occasion of discussing the dualistic propositions [of existing as a thing or not existing as a thing] — means "existing by way of own-entity" (*rang gi ngo bos yod pa*). "Not existing as a thing" (*dngos po med pa*) means "[its entity] not existing at all" (*ngo bo ye med*).

When one delineates that phenomena do not have a particle of establishment as nature in the sense of being established by way of their own entity, the emptiness of nature exists as an attribute (*khyad chos*) of these phenomena, forms and so forth, which serve as the substrata (*khyad gzhi*). Hence, there is no contradiction in both existing as objects of one mind and since that dualistic appearance has not vanished, that emptiness becomes an imputed ultimate truth.

When through cultivating just that view realizing a lack of nature [in the sense of inherent existence] one directly realizes that meaning, in the face of that all mistaken [appearances] that are the appearances of [phenomena as established by] nature — whereas none are established by nature — have vanished. Hence the consciousness that directly actualizes reality does not observe or see the subjects, forms and so forth. Therefore, the pair — the reality and the subjects — does not exist in the face of that awareness. Hence, the positing of those two, reality and substrata, must be done by way of some other conventional awareness.[314]

In that case, the ultimate truth is posited as a mere vanishing of all mistaken appearances that are the appearances of [phenomena] as established by nature [in the sense of inherent existence] — whereas none are established by nature — in addition to (*steng du*) the pacification of all elaborations of the object-to-be-negated, that is to say, establishment by way of a thing's own entity. Hence, although such [an ultimate truth] is asserted, how can it be necessary to assert a [reality] nature that is established by way of its own entity? Candrakīrti's *Clear Words* says:

> That entityness which by its nature becomes the object of those Superiors free from the dimness of ignorance, in the manner of non-perception of the aspects of things that are observed through the force of the dimness of ignorance, is posited as the nature of those [things].

It also says:

> The lack of production which is the [final] nature of things is not anything at all and hence is just a non-thing because it lacks entityness. Therefore, that nature of things does not exist. [868.5]

THIRD, REFUTING THE ASSERTION THAT REALITY IS INDEPENDENT AND POSITIVE

Some [i.e., the Jo-nag-b̄as following Döl-b̄o Shay-rap-gyel-tsen] did not posit the ultimate truth as a mere elimination of the elaborations of the two selves, the object-to-be-negated, and so forth. They asserted that when one realizes the ultimate mode of being, [that entity] appears — as the object of a non-erroneous

---

[314] For instance, an inferential reasoning consciousness realizing emptiness.

mind — in the way that blue, yellow, and so forth appear in the manner of being established independently (*rang dbang du*). They also asserted that the ascertainment of its existing in this way is the view realizing the profound meaning.

Also, they assert that the realization of these external and internal phenomena — which are the bases that sentient beings misapprehend as the two selves — as not existent [by] nature (*rang bzhin* [*gyis*][315] *med pa*), is a place for going astray with respect to the correct view (*lta ba'i gol sa*).

Such assertions are outside the sphere of all the scriptures of the Greater and Lesser Vehicles (*theg pa che chung*) because (1) those [Jo-nang-b̄as] assert that it is necessary to overcome the conception of self that is the root binding persons in cyclic existence, and (2) the bases that are apprehended by this [conception] as self are these [phenomena] realized as not existent by nature. Hence, without overcoming that, they assert that the conception of self is overcome through realizing some other phenomenon unrelated with that [conception of self] as true.[316]

Regarding this, for instance, it is no different than if [some person] conceives there is a snake to the east and becomes distressed, and if [someone else] thinking the distress cannot be overcome by thinking there is no snake to the east — instead says, "Think on the fact that to the west there is a tree. Through this,

---

[315] The particle *gyis* is inserted in the *MCHAN,* 405.6.

[316] *LRC,* 869.1-3:

> *theg pa che chung gi gsung rab thams cad las phyi rol tu gyur pa yin te sems can thams cad 'khor bar ching ba'i rtsa ba bdag du 'dzin pa sdog dgos par ni 'dod la des bdag tu bzung ba'i gzhi de rang bzhin med par rtogs pas de mi ldog par de dang 'brel med kyi chos gzhan zhig bden par song bar rtogs pas bdag tu 'dzin pa ldog par 'dod pa'i phyir ro //*

you will get rid of your conception of a snake in the room and will overcome your distress."

Therefore, those who wish goodness for themselves banish such to the distance and [work vigorously at] the means of eradicating the mode of apprehension of ignorance — that which binds beings in cyclic existence and is the root of all ruin. In dependence on the texts of the superior Nāgārjuna and his sons, which clearly set forth the vast and manifold collections of reasonings that establish deep ascertainment of the scriptures of definitive meaning and show that the meaning of those is not suitable to be interpreted otherwise, one will go beyond the ocean of cyclic existence.

[I, D̄zong-ka-b̄a,] have seen that these refutations of wrong ideas with respect to the object-to-be-negated are very valuable for eliminating the places where one goes wrong in finding the Middle View. Therefore I have explained them at length. [870.1]

DOCUMENT FIVE: FOUR INTERWOVEN ANNOTATIONS

This document is the section of the *Four Interwoven Annotations to (Ḏzong-ka-ḇa's) "Great Exposition of the Stages of the Path"*[317] commenting upon the chapter of Ḏzong-ka-ḇa's text from within the "Special Insight" section entitled, "The Refutation of an Identification of the Object-to-be-negated That Is Too Narrow." The *Four Interwoven Annotations* is a composite interlinear commentary on Ḏzong-ka-ḇa's *Great Exposition of the Stages of the Path* that appears to be an accreted compilation in successive editions. The four annotators are Jam-ȳang-shay-ḇa (*'jam dbyangs bzhad pa,* 1648-1721), Ba-so Chö-gyi-gyel-tsen (*ba so chos kyi rgyal mtshan,* 1402-1473; dates uncertain), De-druk-ken-chen Nga-w̄ang-rap-den (*sde drug mkhan chen ngag dbang rab rten,* 17th century), and Dra-d̄i Ge-shay Rin-chen-dön-drup (*bra sti dge bshes rin chen don grub,* 17th century).

The Tibetan text employs the typographical device of large and small font sizes often identified with the first initial of the annotator. As Napper points out, a literal translation of the *Four Interwoven Annotations* is unfeasible, due to the repetitious complexity of the interwoven commentarial voices. Therefore, I have presented the translation here as a coherent whole — as it would be read by a Tibetan scholar — without attempting to identify

---

317 The Chos-'phel-legs-ldan 1972 edition translated here is referred to as the New Delhi edition. It is a two-volume reproduction (with tracing of the faint original) of a print of the corrected Tshe-mchog-gling blocks of 1842 by Chos-'phel-legs-ldan. The 1842 blocks were themselves a corrected edition of the original 1802 blocks. Numerous errors remain.

the individual commentators or differentiate D̄zong-ka-b̄a's original words within the interwoven text.[318]

In the past there were editions of the text that contained only the annotations of one, two, and three of the authors. Although the earlier editions with fewer commentators are not now extant, the current text including the annotations of all four authors survives in two editions, the New Delhi edition employed here and a Chinese edition with no publication data.

Page numbers to the New Delhi edition of the Tibetan text are inserted into the text in square brackets. The three major subject headings are from D̄zong-ka-b̄a's text; subheadings are supplied from Jam-ȳang-shay-b̄a's commentary in the *Four Interwoven Annotations.*

THE REFUTATION OF AN IDENTIFICATION OF THE OBJECT-TO-BE-NEGATED THAT IS TOO NARROW

This section has three parts: (1) refuting the assertion that the object-to-be-negated possesses the three attributes (*khyad chos gsum ldan*); (2) in our system, the nature possessing the three attributes (*khyad par gsum ldan gyi rang bzhin*) is emptiness; and (3) refuting the assertion that reality (*chos nyid, dharmatā*) is independent and positive. [387]

FIRST, REFUTING THE ASSERTION THAT THE OBJECT-TO-BE-NEGATED POSSESSES THE THREE ATTRIBUTES

This section has seven parts: (1) confusing the mode of subsistence of things possessing the three attributes with that which is to be negated; (2) that [the nature of things possessing the three attributes] is not the nature which is the object-to-be-negated; (3)

---

[318] For a discussion of the annotators' differing commentarial styles, see Napper's "Translator's Introduction," *DAE,* 219-228.

the Hearer schools refute such a nature, therefore it is not suitable to be the object-to-be-negated here [in the Middle Way Consequence School]; (4) although it is logically implied that if something is established from its own side then it must be established in a manner possessing these three attributes, that which possesses these three attributes is not the object-to-be-negated; (5) if something is truly established it must not be produced by causes and conditions, and so forth, but non-production by causes and conditions, and so forth, is not the meaning of being truly established; (6) since the innate mode of apprehension does not have such [a mode of apprehension as is involved with these artificial conceptions], although one refuted these [artificial conceptions], there is no benefit [of liberation]; and (7) how the wise are amazed at such.

FIRST, CONFUSING THE MODE OF SUBSISTENCE OF THINGS POSSESSING THE THREE ATTRIBUTES WITH THAT WHICH IS TO BE NEGATED

[387.1] With respect to the mode of refuting too narrow an identification of the object-to-be-negated, if the establishment of things as possessing the three attributes of a nature did occur, it would be an object-to-be-negated of reasoning by a consciousness analyzing the ultimate, and the conception of that would be an artificial conception of true existence. However since those three qualities do exist with the nature or mode of subsistence of phenomena they are [not][319] refuted.

Moreover, in general, just as one must understand "thing" (*dngos po, bhāva*) as having two meanings — one as able to perform a function and the other as the nature that is the object-to-be-negated — so there are many usages of "nature":

---

319 *MCHAN*, 387.2. Text corrected from *yin no* to *min no.*

(1) the mode of subsistence of objects,
(2) the conventional nature of forms and so forth, and
(3) establishment from an object's own side, the object-to-be-negated.

Thus there are many meanings of "nature." One should know which it is by way of the context.

Moreover, regarding the three attributes, (1) non-fabricated means not newly fabricated by causes and conditions and (2) [not] depending on another means [not] depending on causes and conditions. Thus, [the three attributes] are not the meaning of [the object-to-be-negated, i.e.,] establishment by way of its own entity.

[Nevertheless] some Tibetans say:

> On the occasion of this [Consequence School,] that which is to be negated is nature and that [Consequence School object-to-be-negated] nature possesses the three attributes of (1) an entity attribute, that it is not produced by causes and conditions, (2) a state attribute, that it is immutable, and (3) a certification attribute, that it does not depend on another. These three attributes, moreover, are mentioned in the *Treatise on the Middle,* which says that:
>
> > It is not reasonable that the nature[320] should arise from causes and conditions. If such a nature did arise from causes and conditions, that nature would be something made (*byes pa can*). How could it be suitable for something to be both the nature that is how things subsist and something "made up," that is, fabricated by causes and conditions? Since being such a nature and being fab-

---

[320] Dra-di Ge-shay adds the qualifying phrase, "which is the way phenomena abide" (*chos rnams kyi ji ltar gnas pa, MCHAN,* 387.6) to identify Nāgārjuna's thought. The opponent, however, is thinking of this nature as the object-to-be-negated.

> ricated by causes and conditions is very contradictory, such is not suitable. Such natures are non-fabricated, i.e., not produced by causes and conditions, and do not depend on another mind that certifies them.

[*Reply:*] Since these [three attributes] are a feature of emptiness, how could the nature [mentioned in the *Treatise on the Middle*] be suitable as the object-to-be-negated? [388.1] One who propounds such, [i.e., that the object-to-be-negated nature possesses the three attributes] has not identified the object-to-be-negated well. For, like the example of showing the entity of thing (*dngos po, bhāva*) when identifying pot, identifying the uncommon object-to-be-negated of the view [of emptiness] as this nature that possesses the three attributes [is incorrect because] such a nature is wider than that.

SECOND, THAT IS NOT THE NATURE WHICH IS THE OBJECT-TO-BE-NEGATED

In general, if it were asserted that external and internal things such as sprouts and so forth are established as such natures having the three attributes, then Proponents of the Middle also would have to refute such; but the refutation of such a nature is not sufficient. A non-mistaken good identification of the object-to-be-negated is to identify it upon examining the final root of an object-to-be-negated, which is such that, through just refuting it, the Middle Way view realizing just the lack of existence by nature (*rang bzhin gyis med pa nyid*) of phenomena is definitely generated in one's continuum without depending on negating something else. [388.6]

THIRD, THE HEARER SCHOOLS REFUTE SUCH A NATURE, THEREFORE IT IS NOT SUITABLE TO BE THE OBJECT-TO-BE-NEGATED HERE [IN THE CONSEQUENCE SCHOOL]

It being the case that one must make such an identification, your identification of the object-to-be-negated given earlier is just a partial (*phyogs re ba*) identification and thus too narrow (*khyab chung ba*). For, our own schools such as the Great Exposition and Sūtra Schools, and so forth, have already established that products, compounded phenomena, are created by causes and conditions and that they change state by way of disintegrating each moment. Therefore if the object-to-be-negated [is as you say it is, then] there would be the faults that (1) it would not be necessary to prove the lack of existence by nature to those schools — the Great Exposition and Sūtra Schools, and so forth — and (2) those Proponents of the Great Exposition, Proponents of Sūtra, and so forth, even would absurdly cognize the lack of existence by nature of things. Hence, how could your identification be getting at the final uncommon object-to-be-negated for the view realizing emptiness!

FOURTH, ALTHOUGH IT IS LOGICALLY IMPLIED THAT IF SOMETHING IS ESTABLISHED FROM ITS OWN SIDE THEN IT MUST BE ESTABLISHED IN A MANNER POSSESSING THESE THREE ATTRIBUTES, THAT WHICH POSSESSES THESE THREE ATTRIBUTES IS NOT THE OBJECT-TO-BE-NEGATED

The Proponents of True Existence, and so forth, say in general that things have a nature in the sense of establishment by way of their own entities. In response to that, [the Consequentialists] make the logical extension that "if things were established by way of their own entities, then they would not depend on causes and conditions, would be immutable, and so forth." Although there are many such logical extensions in Nāgārjuna's *Treatise,* Candrakīrti's *Clear Words*, and so forth, those are cases of expressing fallacies from the viewpoint of a pervader [something wider]. This is not an identification of the object-to-be-negated from the viewpoint of its own entity.

To someone who, for example, asserts that something that is not a pot is a pot, thinking that if it is refuted that this non-pot is a thing by saying "then it would be a thing" it would perforce refute its being a pot, for "thing" is wider and "pot" is narrower. Thinking such, [an opponent] expresses fallacy from the viewpoint of something wider: "It follows it is a thing." However, this is not a case of identifying pot's own entity, which is narrower. [390] Similarly, if someone asserts that things have establishment by way of their own entity — which is something narrower — this would entail that things have a nature possessing the three attributes, which is wider. Thinking such, from that point of view they draw an unwanted consequence, "They would be natures having the three attributes." They are not identifying the entity of the special object-to-be-negated which is narrower, through the wider expression of fallacy. [390.1]

FIFTH, IF SOMETHING IS TRULY ESTABLISHED IT MUST NOT BE PRODUCED BY CAUSES AND CONDITIONS, AND SO FORTH; BUT NON-PRODUCTION BY CAUSES AND CONDITIONS, AND SO FORTH, IS NOT THE MEANING OF BEING TRULY ESTABLISHED

Another reason is that if something is ultimately established, really established, and truly established, then it must not be produced by causes and conditions — it must be immutable, and so forth; but even if that is so, still, not[321] being produced by causes and conditions and so forth is not posited as the meaning of being ul-

---

[321] *MCHAN*, 390.3. Text amended from *rgyu rkyen gyis skyed pa* to *rgyu rkyen gyis ma skyed pa*.

timately established and so forth. For example, although impermanence pervades pots, impermanence is not suitable as the meaning of pot; whereas that which is a bulbous thing, and so forth, and can serve as a pot without being confused with any other object, must be posited as the meaning of pot.

Similarly, if something is ultimately established and so forth, then it would have to be a partless thing. Still, partless thing is not asserted to be the object to be negated here. Since such partless things are just imputed by the uncommon conceptions of proponents of [false] tenets, such a conception exists only among those whose mental continua are affected by tenets, and thus is not the root that binds the embodied in cyclic existence. [390.5] Although one meditated on partless things as empty of inherent existence upon delineating [such a view], that would not damage at all the innately ignorant conception (*ma rig pa'i 'dzin pa*) that has operated since beginningless time. Hence, even though one brought to completion the direct realization of that meaning [i.e., the lack of inherent existence of partless things, and so forth], this would not at all damage ignorance or the innate afflictive emotions (*lhan skyes kyi nyon mongs*) as well. [391.1]

SIXTH, SINCE THE INNATE MODE OF APPREHENSION DOES NOT HAVE SUCH [A MODE OF APPREHENSION AS IS INVOLVED WITH THESE ARTIFICIAL CONCEPTIONS], ALTHOUGH ONE REFUTED THESE [ARTIFICIAL CONCEPTIONS], THERE IS NO BENEFIT

Due to the aforementioned reasons, when delineating the nature of phenomena by way of the view, one takes as the main point just that fact that what is conceived by an innately ignorant consciousness does not exist. As a branch of that, one refutes the objects apprehended by the artificial conceptions of true existence and the conception of a permanent, unitary, independent self, and so forth. [391.4]

The meaning of [Ḏzong-ka-ḇa's statement that], "When the view is delineated, one is to consider the refutation of the conceived object of innate ignorance to be the main point, and refute the conceived object of artificial ignorance as a branch of that," is that: since most artificial conceptions of true existence are fully qualified conceptions of true existence, one refutes the innate conceived object through designating it [i.e., the negation of the conceived object of the artificial conception of true existence,] as the reason, as for example in the statement, "Such-and-such lacks true existence because of not being established as able to bear analysis by reasoning." This is like the statement [in Candrakīrti's *Introduction*]:

> Therefore this reasoning of dependent-arising
> Cuts the extremes, the nets of bad views.[322] [391.3][323]

If, not knowing that this mode [of refuting the objects apprehended by the artificial conceptions of true existence and the conception of a permanent, unitary, independent self, and so forth, is a branch of refuting the innate conception,] one forsakes refuting the mode of apprehension of an innately ignorant consciousness, and at the time of refuting a self of persons refuted a permanent, unitary, independent self and at the time of refuting a self of phenomena refuted (1) apprehended objects that are partless particles, (2) apprehending consciousnesses that are partless moments, and (3) the nature possessing the three attributes, and so forth — that are imputed only by proponents of tenets — then such refutations are unsuitable in all ways. [392]

---

322 *Introduction*, VI.115 [228.3].

323 The material from, "The meaning of [Ḏzong-ka-ḇa's statement that]..." [*MCHAN*, 391.1] to here [*MCHAN*, 391.3], appears before the heading in the Tibetan text as a "prior commentary" (*snga 'grel*). In the English translation, these lines have been placed after the heading.

If it were not unsuitable, then, since when delineating the view one delineated nothing beyond the non-existence of a permanent, unitary, and independent [self of persons], and so forth,[324] then at the time of meditation also one would have to meditate only on such. Why? Delineation of the view is for the sake of meditation. [392.2]

SEVENTH, HOW THE WISE ARE AMAZED AT SUCH

Therefore, even if one manifested such a selflessness upon meditation, and completed familiarization with it, that would be exhausted as only manifestly perceiving the non-existence of a permanent, unitary, and independent self, and so forth. If one did assert in that way, as explained above, that merely directly perceiving the non-existence of the two selves only as they are imputed by artificial conceptions can overcome and abandon the innate afflictions — desire, and so forth — that would be extremely absurd. The reason for this is that Candrakīrti's *Introduction* states: [392.4]

> When they assert that the selflessness of persons is directly realized, they do their abandonment by way of perceiving the non-existence only of a permanent self but they do not assert this permanent self as the basis that is the object of observation or as the basis of the subjective aspect of the innate conception of "I." Therefore the proposition that the innate view of a self is thoroughly removed by knowing the non-

---

[324] In this discussion, the frequent use of "and so forth" (*la sogs pa*) in the phrase, "permanent, unitary, and independent self, and so forth," indicates a self of phenomena misconceived as (1) apprehended objects that are partless particles, (2) apprehending consciousnesses that are partless moments, and (3) the nature possessing the three attributes.

> existence of only a permanent self is a source of much amazement.[325] [392.6]

Candrakīrti's *Auto-Commentary* says:

> In order to illuminate by way of an example this senseless proposition that the innate conception of a self is abandoned through only refuting a permanent self, the root text says that: [393.1]
>
>> When an ignorant person sees a snake living inside the wall of the house and is frightened, another person says, "Do not be frightened by that snake. There is no elephant inside the wall." Alas, the assertion that fears of a snake could be removed by the words that there is no elephant is source of laughter by others — i.e., the intelligent — when they see this.

Even though this is mentioned with respect to the selflessness of persons, it also should be applied to the selflessness of phenomena. With respect to how to apply [this to the selflessness of phenomena]:

> When they assert that the selflessness of phenomena is directly realized, they do their abandonment by way of perceiving the non-existence only of an artificial self of phenomena, but they do not assert this artificial self of phenomena as the basis that is the object of observation or as the basis of the subjective aspect of innate ignorance. Therefore the proposition that the innate ignorance is thoroughly removed by knowing the non-existence of only the artificial self of phenomena is a source of much amazement.

---

[325] *Introduction,* VI.140 [264.2-5].

SECOND, IN OUR SYSTEM THE NATURE POSSESSING THE THREE ATTRIBUTES IS THE MODE OF SUBSISTENCE, EMPTINESS

This section has thirteen parts. [393.5]

FIRST, THE MEANING OF THAT SCRIPTURE

[*Objection:*] If the triply-qualified mode of subsistence does not exist, there would be no hearing, thinking, and meditating [on it]. When the master Nāgārjuna set forth non-fabrication and non-dependence on another as the characteristics of the entity of nature, did he speak hypothetically or does such a nature exist in fact?

Response: A nature having those three attributes is refuted with respect to certain substrata, i.e., compounded phenomena, but in general does exist. Although emptiness — the mode of subsistence — exists as that nature which is the nature having the three attributes, it does not exist as a nature that is established by way of its own entity. The *Clear Words* says that:

> That factor which is non-erroneous with respect to fire in the three times is the nature of fire, its emptiness. Fire is only empty of nature [i.e., inherent existence] over the three times, and therefore this fundamental entity which existed from the start and which:
>
> (1) is not newly fabricated by causes and conditions,
> (2) is not a new arising of what did not exist before, and
> (3) from the beginning does not depend on another — unlike the heat of water, which depends on fire as a condition and does not depend on a positing factor because it does not pass beyond a natural emptiness from the very start, without being like positing here and there, long and short, and so forth, in dependence on any [comparative] basis

is the nature of fire [i.e., its emptiness]. [394.3]

The natural emptiness in the entity of fire is not existent by way of its own entity and is also not non-existent conventionally. Though indeed it does not exist by way of its own entity, in order to relieve listeners of fear it is said that it conventionally exists as only an imputation by thought. [394.4]

Response: The reality which is mentioned in the Perfection of Wisdom Sūtras in the phrase "whether the Tathāgatas appear or not the reality of phenomena just abides" is posited as the nature. This is non-fabricated and does not depend on another. That nature does exist. [Candrakīrti] proves that it exists together with a source for this in his *Auto-Commentary:*

> *Objection:* Does the Master Nāgārjuna assert that a nature qualified in such a way exists or not?
>
> *Response:* That reality in terms of which the Supramundane Victor says in the Perfection of Wisdom Sūtras, "Whether the Tathāgatas appear or not the reality of phenomena just abides" just definitely exists.
>
> *Objection:* Also, what is this reality?
>
> *Response:* It is the final mode of abiding of these phenomena, eyes, and so forth. [395.2]
>
> *Objection:* What is the nature that is the mode of abiding of these like?
>
> *Response:* It is their non-fabricatedness, i.e., non-falsity, their mode of abiding or subsistence which does not depend on other causes and conditions. Furthermore, that mode of subsistence is the entity realized by a Superior's knowledge of meditative equipoise free from the visual dimness of ignorance and its predispositions by way of not being polluted by those.
>
> *Objection:* Does that nature exist?
>
> *Response:* Who could say that it does not exist? If it did not exist, for what purpose would Bodhisattvas cultivate the

> path of the perfections? Bodhisattvas initiate hundreds of efforts for the sake of realizing such a reality. [395.7]

SECOND, THOUGH THE NATURE REFUTED FORMERLY AND THE NATURE WHICH IS THE MODE OF SUBSISTENCE OF THINGS HAVE THE SAME NAME, THE MEANING IS DIFFERENT

Objection: Did you not earlier refute an establishment by nature with respect to all phenomena?

Response: Did we not say earlier many times that there does not exist in phenomena even a particle of the nature that is establishment by way of a thing's own entity (*rang gi ngo bos grub pa'i rang bzhin*) and that does not depend on internal mental imputation? Therefore what need is there to say anything about other phenomena, products and so forth, as being established as a nature in the sense of being established by way of their own entities without depending on internal imputation! Even the reality of things, the ultimate truth, is not in the least established as such a nature. The *Clear Words*, upon refuting a nature established by way of its own entity, says that it exists conventionally. Earlier Candrakīrti said [in the *Clear Words*] that:

> Because the heat of fire is produced by other causes and conditions, it is not the nature of fire.

Thereupon, in order to identify the nature of fire he says that:

> That which abides non-erroneously in fire throughout the three times — past, future, and present — which is the fundamental entity of fire — i.e., the basic entity or basic disposition of fire:
>
> (1) which is not fabricated by causes and conditions, not being something that did not arise before and arose newly due to some other causes like, for example, the heat of water,
>
> (2) and which does not depend on causes and conditions, like for example here and there or long and

> short — which have a mode of mutual dependence on each other —

is called nature. [396.4]

Objection: Does there exist such a non-fabricated and non-relative entity of fire?

Response: Such a nature is not existent by way of its own entity and also is not utterly non-existent either. Though it is so, in order to get rid of the fear of the listeners, when it is taught it is said upon making a superimposition that it exists conventionally. The conventions of "nature" and "reality" which did not exist before [for those listeners] are newly associated [with the reality nature].

THIRD, ABANDONING OBJECTIONS

Objection: Since Candrakīrti says that it [i.e., the non-fabricated entity of fire] is taught to be conventionally existent *upon making a superimposition* in order to get rid of the fear of listeners, the Master [Candrakīrti] himself does not assert that it exists.

Response: That is not reasonable. Those which [exist conventionally] upon imputation for the purpose of abandoning the fear of listeners are not just the nature but other phenomena also. If such a nature did not exist, then all other phenomena also would be senseless.

FOURTH, NOT ONLY MUST IT EXIST BUT ALSO BOTH PARTIES CAN ASSERT IT

Therefore, that nature exists because, as quoted earlier in the *Auto-Commentary,* Candrakīrti — expressing the damage that if such a nature did not exist it would absurdly follow that pure behavior would be senseless — proves in this way that it does exist. And also Candrakīrti's *Auto-Commentary* says that:

> It is not just that the master Nāgārjuna asserts this nature; also other persons can be caused to assert the meaning of this

> nature [in debate]. Hence, this nature is also presented as just established for both oneself and others (or, both disputants). [398.2]

FIFTH, IF THE NATURE DID NOT EXIST, THEN SINCE EVEN NIRVĀṆA WOULD NOT BE AN ULTIMATE TRUTH, THERE WOULD BE NO RELEASE

If, other than the existence of that nature, one asserted that it did not exist, in the Middle Way system it would have to be asserted that release could not be attained because the cessation which is an ultimate truth would not exist. The ultimate true cessation would not exist because Candrakīrti's *Commentary on (Nāgārjuna's) "Sixty Stanzas of Reasoning"*[326] states:

> That which is called the attainment of nirvāṇa means the actualization of nirvāṇa, and nirvāṇa on this occasion is described as a true cessation. And that true cessation is the ultimate truth. And because true cessation is the ultimate, the ultimate truth would not exist [if the nature did not exist].[327]

SIXTH, INDICATING THAT WHEN NIRVĀṆA IS ATTAINED ONE MUST ACTUALIZE THE ULTIMATE TRUTH OF CESSATION

Moreover, the source for this — Candrakīrti's *Commentary on (Nāgārjuna's) "Sixty Stanzas of Reasoning"* — proves with much vigor that when nirvāṇa is attained the ultimate truth of cessation must be actualized. [398.5]

---

[326] *rigs pa drug cu pa'i 'grel pa, yuktiṣaṣṭikāvṛtti,* P5265.

[327] Other quotes from Candrakīrti's *Commentary on (Nāgārjuna's) "Sixty Stanzas of Reasoning"* are cited by Nga-w̄ang-b̄el-den in the *Explanation of the Conventional and the Ultimate in the Four Systems of Tenets* (*grub mtha'i bzhi'i lugs kyi kun rdzob dang don dam pa'i don rnam par bshad pa legs bshad dpyid kyi dpal mo'i glu dbyangs*), (New Delhi: Guru Deva, 1972), 169.4-170.1.

SEVENTH, ALTHOUGH [THE EMPTINESS] NATURE HAS ALL THREE ATTRIBUTES, SINCE IT EXISTS CONVENTIONALLY IT IS NOT ESTABLISHED FROM ITS OWN SIDE

As explained above, compounded phenomena such as eyes, and so forth, fulfill neither of the meanings of nature: (1) establishment as a nature in the sense of establishment by way of own-entity or (2) nature meaning reality when reality is posited as nature. Hence, compounded phenomena such as eyes, and so forth, are not established as any nature.

Although the ultimate truth is established as the nature in the sense of positing reality as nature, an ultimate truth is posited — as such a reality that is nature — by way of its two positors, non-fabrication and non-dependence on another, and hence the ultimate does not at all come to be established by way of its own entity. Therefore, since the ultimate must be posited as not in the least established as a nature in the sense of being established by way of its own entity, the ultimate is only established conventionally.

EIGHTH, THE EXPLANATION OF THE MEANING OF THE THREE ATTRIBUTES

Here, being fabricated means not existing earlier and being created later as a new arising, or being produced later contingently. Depending on another means depending on other causes and conditions.[328] [399.3]

---

[328] Here Ḏzong-ka-ḇa says that depending on another means depending on other causes and conditions. However, earlier in the text [*MCHAN,* 387.5] Ḏzong-ka-ḇa spoke of "the certification [attribute], not depending on another" (*rnam 'jog [gyi khyad par] gzhan la mi bltos pa'o*). An annotator glosses this in a note with "not depending on another positing awareness" (*'jog byed kyi blo gzhan la bltos pa med pa*) [*MCHAN,* 388.2].

NINTH, ANSWERING ANOTHER DISPUTANT'S OBJECTION THAT THIS IS CONTRADICTORY

Forms and so forth are not established as either of those two types of nature — neither the reality referred to as nature nor the nature that is establishment from a thing's own side. Hence, by remaining with just forms, and so forth, one does not see the nature that is reality. Since it is not seen that way, one cultivates the path in order to see the nature that is reality. Hence, [Candrakīrti] says that its basis, pure behavior, is not senseless.

Moreover, it is explained that it is not contradictory (1) utterly not to assert a nature of phenomena in the sense of their establishment by way of their own entity and (2) contingently to assert for each phenomena a [reality] nature that is a convention.[329] In the *Auto-Commentary* [Candrakīrti] initially states another's objection that these are contradictory. [It begins with the exclamations] "Incredible!" (*kye ma*), "Amazing!" (*ma la*).[330] From among the many usages of "incredible" this is a term of derision. "Amazing"[331] is like saying in common language, "improper from the base" (*gzhi nas ma 'grig*) or, "not established from the root"

[329] *rang rang gi tha snyad kyi rang bzhin* [*MCHAN*, 399.5]. This note serves to emphasize that emptiness is not inherently existent.

[330] Alexander Csoma de Koros, *Sanskrit-Tibetan-English Vocabulary* (Delhi: Sri Satguru Publications, 1980), 49:

Ahovata	kye ma, kye hud, ma la, ye ma, ya la la	Oh! strange, wonderful
Hā	kye, kye ma, kye hud	O! Oh! Alas!

[331] The commentary [*MCHAN*, 400.1] gives a gloss of "amazing" (*ma la*) as "from the base" (*gzhi nas*) or "from the bottom" (*ma nas*).

(*rtsa ba nas ma byung*), or like saying "not established from the foot!" (*rkang nas ma byung*). The *Auto-Commentary* states:

> *Objection:* Incredible! Amazing! You persons who assert there are no inherently existent things at all and who also contingently, i.e., conventionally, assert a nature that is non-fabricated and not dependent on others are propounding something that is mutually contradictory and senseless.
>
> *Response:* You who say such do not understand that the thought of these statements in [Nāgārjuna's] *Treatise* is that if just these entities of eyes, and so forth, which are dependent-arisings produced by causes and conditions and which are apprehendable by way of being directly realizable even by childish ordinary beings were the final nature of those entities of eyes and so forth, then such a nature would be directly realized even by those who are erroneous, i.e., mistaken. In that case, cultivating the path for the sake of directly seeing that nature and maintenance of purity would be senseless. Therefore, just these entities of eyes and so forth are not the final nature, and hence cultivation of the path and maintenance of purity for the sake of viewing that final nature are purposeful and fruitful.
>
> Regarding how it conventionally exists having the three attributes, Candrakīrti himself says in terms of contingent conventions that the final nature is not fabricated in the sense of being something that formerly did not exist and newly arose and says that the final nature is not dependent on other causes and conditions.
>
> That entity which is not something seen by childish ordinary beings is suitable to be the final nature. Due to just those positors of this as a nature — being non-fabricated, and so forth and not being an object seen [by childish beings] — just that ultimate is not a thing (*dngos po, bhāva*) in the sense of being truly established or being established by way of its own character and is also not a non-thing in the sense of its entity not existing at all, because that ultimate is by nature devoid and pacified of all elaborations. [401.3]

TENTH, THE MEANING OF THAT IS THAT THE ULTIMATE DOES NOT EXIST BY WAY OF ITS OWN ENTITY AND IS NOT UTTERLY NON-EXISTENT

Here in this context [of the above quotation from Candrakīrti's *Auto-Commentary*], "existing as a thing" (*dngos po yod pa*) — as explained before on the occasion of discussing the dualistic propositions of existing as a thing or not existing as a thing — must be taken as meaning "existing by way of own-entity" (*rang gi ngo bos yod pa*). "Not existing as a thing" (*dngos po med pa*) must be taken as referring to its "entity not existing at all" (*ngo bo ye med*). [401.4]

ELEVENTH, THE IMPUTATIONAL ULTIMATE[332]

At this time of initially delineating the view now while a common being, when one delineates that phenomena do not have a particle of establishment as nature in the sense of being established by way of their own entity, the emptiness of nature which is delineated exists as an attribute (*khyad chos*) of these phenomena, forms and so forth, which serve as the substrata (*khyad gzhi*). Hence, there is no contradiction in both the substrata — forms and so forth — and the attribute — emptiness — existing as objects of one mind.

To that [inferential consciousness realizing emptiness] there is the dualistic appearance of [a phenomenon] appearing to exist by way of its own nature, whereas [phenomena] do not exist by way of their own nature and since that dualistic appearance has not vanished, that emptiness — which for that mind is together with appearance — becomes an imputed, but not metaphorical, ultimate truth. [401.2]

---

[332] Text correction from *brtags* to *btags* [*MCHAN,* 401.4] based on the Berkeley edition, 117.2.

However it is very important to distinguish between the emptiness in the face of the ascertainment factor of that awareness and the emptiness in the face of the appearance factor of that awareness. For, the emptiness in the face of the ascertainment factor of that awareness [i.e., an inferential consciousness realizing emptiness] is an actual emptiness.

What is being said [here in the *Great Exposition of the Stages of the Path*] is: in that way the emptiness which is an emptiness of nature [in the sense of establishment by way of own-entity] with respect to forms, and so forth, exists as an attribute of forms, and so forth. The collection of such a substratum and attribute — for instance the collection of a sprout and the lack of true existence of that sprout — exists in the face of an inferential reasoning consciousness realizing the selflessness of a sprout. Since such dualistic appearance has not vanished, emptiness in the face of that inferential consciousness is an imputed ultimate truth. However, such dualistic appearance has vanished in the face of a Superior's meditative equipoise directly realizing the selflessness of a sprout and hence, since the positing of those two — substratum and attribute — is not feasible in the face of such an awareness, another awareness must posit them. [402.3]

The meaning of this is explained in the *Smaller Exposition of the Stages of the Path:* With respect to that [directly realized] ultimate, although there is no difference in terms of entity, that ultimate — from the point of view of the object — must be one that is endowed with the two features of (1) a pacification of all elaborations of the object-to-be-negated, i.e., establishment by way of its own entity and (2) a pacification of all elaborations of dualistic appearance. [402.4]

Moreover — in the face of a Superior's exalted wisdom of meditative equipoise realizing the lack of true existence — the lack of true existence of a sprout is both. However, the elaborations of dualistic appearance have not vanished for an inferential consciousness realizing a sprout as selfless. In the face of that inferential cognition, the lack of true existence of the sprout is a suchness that involves a pacification of the elaborations of the object-to-be-negated, but is not a suchness that involves a pacification of the elaborations of dualistic appearance. Therefore, from that point of view, it is an imputed ultimate truth in the face of that consciousness, but in general it is not an imputed ultimate truth in the face of that consciousness. However, it is said that through this, distinctions may need to be made also with respect to the *Great Exposition of the Stages of the Path.* [402.6]

TWELFTH, THE WAY THE ACTUAL ULTIMATE IS FREE FROM ELABORATIONS

When through cultivating just that view realizing a lack of nature [in the sense of inherent existence] one directly realizes that meaning, in the face of that direct realization all mistaken [appearances] that are the appearances of [phenomena] as established by nature — whereas none are established by nature — have vanished. Hence the consciousness that directly actualizes reality does not observe or see the subjects,[333] forms, and so forth. Therefore, the pair — the emptiness which is such a reality and the subjects, forms, and so forth — does not exist in the face of that awareness.[334] Since the pair does not exist in the face of it, the positing of those two, reality and substrata, as reality and substrata is not done by that awareness directly realizing reality and therefore must be done by way of some other conventional awareness. [403.3]

---

[333] Here "subjects" refers to the substrata, those things that are empty.

[334] That is to say, the two as a pair do not appear to a Superior's wisdom consciousness directly realizing emptiness, because only emptiness

THIRTEENTH, ALTHOUGH THE ULTIMATE IS FREE FROM ELABORATIONS IT NEED NOT BE ESTABLISHED FROM ITS OWN SIDE

In that case, the ultimate truth is posited as a mere vanishing of all mistaken appearances that are the appearances of [phenomena] as established by nature [in the sense of inherent existence] — whereas none are established by nature — in addition to (*steng du*) the pacification of all elaborations of the object-to-be-negated, that is to say, establishment by way of a thing's own entity. Hence, although such an ultimate truth is asserted, how can it be necessary to assert a [reality] nature that is established by way of its own entity?

[In the citation from the *Clear Words* below] Candrakīrti says that "things are observed through the force of the dimness of ignorance;" this means "things that are observed through the force of the dimness of ignorance." With respect to the meaning of many such occurrences, on learner paths there do not exist consciousnesses that are not polluted by the dimness of ignorance except for a Superior's non-contaminated wisdom of meditative equipoise. Therefore, thinking that the pollution of ignorance exists in the conventional consciousnesses that are the positors of conventionalities, forms and so forth, it is said — with respect to conventionalities — on many occasions that they are "posited by ignorance," they are "produced by ignorance," and they are "observed by ignorance." Moreover, Candrakīrti's *Clear Words* says that:[335]

---

appears to that consciousness.

[335] These two citations are from *PP* 265.2-8 [*TSHIG*, 43.1.6; *D-TSHIG*, 228.6-14].

> Just that entity or nature of things becomes an object of meditative equipoise of Superiors — who are not polluted by ignorance and are free from its predispositions — in the manner of the non-perception of false entities since it does not become an object by way of the aspects of things — that is to say, the false entities of forms, and so forth, from between the two [i.e., conventional and ultimate] entities — that appear and are observed to be established by nature [in the sense of being inherently existent] through the force of the dimness of ignorance. This entity is posited as just the final nature (*rang bzhin mthar thug nyid*) of those things.

And it says:

> The emptiness which is the lack of production by nature and which is the final nature that is the mode of subsistence of things such as forms — as it appears in meditative equipoise devoid of all the two elaborations[336] — is not anything at all in the sense that it is not explicitly provable to others — in accordance with how it appears — through analyses, verbalizations, examples, and reasons and hence it is just a non-thing in that it is the vanishing of things such as forms. Therefore in the face of that meditative equipoise, its entity is not apprehendable.[337] Hence, that nature of things abides in this way, and that nature does not exist in the face of that meditative equipoise in the manner of things such as forms being the support and the nature being the supported. [404.6]

---

336 The elaborations of true existence (*dgag bya'i spros pa*) and the elaborations of mistaken appearances (*'khrul snang gi spros pa*).

337 That is, it cannot be explained to others through analyses, verbalizations, and so forth.

THIRD, REFUTING THE ASSERTION THAT REALITY IS INDEPENDENT AND POSITIVE

This section has three parts: (1) in any Mind Only or Middle Way system a negative phenomenon must be imputedly existent, therefore the assertion that reality is a positive independent phenomenon that does not depend upon the elimination of an object-to-be-negated is wrong; (2) advice that those who want goodness for themselves should abandon this extremism; and (3) the value of the unmistaken object-to-be-negated.

FIRST, IN ANY MIND ONLY OR MIDDLE WAY SYSTEM A NEGATIVE PHENOMENON MUST BE IMPUTEDLY EXISTENT; THEREFORE THE ASSERTION THAT REALITY IS POSITIVE AND INDEPENDENT AND DOES NOT DEPEND UPON THE ELIMINATION OF AN OBJECT-TO-BE-NEGATED IS WRONG

The Jo-nang-b̄as, who pretended[338] to take as their source the Kālacakra and Maitreya's *Treatise on the Later Scriptures of the Mahāyāna,*[339] or some Tibetans who profess to be wise,[340] did not posit the ultimate truth as a mere elimination of the elaborations of the two selves of persons and phenomena, the object-to-be-negated, and so forth. They asserted that even when one realizes the ultimate mode of being, that entity appears — as the object of a non-erroneous mind — in the way that blue, yellow, and so forth appear to the mind as unmixed diverse substances in the manner of its entity being established independently (*rang dbang du*), unmixed with any other, from its own side, and not dependent on another. [405.3] They also asserted that what appears in

---

[338] The verb Jam-ȳang-shay-b̄a uses is *khul.* See note 242.

[339] Maitreya[nātha] (*byams mgon*), *theg pa chen po rgyud bla ma'i bstan bcos, mahāyānottaratantraśāstra,* P5525.

[340] These two identifications are by different annotators. See note 244.

this way exists in accordance with its appearance and that the ascertainment of its existing in this way is the final view realizing the profound meaning in the Kālacakra system and in Asaṅga's system.

Also, they assert that the realization by Nāgārjuna, Haribhadra, and so forth, of these external and internal phenomena — which are the bases that sentient beings misapprehend as the two selves of persons and phenomena — as not existent by nature (*rang bzhin gyis med pa*), is a view of annihilation and a place for going astray with respect to the correct view (*lta ba'i gol sa*). [405.5] The meaning of "place for going astray" is "opposite (*log*) [view]" or "wrong (*nor*) [view]." The phrase, "place for going astray with respect to the correct view" comes to mean, "direction opposite to the correct view" (*yang dag pa'i lta ba'i log phyogs*), "a place deviating from the view" (*lta ba log sa*), or, "a wrong view" (*log lta*). For example, this is like saying, "went on an opposite path" (*lam log sar phyin pa*) and "went astray from the path" (*lam gol sar phyin pa*), for "having gone on a wrong path" (*lam nor sar phyin pa*). Hence, it needs to be known that just as, "place for going astray from the path" (*lam gyi gol sa*), "place that is wrong on the path" (*lam gyi nor sa*), "place that deviates from the path" (*lam gyi log sa*), and so forth, are equivalent, so "place for going astray from the view" (*lta ba'i gol sa*), "place that is wrong regarding the view" (*lta ba'i nor sa*), "place that deviates from the view" (*lta ba'i log sa*), and so forth, are equivalent. [406.1]

Regarding how those [assertions that (1) when one realizes the ultimate mode of being, that entity appears unmixed, independent, established under its own power, and so forth, and that (2) realizing phenomena as not existent by nature is a view of annihilation and a place for going astray with respect to the correct view] are not even among Buddhist systems:

Such assertions are outside the sphere of all the scriptures of the Greater and Lesser Vehicles (*theg pa che chung*) because (1) those [Jo-nang-b̄as] themselves very much assert that it is necessary to overcome the conception of self that is the root binding persons in cyclic existence and (2) the bases that are apprehended by this [conception] as self in the sense of establishment by nature (*rang bzhin gyis grub pa nyid*) are these phenomena which are the external and internal aggregates, and so forth, and hence in dependence on apprehending those bases as established by nature one is bound in cyclic existence by attachment, having been deceived by the appearance of those [bases] as existent by way of nature, whereas they are not existent by nature.

Hence, these bonds must be cut through realizing that just these bases are without nature, and, whereas this is the case, they assert that realizing such does not overcome the conception of self which is such a bond. [406.4] Also, they assert the wrong opinion that through realizing some other phenomenon — which is independent and unrelated with the conception of self in the sense that it does not exist as an object of that conception of self or in its sphere — the conception of self is overcome. [406.5]

These assertions are very amazing. For instance, it is no different than if some person conceives there is a snake to the east and becomes distressed, and if someone else as a technique for removing this distress — thinking the distress cannot be overcome by thinking there is no snake to the east — instead says, "Think on the fact that to the west there is a tree. If you think about this you will get rid of your conception of a snake in the room and will overcome your distress." [407.2]

SECOND, THE ADVICE THAT THOSE WHO WANT GOODNESS FOR THEMSELVES BANISH THIS [VIEW] TO THE DISTANCE

Therefore those beings who wish to accomplish goodness for themselves banish such wrong views to the distance and work vigorously at the unmistaken means of eradicating the mode of apprehension of ignorance — that which binds beings in cyclic existence and is the root of all ruin, i.e., loss or dimunition. In dependence on the texts of the superior Nāgārjuna and his sons — the *Treatise on the Middle* and its commentaries — that clearly set forth the vast and manifold collections of reasonings that establish deep ascertainment of the scriptures of definitive meaning and show that the meaning of those scriptures is not suitable to be interpreted otherwise, those beings go beyond the ocean of cyclic existence through knowing those meanings and meditating on them. [407.7]

THIRD, THE VALUE OF NOT MISTAKING THE OBJECT-TO-BE-NEGATED

[I, D̄zong-ka-b̄a,] have seen that these aforementioned refutations of wrong ideas with respect to the object-to-be-negated are very valuable and helpful for eliminating the places where one goes wrong in the process of finding the Middle View. Therefore I have explained them at length. What has preceded here has been the mode of refuting wrong conceptions by others with respect to the object-to-be-negated. [408.1]

TRANSLATION EQUIVALENTS

The following table of translation equivalents details a variety of technical terms concerned with the study of nature. I give paradigmatic examples in notes. These terms include most of those in the *Treatise on the Middle* (XV) and the corresponding chapter in the *Clear Words,* as well as terms relating to the topic of nature encountered in this work.

English	Sanskrit	Tibetan
absence of nature[341]	svābhāvābhāva	rang bzhin med pa
aspects of things[342]	bhāvajātam	dngos po'i rnam pa
by way of own-entity[343]	svarūpataḥ	rang gi ngo bas
causal contributors[344]	upādāna	nye bar len pa

341 "...because of a wish to express a non-affirming negative, 'lacking being' means an absence [or "a lack"] of nature"; *abhāvapratiṣedhavivakṣatatvāt bhāvābhāvārtha eva svabhāvābhāvārthaḥ* [*PP*, 279.3]; *med par dgag pa brjod par 'dod pa'i phyir dngos po med pa'i don ni rang bzhin med pa'i don yin no* [*TSHIG*, 45.1.8; *D-TSHIG*, 239.3-5]. See page 158.

342 "...the aspects of things that are observed through the force of the opthomalia of ignorance"; *avidhyātimiraprabhāvopalabdhaṃ bhāvajātaṃ* [*PP*, 265.3]; *dngos po'i rnam pa ma rig pa'i rab rib kyi mthus dmigs pa* [*TSHIG*, 43.1.6; *D-TSHIGS*, 228.8-9]. See page 143.

343 "Such a nature is not existent by way of its own entity"; *na tadasti...svarūpataḥ* [*PP*, 264.3]; *de ni rang gi ngo bos yod pa ma yin pa* [*TSHIG*, 42.5.8; *D-TSHIG*, 227.8]. See page 146.

344 "A nature of things just exists because of the causal contributors — the causes and conditions that produce them"; *atrāha vidhyate eva bhāvānāṃ svabhāvastanniṣpādakahetupratyayopādānāt* [*PP*, 259.1]; *'dir smras pa dngos po rnams kyi rang bzhin ni yod pa nyid de de dag skyed par byed pa'i rgyu dang rkyen nye bar len pa'i phyir ro* [*TSHIG*, 42.1.8; *D-*

conventional own-entity[345]	sāṃvṛtam svarūpam	rang gi ngo bo kun rdzob pa
entity[346]	bhāva[347]/rūpam[348]	ngo bo
entity of suchness[349]	tathābhāva	de bzhin nyid kyi ngo bo

TSHIG, 223.1-2]. See page 79.

345 "The Supramundane Victor, in the *abhidharma,* made a presentation of a conventional own-entity"; *bhagavatā tadevaiṣām sāṃvṛtaṃ svarūpamabhidharma vyavasthāp itaṃ* [*PP,* 261.5.6]; *bcom ldan 'das kyi kyang chos mngon par de dag gi rang gi ngo bo kun rdzob pa* [*TSHIG,* 42.4.4; D-*TSHIG,* 225.15-16]. See page 143.

346 The term "entity" (*ngo bo*) can be the translation of either *bhāva* or *rūpam.* See next two notes.

347 "It is that entity of suchness that does not change and always abides"; *keyam tathatā tathābhāvo 'vikāritvam sadaiva svāyitā* [*PP,* 264.11]; *de bzhin nyid 'di yang gang zhig ce na de bzhin nyid kyi ngo bo 'gyur ba med pa nyid* [*TSHIG,* 43.1.5; *D-TSHIG,* 228.4]. See page 147.

348 "...that which is the entity that is the "mine" of whatsoever thing is said to be its nature"; *iha svo bhāvaḥ svabhāva iti yasya padārthasya yadātmīyaṃ rūpaṃ tattasya svabhāva iti vyapadiśyate // kiṃ ca kasyātmīyaṃ yadhyasyākṛtrimaṃ* [*PP,* 262.12]; *'di ni rang gi dngos po ni rang bzhin no zhes bya bas gang zhig dngos po gang gi bdag gi ba'i ngo bo yin pa de ni rang bzhin yin no zhes brjod do // gang zhig gang gi bdag gi ba yin zhe na gang gis gang ma bcos pa'o* [*TSHIG,* 42.5.2; *D-TSHIG,* 226.13]. See page 145.

349 "It is that entity of suchness that does not change and always abides"; *keyam tathatā tathābhāvo 'vikāritvam sadaiva svāyitā* [*PP,* 264.11]; *de bzhin nyid 'di yang gang zhig ce na de bzhin nyid kyi ngo bo 'gyur ba med pa nyid* [*TSHIG,* 43.1.5; *D-TSHIG,* 228.4]. See page 147. Also see footnote 224.

entityness[350]	rūpatvā[351]	ngo bo nyid
entityness	svabhāva[352]	ngo bo nyid
entityness	svarūpam[353]	ngo bo nyid
establishment by way of own-entity[354]	*svabhāvasiddha[355]	rang gi ngo bos grub pa
existence by way of just nature[356]	svabhāvata evāstit-vaṃ	rang bzhin kho nas yod pa nyid

[350] The term "entityness" (*ngo bo nyid*) can be the translation of either *rūpatvā, svabhāva,* or *svarūpam.* See next three notes.

[351] "When these pots and so forth are not established as an entityness of being"; *yadā tvamī ghaṭādayo bhāvarūpatvenaivāsiddhāstadā* [*PP*, 267.5]; *gang gi tshe bum pa la sogs pa 'di dag ngnos po'i ngo bo nyid du ma grub pa* [*TSHIG*, 43.3.6; *D-TSHIG*, 230.9-10]. See page 147.

[352] "Since an imputed entityness does not exist in them"; *tasya parikal-pitasvabhāvābhāvād* [*PP*, 274.7]; *de la kun tu brtags pa'i ngo bo nyid med pas...* [*TSHIG*, 44.4.7; *D-TSHIG*, 236]. See page 155. Poussin states, "Akutobhaya traduit *svabhāva* par *ngo bo nyid.*" *PP*, 259.n2.

[353] "That entityness...is posited as the nature of those"; *tadeva svarūpameṣām sbabhāva iti* [*PP*, 265.4]; *ngo bo nyid de dag gi rang bzhin du rnam par bzhag go* [*TSHIG*, 43.1.7; *D-TSHIG*, 228.10]. See page 149.

[354] "If there is no nature, that is to say, establishment by way of own-entity..."; *des na rang gi ngo bos grub pa'i rang bzhin med na...*[*LRC*, 798.5-798.6]. See page 67.

[355] I have not located this term in Sanskrit.

[356] "Even if there were existence by way of their nature of fire and so forth, what fault would there be?"; *yadi punarevamagnyādīnāṃ sva-bhāvata evāstitvaṃ syātko doṣaḥ syāt* [*PP*, 271.19]; *gal te yang de ltar me la sogs pa rang bzhin kho nas yod pa nyid du 'gyur na nyes pa cir 'gyur* [*TSHIG*, 44.1.8; *D-TSHIG*, 233.11-12]. See page 152.

existent/non-existent[357]	asti/nāsti	yod pa/med pa
exists[358]	vidyate	yod pa
fabricated[359]	kṛtrimam	bcos ma yin pa
fabrication[360]	kṛtakas	byas pa can
fundamental[361]	nijam	gnyug ma
fundamental nature[362]	mūlaprakṛti	rtsa ba'i rang bzhin

[357] "Such a nature is not existent by way of its own entity and is not [utterly] non-existent either"; *na tadasti na cāpi nāsti svarūpataḥ* [*PP*, 264.3]; *de ni rang gi ngo bos yod pa ma yin pa med pa yang ma yin no* [*TSHIG*, 42.5.8; *D-TSHIG*, 227.9-10]. See page 146.

[358] "A nature of things just exists because of the causal contributors — the causes and conditions that produce them"; *atrāha vidyata eva bhāvānāṃ svabhāvastanniṣpādakahetupratyayopādānāt* [*PP*, 259.1]; *'dir smras pa dngos po rnams kyi rang bzhin ni yod pa nyid de de dag skyed par byed pa'i rgyu dang rkyen nye bar len pa'i phyir ro* [*TSHIG*, 42.1.8; *D-TSHIG*, 223.1-2]. See page 141.

[359] "That which is fabricated is not its 'mine'"; *yattu kṛtrimaṃ na tattasyātmīyaṃ* [*PP*, 263.1]; *gang zhig bcos ma yin pa de ni de'i bdag gi ba ma yin* [*TSHIG*, 42.5.3; *D-TSHIG*, 226.16]. See page 145.

[360] "A nature produced by causes and conditions would have a nature of fabrication"; *hetupratyayasaṃbhūtaḥ svabhāvaḥ kṛtako bhavet* [*MMK*, 19]; *rgyu dang rkyen las byung ba yi // rang bzhin byas pa can du 'gyur* [*DBU*, 6.3.1]. See page 134.

[361] "That which abides non-erroneously in fire throughout the three times and that which is the fundamental non-fabricated entity of fire"; *yataśyetadevamato yadevāgneḥ kālatraye 'pyavyabhicāri nijaṃ rūpamakṛtriyaṃ* [*PP*, 263.13-264.1]; *dus gsum du yang me la mi 'khrul ba gnyug ma'i ngo bo* [*TSHIG*, 42.5.6; *D-TSHIG*, 227.5-6]. See page 206.

[362] Deussen, 48.

general character[363]	samānyalakṣaṇam	sbyi'i mtshan nyid
mutually contradictory[364]	parasparavirūddha	phan tshun 'gal ba
nature[365]	prakṛti[366] [367]	rang bzhin
nature[368]	ātmā/ātmaka	bdag/rang bzhin
nature/own-being[369]	svabhāva[370] [371] [372]	rang bzhin

363 "...that which is shared, impermanence and so forth, is their general character"; *sādhāraṇaṃ tvanityatvādikaṃ samānyalakṣaṇam* [*PP*, 261.6]; *mi rtag pa la sogs pa thun mong ba ni sbyi'i mtshan nyid do* [*TSHIG*, 42.4.4; D-*TSHIG*, 225.15-16]. See page 144.

364 "Since they are mutually contradictory, to say something is a product and is also nature is a meaningless statement"; *kṛtakaśca svabhāvaśceti parasparavirūddhatvādasaṃgatārthameva* [*PP*, 260.4]; *byas pa yang yin la rang bzhin yang yin no zhes bya ba 'di ni phan tshun 'gal ba'i phyir 'brel ba med pa'i don yin no* [*TSHIG*, 42.3.1; *D-TSHIG*, 224.5-7]. See page 142.

365 The terms "nature" and "other-being" (*rang bzhin*) can be the translations of either *svabhāva* or *prakṛtiḥ*. See the following notes. The terms *ātmā* and *ātmaka* are also sometimes translated as "nature" (*rang bzhin*). See footnote 75.

366 "Change of a nature is never feasible"; *prakṛter anyathābhāvo na hi jātūpapadyate* [*MMK*, XV.8cd, 19]; *rang bzhin gzhan du 'gyur ba ni // nam yang 'thad par mi 'gyur ro* [*DBU*, 6.3.5-6]. See page 36.

367 The *Bhagavat Gītā*, IX.7, 88:

sarvabhūtānikaunteya prakṛti yānti māmikām //

368 "this lack of production, which is the nature of things"; *bhāvānām-anutpādātmakaḥ* [*PP*, 265.7-8]; *dngos po rnams kyi rang bzhin du gyur pa skye ba med pa* [*TSHIG*, 43.1.8; *D-TSHIG*, 228.13-15]. See page 147.

369 "Nature is non-fabricated"; *akṛtrimaḥ svabhāvo* [*MMK*, XV.2cd]; *rang bzhin dag ni bcos min* [*DBU*, 6.3.2]. See page 35.

370 Candrakīrti explains that, "the etymology of 'nature' (*rang bzhin*,

negative[373]	pratiṣedha	dgag pa
non-entityness	*naiḥsvabhāvatā	ngo bo nyid med pa
non-existent	abhāva	dngos po med pa
non-fabricated[374]	akṛtrimaḥ	bcos ma min pa
non-production of a nature[375]	svabhāvanutpattim	rang bzhin gyis ma skyes pa
non-related things[376]	asamgatārtha	'brel ba med pa'I don
not existent by nature[377]	No Sanskrit source	rang bzhin gyis med pa

---

svabhāva) is 'own-entity'" (*rang gi ngo bo, svo bhāvaḥ*) [*PP* (260.4); *TSHIG,* 43.2.1; *D-TSHIG,* 221.6-7]. See page 142.

371 "Nature in the *'vetāśvatara* Upaniṣad refers to "the specific character" of things." *Śvetāśvatara* (VI.1), 149:

svabhāvameke kavayo vadanti //

372 "A nature (*svabhāva*) that is the own-being of each individual, determining caste." The *Bhagavat Gītā,* XVIII.40, 168:

brāhmaṇakṣatriyaviśāṃ śūdrānāṃ ca parantapa //
karmāṇi pravibhaktāni svabhāvaprabhavair guṇaiḥ //

373 See "absence of nature."

374 "Nature is non-fabricated"; *akṛtrimaḥ svabhāvo* [*MMK,* XV.2cd]; *rang bzhin dag ni bcos min* [*DBU,* 6.3.1]. See page 35.

375 "Great Intelligent One, thinking of the non-production of a nature..."; *svabhāvānutpattim saṃdhāya mahāmate* [*PP,* 262.6]; *blo gros chen po rang bzhin gyis ma skyes pa la dgongs nas...* [*TSHIG,* 42.4.6; *D-TSHIG,* 226.6-7]. See page 144.

376 See footnote 364.

377 "...the realization...of these external and internal phenomena — which are the bases that sentient beings misapprehend as the two selves of persons and phenomena — as not existent by nature"; *bdag gnyis su zhen pa'i gzhir gyur pa'i phyi nang gi chos 'di rnams rang bzhin gyis med par rtogs pa* [*MCHAN,* 405.5]. See page 218.

object-to-be-negated[378]	pratiṣedya	dgag bya
other-being[379]	parabhāva	gzhan gyi dngos po
own-character[380]	svalakṣaṇam	rang gi mtshan nyid
own-entity[381]	svaḥ bhavaḥ	rang gi ngo bo
own-entity[382]	svarūpam	rang gi ngo bo
person/being[383]	puruṣa	bdag/skyes bu

378 "...thus propounds non-existence due to the non-existence of the object-to-be-negated"; *nāstiti brūyātpratiśedhyābhāvāt* [*PP*, 274.2]; *med par smra par 'gyur te dgag lta med pa'i phyir ro* [*TSHIG*, 44.4.2; *D-TSHIG*, 236.10]. See page 155.

379 "If they had an other-being, they would also have own-being"; *sati ca parabhāve svabhāvo 'pi bhaviṣyati* [*PP*, 265.15]; *gzhan gyi dngos po yod na ni rang bzhin yang yod par 'gyur* [*TSHIG*, 43.2.3; *D-TSHIG*, 229.1]. See page 148.

380 "Due to being uncommon because of not being observed separately [from fire], the nature, that is to say, own-character, of fire is heat"; *svabhāvatvenābhiniviṣṭā yathābhiniveśaṃ lakṣaṇamācakśate agnerauṣṇyaṃ svalakṣaṇam* [*PP*, 261.4]; *gzhan du ma dmigs pa las thun mong ma yin pa nyid kyis me'i rang bzhin gyi rang gi mtshan nyid ni tsha ba'o zhes bya bar mngon par zhen pa ji lta ba bzhin mtshan nyid smra* [*TSHIG*, 42.4.2; *D-TSHIG*, 225.12-13]. See page 143.

381 See footnote 370.

382 "That which is the own-entity of those, called the reality of phenomena is that [nature]"; *yā sā dharmāṇām dharmatā nāma saiva tat svarūpam* [*PP*, 264.11]; *de'i rang gi ngo bo ni chos rnam kyi chos nyid ces bya ba gang yin pa de nyid yin no* [*TSHIG*, 43.1.6; *D-TSHIG*, 227.17]. See page 147. I find no instance of *svarūpam* being translated into Tibetan as *rang gi gzugs*.

383 See Deussen, 48.

reality[384]	dharmatā	chos nyid
suchness[385]	tathatā	de kho na nyid
superimposition[386]	samāropya	sgro btags nas
the "mine"[387]	ātmitaṃ	bdag gi ba
the innermost entity[388]	ātmīyam rūpam	bdag gi ba'i ngo bo
without a nature	asvabhāvatā[389]	ngo bo nyid med pa

---

[384] See footnote 382.

[385] "What is this suchness? It is that entity of suchness that does not change and always abides"; *keyam tathatā tathābhāvo śvikāritvam sadaiva svāyitā* [*PP*, 265.1-2]; *de bzhin nyid 'di yang gang zhig ce na de bzhin nyid kyi ngo bo 'gyur ba med pa nyid dang rtag tu gnas pa nyid* [*TSHIG*, 43.1.5; *D-TSHIG*, 228.3-5]. See page 147.

[386] "In that it is said that [nature] exists upon superimposition, what is it like?"; *yadi khalu tadadhyāropāddhavaddhirastītyucyate kīdṛaśaṃ* [*PP*, 264.11]; *gal te sgro btags pa las de yod do zhes brjod na de ci 'dra ba zhig yin zhe na* [*TSHIG*, 43.1.3; *D-TSHIG*, 227.17-18]. See page 147.

[387] See note 359.

[388] "That which is the entity that is the "mine" of whatsoever thing is said to be its nature"; *iha svo bhāvaḥ svabhāva iti yasya padārthasya yadātmīyaṃ rūpaṃ tattasya svabhāva iti vyapadiśyate // kiṃ ca kasyātmīyaṃ yadhyasyākṛtrimaṃ* [*PP*, 262.12]; *'di ni rang gi dngos po ni rang bzhin no zhes bya bas gang zhig dngos po gang gi bdag gi ba'i ngo bo yin pa de ni rang bzhin yin no zhes brjod do // gang zhig gang gi bdag gi ba yin zhe na gang gis gang ma bcos pa'o* [*TSHIG*, 42.5.2-42.5.3; *D-TSHIG*, 226.13]. See page 84.

[389] From Buddhist Sanskrit Texts, No. 4, *Aṣṭasāhasrikā Prajñāpāramitā with Haribhadra's Commentary called Āloka*, edited by P.L. Vaidya (Darbhanga: The Mithila Institute, 1960), 125.18-19:

śūnyatāsvabhāvā hi subhūte pañca skandhāḥ asvabhāvatvāt //

BIBLIOGRAPHY

For works found in the Tibetan canon, 'P' refers to the Tibetan Tripitaka (Tokyo-Kyoto: Suzuki Research Foundation, 1955), which is a reprint of the Peking edition. For modern editions of Sanskrit texts of the Middle Way School and their Tibetan versions, as well as a more complete list of translations, see D.S. Ruegg's *The Literature of the Madhyamaka School of Philosophy in India* (Wiesbaden: Otto Harrasowitz, 1981).

SŪTRAS

Condensed Perfection of Wisdom Sūtra / shes rab kyi pha rol tu phyin pa sdud pa, sañcayagathaprajñāpāramitā. P735.

Descent into Laṅkā Sūtra / lang kar gzhegs pa'i mdo, laṅkavatārasūtra. P775, Vol. 29. Sanskrit edition: P.L.Vaidya, ed. *Saddharmalaṅkāvatārasūtram.* Buddhist Sanskrit Texts No. 3. Darbhanga: Mithila Institute, 1963. English edition: D.T. Suzuki. *The Lankavatara Sutra.* London: Routledge, 1932.

Eight Thousand Stanza Perfection of Wisdom Sūtra / shes rab kyi pha rol tu phyin pa brgyad stong pa'i mdo, aṣṭasāhasrikāprajñāpāramitā-sūtra. P734. Sanskrit edition: P.L.Vaidya, ed. *Aṣṭasāhasrikā Prajñāpāramitā with Haribhadra's Commentary called Āloka.* Buddhist Sanskrit Texts No. 4. Darbhanga: Mithila Institute, 1960.

Perfection of Wisdom Sūtra in Twenty-Five Thousand Lines / pañcaviṃśatisāhasrikā. P731.

Sūtra on the Ten Grounds / mdo sde sa bcu pa, daśabhūmikasūtra. P761.31, Vol. 25. Sanskrit edition: P.L. Vaidya, ed. *Daśabhūmikasūtram.* Buddhist Sanskrit Texts No. 7. Darbhanga: Mithila Institute, 1967. English translation: M. Honda. "An Annotated Translation of the '*Daśabhūmika*'," in D. Sinor, ed.

Studies in Southeast and Central Asia. Satapitdaka Series 74. New Delhi: 1968: 115-276.

Sūtra Unravelling the Thought / mdo sde dgongs 'grel / dgongs pa nges par 'grel pa'i mdo, saṃdinirmochanasūtra. P 774. Tibetan edition and French translation: Étienne Lamotte. *Samdhinirmocanasūtra: l'explication des mysteres.* Louvain, Paris, 1935.

Teaching of Akṣhayamati Sūtra / blo gros mi zad pas bstan pa'i mdo, akṣayamatinirdeśasūtra. P842, Vol. 34.

OTHER SANSKRIT AND TIBETAN SOURCES

• A-gya-yong-dzin (*dbyangs can dga' ba'i blo gros, a kya yongs 'dzin,* 18th century)

A Brief Explanation of Terminology Occuring in (Dzong-ka-ba's) "Great Exposition of the Path" (byang chub lam gyi rim pa chen mo las byungs ba'i brda bkrol nyer mkho bsdus pa). The Collected Works of A-kya Yoṅs ḥdzin, Vol. 1. New Delhi: Lama Guru Deva, 1971.

• Bu-dön (*bu ston,* 1290-1364)

History of the Doctrine (bde bar gshegs pa'i bstan pa'i gsal byed chos kyi 'byung gnas gsung rab rin po che'i mdzod). Lha-sa: zhol bka' 'gyur spar khang, n.d. English translation: E. Obermiller. *History of Buddhism.* Heidelberg: Harrasowitz, 1932; reprint, Suzuki Research Foundation.

• Candrakīrti (*zla ba grags pa,* 6th–7th C.E.)

Auto-Commentary on the "Introduction to (Nāgārjuna's) 'Treatise on the Middle'" (dbu ma la 'jug pa'i bshad pa / dbu ma la 'jug pa'i rang 'grel, madhaymakāvatārabhāṣya). P5263, Vol. 98. Also: Dharmsala edition. Dharmsala: Council of Religious and Cultural Affairs, 1968. Tibetan edition: Louis de la Vallée Poussin, ed. *Madhyamakāvatāra par Candrakīrti.* Bibliotheca

Buddhica IX. Osnabrück: Biblio Verlag, 1970. French translation (to VI.165): Louis de la Vallée Poussin. *Muséon* 8 (1907): 249-317; *Muséon* 11 (1910): 271-358; *Muséon* 12 (1911): 235-328. German translation (to VI.166-226): Helmut Tauscher. *Candrakīrti: Madhyamakāvatāraḥ und Madhyamakāvatārabhāṣyam.* Wien: Wiener Studien zur Tibetologie und Buddhismuskunde, 1981.

Clear Words Commentary on (Nāgārjuna's) "Treatise on the Middle" (dbu ma rtsa ba'i 'grel pa tshig gsal ba, mūlamadhyamikavṛtti prasannapadā). P5260, Vol. 98; cited as *TSHIG*. Tibetan edition: Dharamsala, Tibetan Publishing House, 1968, cited as *D-TSHIG*. Sanskrit: *Mūlamadhyamikakakārikā de Nāgārjuna avec la Prasannapadā Commentaire de Candrakīrti.* Louis de la Vallée Poussin. *Bibliotheca Buddhica* IV. Osnabrück: Biblio Verlag, 1970.

Commentary on (Āryadeva's) "Four Hundred Stanzas on the Yogic Deeds of Bodhisattvas" (bodhisattvayogacaryācatuḥśatakaṭīkā, byang chub sems dpa'i rnal 'byor spyod pa gzhi brgya pa'i rgya cher 'grel pa). P5266.

Introduction to (Nāgārjuna's) "Treatise on the Middle" (dbu ma la 'jug pa, madhyamakāvatāra). P5261, Vol. 98; P5262, Vol. 98. French translation: Louis de la Vallée Poussin, ed., *Madhyamakāvatāra par Candrakīrti.* Bibliotheca Buddhica IX. Osnabrück: Biblio Verlag, 1970. Also, French translation (to VI.165): Louis de la Vallée Poussin. *Muséon* 8 (1907): 249-317; *Muséon* 11 (1910): 271-358; *Muséon* 12 (1911): 235-328. English translation (Chapter VI): Geshe Rabten. *Echoes of Voidness.* London: Wisdom, 1983, 47-92.

- Döl-b̄o S̄hay-rap-gyel-tsen (*dol po pa shes rab rgyal mtshan,* 1292-1361)

The Mountain Doctrine: Ocean of Definitive Meanings (*ri chos nges don rgya mtso zhes bya ba'i bstan bcos dang bsdus don*), Bir: D. Tsondu Senghe, 1984.

- D̄zong-ka-b̄a (*tsong kha pa,* 1357-1419)

The Essence of Good Explanations, Treatise Discriminating the Interpretable and the Definitive (*drang ba dang nges pa'i don rnam par phye ba'i bstan bcos legs bshad snying po*). P6142, Vol. 153. Sarnath: Pleasure of Elegant Sayings Press, 1973.

Four Interwoven Annotations on (*D̄zong-ka-b̄a's*) *"Great Exposition of the Stages of the Path," The Lam rim chen mo of the incomparable Tsong-kha-pa* (*lam rim mchan bzhi sbrags ma / mnyam med rje btsun tsong kha pa chen pos mdzad pa'i byang chub lam rim chen mo'i dka' ba'i gnad rnams mchan bu bzhi'i sgo nas legs par bshad pa theg chen lam gyi gsal sgron*), *with the interlineal notes of Ba-so Chos-kyi-rgyal-mtshan, Sde-drug Mkhan-chen, Ngag-dbang-rab-rtan, 'Jam-dbyangs-bshad-pa'i-rdo-rje, and Bra-sti Dge-bshes Rin-chen-don-grub.* New Delhi: Chos-'phel-legs-ldan, 1972. English translation (sections on calm abiding and special insight): Alex Wayman. *Calming the Mind and Discerning the Real.* New York: Columbia University Press, 1978; reprint New Delhi: Motilal Banarsidass, 1979. English translation, first part of the "Great Exposition of Special Insight" in: Elizabeth Napper. *Dependent Arising and Emptiness.* London: Wisdom Publications, 1990.

Great Exposition of the Stages of the Path / Stages of the Path to Enlightenment Thoroughly Teaching All the Stages of Practice of the Three Types of Beings (*lam rim chen mo; skyes bu gsum gyi rnyams su blang ba'i rim pa thams cad tshang bar ston pa'i byang chub lam gyi rim pa*). P6001, Vol. 152. Also: Dharmsala: Shes rig par khang, no date. English translation: Robert Thurman. *Tsong Khapa's Speech of Gold in the Essence of True Eloquence.* Princeton: Princeton University Press, 1984.

The Illumination of the Thought, Extensive Explanation of (Candrakīrti's) "Supplement to (Nāgārjuna's) 'Treatise on the Middle'" (dbu ma la 'jug pa'i rgya cher bshad pa dgongs pa rab gsal). P6143, Vol. 154. Also: Sarnath, India: Pleasure of Elegant Sayings Press, 1973.

Medium Exposition of the Stages of the Path (lam rim 'bring). P6002, Vol. 152-3. Dharamsala: Shes rig par khang, 1968.

Ocean of Reasonings, Explanation of (Nāgārjuna's) "Treatise on the Middle" (dbu ma rtsa ba'i tshig le'ur byas pa shes rab ces bya ba'i rnam bshad rigs pa'i rgya mtsho). P6153, Vol. 156. Drashi-hlun-bo edition, Vol. *ba,* 316.5-333.6. Also: Sarnath, India: Pleasure of Elegant Sayings Printing Press, 1973.

• Ḡön-chok-jik-may-w̄ang-b̄o (*dkon mchog 'jigs med dbang po,* 1728-1791)

Precious Garland of Tenets / Presentation of Tenets, A Precious Garland (grub pa'i mtha'i rnam par bzhag pa rin po che'i phreng ba). The Collected Works of dkon-mchog-'jigs-med-dbaṅ-po, Vol. 6. New Delhi: Ngawang Gelek Demo, 1972, 485-535. English translation: Geshe Sopa and Jeffrey Hopkins. *Cutting Through Apearances.* Ithaca: Snow Lion Publications, 1994.

• Jam-ȳang-shay-b̄a (*'jam dbyangs bzhad pa,* 1648-1721)

Great Exposition of Tenets; Explanation of "Tenets," Sun of the Land of Samantabhadra Brilliantly Illuminating All of Our Own and Others' Tenets and the Meaning of the Profound [Emptiness], Ocean of Scripture and Reasoning Fulfilling All Hopes of All Beings (grub mtha' chen mo / grub mtha'i rnam bshad rang gzhan grub mtha' kun dang zab don mchog tu gsal ba kun bzang zhing gi nyi ma lung rigs rgya mtsho skye dgu'i re ba kun skong). Musoorie: Dalama, 1962. English translation (beginning of the Prāsaṅgika chapter) in: Jeffrey Hopkins. *Meditation on Emptiness.* London: Wisdom Publications, 1983.

Great Exposition of the Middle; Analysis of (Candrakīrti's) "Supplement to (Nāgārjuna's) 'Treatise on the Middle,'" Treasury of Scripture and Reasoning, Thoroughly Illuminating the Profound Meaning, Entrance for the Fortunate (*dbu ma chen mo / dbu ma 'jug pa'i mtha' dpyod lung rigs gter mdzod zab don kun gsal skal bzang 'jug ngogs*). Buxaduor: Gomang, 1967.

- J̄ang-ḡya (*lcang skya rol pa'i rdo rje,* 1717-1780)

Presentation of Tenets / Clear Exposition of the Presentations of Tenets, Beautiful Ornament for the Meru of the Subduer's Teachings (*grub pa'i mtha'i rnam par bzhags pa gsal bar bshad pa thub bstan lhun po'i mdzes rgyan*). Varanasi: Pleasure of Elegant Sayings Press, 1970.

- Kay-drup Ge-lek-b̄el-sang-b̄o (*mkhas sgrub dge legs dpal bzang po,* 1385-1438)

Thousand Dosages / Opening the Eyes of the Fortunate, Treatise Brilliantly Clarifying the Profound Emptiness (*stong thun chen mo / zab mo stong pa nyid rab tu gsal bar byed pa'i bstan bcos skal bzang mig 'byed*). *From The Collected Works of the Lord Mkhas-grub rje dge-legs-dpal-bzan-po,* Vol. 1, 179-702. New Delhi: Mongolian Lama Gurudeva, 1980.

- Kamalashīla (c. 740-795)

Illumination of the Middle (*dbu ma snang ba, madhyamakāloka*) P5287, Vol.101.

- L̄ong-chen Rab-jam-b̄a (*klong chen rab 'byams pa.* 1308-1363). *Treasury of Tenets* (*grub mtha' mdzod*). Volume 6 of the Sde-ge edition of the Seven Treasuries.

- L̄o-sang-dor-j'ay (*blo bzang rdo rje,* 19th century). *Ship for Entering into the Ocean of Textual Systems, Decisive Analysis of (D̄zong-ka-b̄a's) "Stages of the Path to Enlightenment"* (*byang chub lam gyi rim pa'i mtha' dpyod gzhung lugs rgya mtshor 'jug pa'i gru gzings zhes bya ba la lhag mthong gi mtha' dpyod*). New Delhi: Mongolian Lama Gurudeva, 1980.

- L̄o-sang-ḡön-chok (*blo bzangs dkun mchok,* dates unknown)

Word Commentary on the Root Text of (Jam-ȳang-shay-b̄a's) "Tenets" (*grub mtha' rtsa ba'i tshig ṭīk shel dkar me long,* in *Three Commentaries on the grub mtha' rtsa ba gdon lna'i sgra dbyaṅs* of *'jam-dbyaṅs-bzad-pa'i-rdo-rje ṅag-dbaṅ-brtson-'grus.* Delhi: Chophel Lekden.

- Maitreya[nātha] (*byams mgon,* dates unknown)

Differentiation of the Middle and the Extremes (*madhyāntavibhaṅga, dbus dang mtha' rnam par 'byed pa*). P5522, Vol. 108.

Treatise on the Later Scriptures of the Mahāyāna (*theg pa chen po rgyud bla ma'i bstan bcos, mahāyānottaratantraśāstra*). P5525, Vol. 108. English translation: E. Obermiller. *Sublime Science of the Mahāyāna to Salvation* (*Acta Orientalia,* XI, ii, iii, and iv); also J. Takasaki. *A Study on the Ratnagotravibhāga.* Rome: IS.M.E.O., 1966; and by Jeffrey Hopkins. *"Mahāyāna Treatise on the Sublime Continuum" by Maitreya, with Amplification by Mi-pam-gya-tso (1846-1912).* Unpublished manuscript, 1987.

- Nāgārjuna (*klu sgrub*)

Fundamental Treatise Called "Wisdom" (*dbu ma rtsa ba'i tshig le'ur byas pa shes rab ces bya ba, prajñānāmamūlamadyamakakārikā madhyamakaśāstra*). P5224, Vol. 95. Sanskrit edition: J.W. de Jong, ed. *Nāgārjuna, Mūlamadhyamakakārikāḥ.* Adyar: Adyar Library and Research Centre, 1977. Also: Christian Lindtner. *Nāgārjuna's Filosofiske Vaerker.* Indiske Studier 2, 177-215.

Copenhagen: Akademisk Forlag, 1982. English translations: Jay Garfield, *The Fundamental Wisdom of the Middle Way.* Oxford: Oxford University Press, 1995. Frederick Streng. *Emptiness: A Study in Religious Meaning.* Nashville, New York: Abingdon Press, 1967. Kenneth Inada. *Nāgārjuna: A Translation of his Mūlamadyamakakārikā.* Tokyo: The Hokuseido Press, 1970. David Kalupahana. *Nāgārjuna: The Philosophy of the Middle Way.* Albany: State University of New York Press, 1986. Italian translation: R. Gnoli. *Nāgārjuna: Madhyamaka Kārikā, Le stanze del cammino di mezzo.* Enciclopedia di autori classici 61. Turin: P. Boringhieri, 1961. Danish translation: Christian Lindtner. *Nāgārjuna's Filosofiske Vaerker.* Indiske Studier 2. Copenhagen: Akademisk Forlag, 1982. For more detail on published editions and translations, see Ruegg's *Literature of the Madhyamaka School of Philosophy in India,* 126-7.

The Precious Garland (*rgyal po la gtam bya ba zrin po che'i phreng ba'i rgya cher bshad pa, rājaparikathāratnāvalī*). P5658; sde dge bstan-'gyur series (Karmapa edition) Vol. 172. Sanskrit, Tibetan, and Chinese translations in: Michael Hahn. *Nāgārjuna's Ratnāvalī, Vol. 1, The Basic Texts.* Bonn: Indica et Tibetica Verlag, 1982.

Sixty Stanzas of Reasoning (*yuktiatikākārikā, rigs pa drug cu pa'i tshig le'ur byas pa*) P5225, Vol. 95; Toh 3825, Tokyo sde dge Vol. 1. Tibetan edition with Sanskrit fragments and English translation: Christian Lindtner in *Nagarjuniana.* Indiske Studier 4. Copenhagen: Akademisk Forlag, 1982.

- Nga-w̄ang-b̄el-den (*ngag-dbang-dpal-ldan,* b. 1797; also known as B̄el-den-chö-jay (*dpal ldan chos rje*)

Annotations for (*Jam-ȳang-shay-b̄a's*) *"Great Exposition of Tenets," Freeing the Knots of the Difficult Points, Precious Jewel of Clear Thought* (*grub mtha' chen mo'i mchan 'grel dka' gnad mdud grol blo gsal gces nor*). Sarnath: Pleasure of Elegant Sayings Printing Press, 1964. English translation (first chapter): John Buescher. "The Buddhist Doctrine of Two Truths in the Vaibhāṣika and Theravāda Schools." Ann Arbor: University Microfilms, 1982.

Explanation of the Conventional and the Ultimate in the Four Systems of Tenets (*grub mtha'i bzhi'i lugs kyi kun rdzob dang don dam pa'i don rnam par bshad pa legs bshad dpyid kyi dpal mo'i glu dbyangs*). New Delhi: Guru Deva, 1972.

• N̄ya-cha-wa Tsön-drü-s̄eng-gay (*rmya bya ba brston grus seng ge*, 12th century)

The Ornament of Correctness, Commentary on (Nāgārjuna's) "Fundamental Treatise Called 'Wisdom'" (*dbu ma rtsa ba shes rab kyi 'grel pa 'thad pa'i rgyan*). Rumtek, Sikkim: Chakra Center, 1975.

• Kalkī Puṇḍarīka (*rigs ldan pad ma dkar po*)

Great Commentary on the "Kālachakra Tantra," the Stainless Light (*bsdus pa'i rgyud kyi rgyal po dus kyi 'khor lo'i 'grel bshad rtsa ba'i rgyud kyi rjes su 'jug pa stong phrag bcu gnyis pa dri ma med pa'i 'od ces bya ba, vimālaprabhānāmamūlatantrānusāriṇīdvādaśasāhasrikālaghukālacakratantrarājaṭīkā*). P2064.

• Śāntideva (*zhi ba lha*, 8th century)

Engaging in the Bodhisattva Deeds (*bodhisattvacaryāvatāra, byang chub sems dpa'i spyod pa la 'jug pa*). P5272.

WORKS OF MODERN SCHOLARSHIP

Ames, William. "The Notion of *Svabhāva* in the Thought of Candrakīrti." *Journal of Indian Philosophy* 10 (1982).

Boquist, Ake. "Trisvabhāva: A Study of the Development of the Three-nature-theory in Yogācāra Buddhism." Tord Olsson ed.,

Lund Studies in African and Asian Religions, Vol. 8. Lund: University of Lund, 1993.

Candra, Lokesh. *Eminent Tibetan Polymaths of Mongolia.* New Delhi: International Academy of Indian Culture, 1961.

Conze, Edward. *Buddhist Texts Through the Ages.* New York: Harper, 1964.

Conze, Edward. *Buddhist Thought in India.* Ann Arbor: University of Michigan Press, 1967.

Conze, Edward. *Materials for a Dictionary of the Prajnāpāramitā Literature.* Tokyo: Suzuki Research Foundation, 1973.

Conze, Edward. *The Perfection of Wisdom in Eight Thousand Lines & its Verse Summary.* Berkeley: Four Seasons Foundation, 1973.

Conze, Edward. *The Prajñāpāramitā Literature.* London: 1960.

Csoma de Koros, Alexander. *Sanskrit-Tibetan-English Vocabulary.* Delhi: Sri Satguru Publications, 1980.

Das, Sarat Candra. *A Tibetan-English Dictionary.* New Delhi: Gaurav Publishing House, 1985.

Deussen, Paul. *Sixty Upaniṣads of the Veda.* Delhi: Motilal Banarsidass, 1980.

Dreyfus, Georges. *Recognizing Reality.* Albany: SUNY, 1997.

Eckel, David. *Jñānagarbha's "Commentary on the Distinction Between the Two Truths."* Albany: SUNY Press, 1987.

Festinger, Leon. *When Prophecy Fails.* Minneapolis: University of Minnesota Press, 1956.

Garfield, Jay, L. "Dependent-arising and the Emptiness of Emptiness: Why Did Nāgārjuna Start with Causation?" *Philosophy East and West* 44 No. 2 (April, 1994).

Garfield, Jay, L. *The Fundamental Wisdom of the Middle Way.* Oxford: Oxford University Press, 1995.

Geertz, Clifford. "Religion as a Cultural System," in *The Interpretation of Cultures; Selected Essays.* New York: Basic Books, 1973.

Hayes, Richard P. "Nāgārjuna's Appeal," *Journal of Indian Philosophy* 22 (1994): 229-378.

Hopkins, Jeffrey. *Buddhist Advice For Living & Liberation: Nāgārjuna's Precious Garland.* Ithaca: Snow Lion Publications, 1998.

Hopkins, Jeffrey. *Meditation on Emptiness.* London: Wisdom Publications, 1983; 2nd edition, 1996.

Hopkins, Jeffrey. "Special Insight: From D̄zong-ka-b̄a's *Middling Exposition of the Stages of the Path to Enlightenment Practised by Persons of the Three Capacities* with supplementary headings by Trijang Rinbochay." Unpublished manuscript, 1979.

Ichimura, Shohei. "Nāgārjuna's Philosophy of Sunyata and his Dialectic." University of Chicago unpublished dissertation, 1972.

Katz, Nathan. "Prasanga and Deconstruction: Tibetan Hermeneutics and the yāna Controversy." *Philosophy East and West* 34 (April 1984).

Klein, Anne. *Path to the Middle.* Albany: SUNY Press, 1994.

Lamotte, Étienne. *L'enseignement de Vimalakīrti.* Louvain: Muséon, 1962.

Lancaster, Lewis. "The Oldest Mahāyāna Sūtra: Its Significance for the Study of Buddhist Development." *The Eastern Buddhist* 8 (1975).

Lang, Karen. "A Dialogue on Death: Tibetan Commentators on the First Chapter of Āryadeva's *Catuḥśatika,*" in *Tibetan Buddhism: Revelation and Reason,* ed. Steven Goodman and Ronald Davidson. Albany: SUNY Press, 1992.

Larson, Gerald J. and Bhattacharya, Ram Shankar, editors. *Sāṃkhya: a Dualist Tradition in Indian Philosophy* (volume 4 of the

Encyclopedia of Indian Philosophies). Princeton: Princeton University Press, 1987.

Lopez, Donald S. *A Study of Svātantrika.* Ithaca: Snow Lion Publications, 1987.

Murti, T.R.V. *The Central Philosophy of Buddhism.* London: Unwin Publishers, 1980.

Napper, Elizabeth. *Dependent Arising and Emptiness.* London: Wisdom Publications, 1989.

Newland, Guy. *The Two Truths.* Ithaca: Snow Lion Publications, 1994.

Obermiller, E. *Sublime Science of the Mahāyāna to Salvation.* Acta Orientalia, 1931.

Powers, C. John. *Wisdom of Buddha: the Saṃdinirmocana Mahāyāna Sūtra.* Berkeley: Dharma Publishing, 1995.

Purohit Swami. *The Bhagavad Gita: The Gospel of Lord Shri Krishna.* New York: Vintage Books, 1977.

Rabten, Geshe. *Echoes of Voidness.* London: Wisdom Publications, 1983.

Radhakrishnan. *Indian Philosophy.* London: George Allen and Unwin, 1923, Vol. I.

Robinson, Richard H. "Did Nāgārjuna Really Refute All Philosophical Views?" *Philosophy East and West* 22 (1972).

Roerich, George N. *The Blue Annals.* Delhi: Motilal Banarsidass, 1976.

Ruegg, David S. "The Jo Naṅ Pas: A School of Buddhist Ontologists According to the Grub Mtha' Sel Gyi Me Loṅ." *Journal of the American Oriental Society* (January, 1963).

Ruegg, David S. *The Literature of the Madhyamaka School of Philosophy in India.* Wiesbaden: Otto Harrassowitz, 1981.

Ruegg, David S. "The Uses of the Four Positions of the Catuṣkoṭi." *The Journal of Indian Philosophy* 5 nos. 1/2, 1-71.

Saraswati, Kriyananda. *Nine Principal Upanishads.* Bihar: Bihar

School of Yoga Press, 1975.

Sonam, Ruth. *Yogic Deeds of Bodhisattvas.* Ithaca: Snow Lion Publications, 1994.

Stearns, Cyrus R. "The Buddha From Dol po and His Fourth Council of the Buddhist Doctrine." University of Washington unpublished dissertation, 1996.

Suzuki, Daisetz. *The Lankavatara Sutra.* London: Routledge and Kegan Paul Ltd., 1968.

Thurman, Robert. *Tsong Khapa's Speech of Gold in the Essence of True Eloquence.* Princeton: Princeton University Press, 1984.

Wayman, Alex. *Calming the Mind and Discerning the Real.* New York: Columbia University Press, 1978.

Williams, Paul. *Mahāyāna Buddhism.* London: Routledge, 1989.

Wylie, Turrell. "A Standard System of Tibetan Transcription." *Harvard Journal of Asiatic Studies* 22 (1959): 261-7.

INDEX

TIBETAN TEXT: དགག་བྱ་ངོས་འཛིན་ཁྱབ་ཆུངས་པ་དགག་པ་

This section presents the Tibetan text of D̄zong-ka-b̄a's *Great Exposition of the Stages of the Path* portion entitled, "The Refutation of an Identification of the Object-to-be-negated That Is Too Narrow." The digitized text was downloaded from the Asian Classics Input Project internet site and reformatted to conform to the current style.

See the English translation of this section, pages 179-192. Page references to the Dharamsala edition of the Tibetan text [860.4-870.1] are inserted into the digitized Tibetan in square brackets.

།གཉིས་པ་དགག་བྱ་ངོས་འཛིན་ཁྱབ་ཆུངས་པ་དགག་པ་ནི། [860.4]

ཁ་ཅིག་ན་རེ། དགག་བྱ་ནི་རང་བཞིན་ཡིན་ལ་དེ་ཡང་ཁྱད་པར་གསུམ་དང་ལྡན་པ་སྟེ་ངོ་བོ་རྒྱུ་དང་རྐྱེན་གྱིས་མ་བསྐྱེད་པ་དང་གནས་སྐབས་གཞན་དུ་མི་འགྱུར་བ་དང་རྣམ་འཇོག་གཞན་ལ་མི་ལྟོས་པའོ། །དེ་ཡང་དབུ་མའི་རྩ་བ་ལས།

།རང་བཞིན་རྒྱུ་དང་རྐྱེན་ལས་ནི།
།འབྱུང་བར་རིགས་པ་མ་ཡིན་ནོ།
།རྒྱུ་དང་རྐྱེན་ལས་བྱུང་ན་ནི།
།རང་བཞིན་བྱས་པ་ཅན་དུ་འགྱུར།
།རང་བཞིན་བྱས་པ་ཅན་ཞེས་བྱར།
།ཇི་ལྟ་བུར་ན་རུང་བར་འགྱུར།

།རང་བཞིན་དག་ནི་བཅོས་མིན་དང་། [861]

།གཞན་ལ་ལྟོས་པ་མེད་པ་ཡིན།

།ཞེས་གསུངས་པའི་ཕྱིར་རོ་ཞེས་ཟེར་རོ། །སྤྱིར་མྱུ་གུ་ལ་སོགས་པའི་ཕྱི་ནང་གི་དངོས་པོ་རྣམས་རང་བཞིན་དེ་འདྲ་བ་ཞིག་ཏུ་གྲུབ་པར་འདོད་ན་དབུ་མ་པས་དགག་པར་བྱ་དགོས་མོད་ཀྱང་འདིར་དགག་བྱ་ངོས་འཛིན་པ་ནི། གང་ཞིག་བཀག་ན་ཆོས་རྣམས་རང་བཞིན་མེད་པ་ཉིད་དུ་རྟོགས་པའི་དབུ་མའི་ལྟ་བ་རྒྱུད་ལ་སྐྱེ་བའི་དགག་བྱའི་རྩ་བ་དེ་ངོས་འཛིན་པ་ཡིན་ནོ། །དེ་ལྟར་ན་འདུས་བྱས་རྣམས་རྒྱུ་རྐྱེན་གྱིས་བསྐྱེད་པ་དང་གཞན་དུ་འགྱུར་བ་ནི་རང་གི་སྡེ་པ་རྣམས་ཀྱིས་གྲུབ་ཟིན་པས་དེ་དག་ལ་རང་བཞིན་མེད་པ་བསྒྲུབ་མི་དགོས་པར་འགྱུར་བ་དང་། དེ་དག་གིས་ཀྱང་དངོས་པོ་རྣམས་རང་བཞིན་མེད་པར་རྟོགས་པར་འགྱུར་བ་སོགས་ཀྱི་སྐྱོན་ཡོད་པས་དེ་ཐུན་མོང་མ་ཡིན་པའི་དགག་བྱ་ག་ལ་ཡིན། རང་གི་ངོ་བོས་གྲུབ་པའི་རང་བཞིན་དུ་གྲུབ་ན་རྒྱུ་རྐྱེན་ལ་མི་ལྟོས་པ་དང་གཞན་དུ་མི་འགྱུར་བ་སོགས་སུ་འགྱུར་དགོས་སོ་ཞེས་འཕངས་པ་ནི་དབུ་མའི་གཞུང་རྣམས་སུ་དུ་མ་ཞིག་ཡོད་ཀྱང་དེ་དག་ནི་ཁྱབ་བྱེད་ཀྱི་ངོས་ནས་སྐྱོན་བརྗོད་པ་ཡིན་གྱི། དགག་བྱ་རང་གི་ངོ་བོའི་སྒོ་ནས་ངོས་བཟུང་བ་མིན་ནོ།

།གཞན་ཡང་དོན་དམ་པར་དང་ཡང་དག་པར་གྲུབ་པ་དང་བདེན་པར་གྲུབ་ན་འང་རྒྱུ་རྐྱེན་གྱིས་མ་བསྐྱེད་པ་སོགས་སུ་འགྱུར་དགོས་ན་འང་དེ་དག་ནི་དོན་དམ་པར་གྲུབ་པ་སོགས་ཀྱི་དོན་མིན་ཏེ། དཔེར་ན། བུམ་པ་ལ་མི་རྟག་པས་ཁྱབ་ཀྱང་མི་རྟག་པ་བུམ་པའི་

དོན་དུ་མི་རུང་གི། ལྟོ་ལྦྱིར་བ་དེའི་དོན་དུ་བཞག་དགོས་པ་བཞིན་ནོ། །དེ་བཞིན་དུ་དོན་དམ་པར་གྲུབ་པ་སོགས་ཡིན་ན་ཆ་མེད་ [862] པའི་དངོས་པོར་འགྱུར་དགོས་ན་འང་ཆ་མེད་ཀྱི་དངོས་པོ་འདིར་རྒྱ་བའི་དགག་བྱ་མི་འདོད་དེ། དེ་ནི་གྲུབ་མཐའ་སྨྲ་བ་རྣམས་ཀྱིས་ཐུན་མོང་མ་ཡིན་པའི་འཛིན་པས་བཏགས་པ་ཙམ་ཡིན་པས་འཛིན་པ་དེ་ལུས་ཅན་འཁོར་བར་འཆིང་བའི་རྒྱ་བ་མིན་པའི་ཕྱིར་དང་། དེ་དག་རང་བཞིན་མེད་པར་གཏན་ལ་ཕབ་ནས་བསྒོམས་ཀྱང་ཐོག་མ་མེད་པའི་མ་རིག་པའི་འཛིན་པ་ལ་ཅི་ཡང་མི་གནོད་པས་དེ་དག་གི་དོན་མངོན་སུམ་དུ་རྟོགས་པ་མཐར་ཐུག་ཀྱང་ལྷན་སྐྱེས་ཀྱི་ཉོན་མོངས་རྣམས་ལྡོག་པར་མི་འགྱུར་བའི་ཕྱིར་རོ། །དེས་ན་ལྟ་བས་གཏན་ལ་འབེབས་པའི་དུས་སུ་ལྷན་སྐྱེས་ཀྱི་མ་རིག་པས་ཇི་ལྟར་བཟུང་བའི་དོན་མེད་པར་གཏན་ལ་འབེབས་པ་གཙོ་བོར་བཟུང་ནས། དེའི་ཡན་ལག་ཏུ་ཀུན་བཏགས་ཀྱི་འཛིན་པའི་ཡུལ་རྣམས་སུན་འབྱིན་པ་མ་ཤེས་པར་ལྷན་སྐྱེས་ཀྱི་མ་རིག་པའི་འཛིན་སྟངས་སུན་འབྱིན་པ་དོར་ནས་གང་ཟག་གི་བདག་འགོག་པ་ན་རྟག་གཅིག་རང་དབང་ཅན་གྱི་བདག་དང་ཆོས་ཀྱི་བདག་འགོག་པ་ན་གཟུང་བརྡུལ་ཕྲན་ཆ་མེད་དང་འཛིན་པ་སྐད་ཅིག་ཆ་མེད་དང་རང་བཞིན་ཁྱད་པར་གསུམ་ལྡན་ལ་སོགས་པ་གྲུབ་མཐར་སྨྲ་བ་པོ་ནས་བཏགས་པ་རྣམས་འགོག་པ་ནི་རྣམ་པ་ཐམས་ཅད་དུ་མི་རུང་སྟེ། དེ་ལྟ་མིན་ན་ལྟ་བས་གཏན་ལ་འབེབས་པའི་དུས་སུ་དེ་ཙམ་ཞིག་ལས་གཏན་ལ་མ་ཕབ་པས་བསྒོམ་པའི་ཚེ་ཡང་དེ་ཙམ་ཞིག་བསྒོམ་དགོས་ཏེ། ལྟ་བས་གཏན་ལ་འབེབས་པ་ནི་བསྒོམ་པའི་དོན་དུ་ཡིན་པའི་ཕྱིར་རོ། །དེའི་ཕྱིར་བསྒོམས་ནས་མངོན་དུ་

གྱུར་པ་དང་གོམས་པ་དེ་མཐར་ཐུག་ནའང་དེ་ཙམ་ཞིག་ཏུ་ཟད་ལ། དེ་ལྟར་ཀུན་བརྟགས་ཀྱི་ [863] འཛིན་པས་བཏགས་པ་ཙམ་གྱི་བདག་གཉིས་མེད་པར་མཐོང་བས་ལྷན་སྐྱེས་ཀྱི་ཉོན་མོངས་རྣམས་ལྡོག་པར་འདོད་ན་ཧ་ཅང་ཐལ་ཏེ། འཇུག་པ་ལས།

།བདག་མེད་རྟོགས་ཚེ་རྟག་པའི་བདག་སྤོང་ཞིང་།
།འདི་ནི་ངར་འཛིན་རྟེན་དུའང་མི་འདོད་པ།
།དེ་ཕྱིར་བདག་མེད་ཤེས་པས་བདག་ལྟ་བ།
།དཔྱིས་ཀྱང་འབྱིན་ཞེས་སྨྲ་བ་ཤིན་ཏུ་མཚར།

།ཞེས་གསུངས་ཤིང་། འགྲེལ་པ་ལས་ཀྱང་།

ཕན་ཚུན་འབྲེལ་པ་མེད་པའི་དོན་འདི་ཉིད་དཔེའི་སྒོ་ནས་གསལ་བར་བྱ་བའི་ཕྱིར་བཤད་པ།

རང་ཁྱིམ་རྩིག་ཕུག་སྦྲུལ་གནས་མཐོང་བཞིན་དུ།
།འདི་ན་གླང་ཆེན་མེད་ཅེས་དོགས་བསལ་ཏེ།
།སྦྲུལ་གྱི་འཇིགས་པ་སྤོང་བར་བྱེད་པ་ནི།
།ཀྱི་མ་གཞན་གྱི་གནམ་པོར་འགྱུར་ཉིད་དོ།

།ཞེས་གསུངས་ཏེ། འདི་གང་ཟག་གི་བདག་མེད་ལ་གསུངས་ཀྱང་ཆོས་ཀྱི་བདག་མེད་ལའང་མཚུངས་ཏེ།

བདག་མེད་རྟོགས་ཚེ་ཀུན་བརྟགས་བདག་སྤོང་ཞིང་།

།འདི་ནི་མ་རིག་རྗེན་དུའང་མི་འདོད་པ།
།དེ་ཕྱིར་བདག་མེད་ཤེས་པས་མ་རིག་པ།
།དཔྱིས་ཀྱང་འབྱིན་ཞེས་སྨྲ་བ་ཤིན་ཏུ་མཚར།

།ཞེས་སྨྲས་སོ། །འོ་ན་སློབ་དཔོན་གྱིས་སྔར་བཤད་པ་ལྟར་མ་བཅོས་པ་དང་གཞན་ལ་ལྟོས་པ་མེད་པ་རང་བཞིན་གྱི་མཚན་ཉིད་དུ་གསུངས་པ་དེ་བརྟག་པ་མཐར་བཟུང་གི་སྒོ་ནས་གསུངས་སམ་རང་བཞིན་དེ་འདྲ་བ་ཞིག་ཡོད་པ་ཡིན་ཞེ་ན། འདི་ནི་ཆོས་རྣམས་ཀྱི་ཆོས་ཉིད་ཅེས་གསུངས་པ་དེ་ལ་རང་བཞིན་ཞེས་བཞག་པ་ཡིན་ཏེ་བཅོས་མ་མིན་པ་དང་གཞན་ལ་རག་ལས་པ་མིན་པའོ། །དེ་ནི་ཡོད་དེ། འཇུག་འགྲེལ་ལས།

ཁྱད་པར་དུ་མཛད་པ་རྣམ་པ་དེ་ལྟ་བུའི་རང་ [864] བཞིན་སློབ་དཔོན་གྱིས་ཞལ་གྱིས་བཞེས་པ་ཞིག་ཡོད་དམ་ཞེ་ན། གང་གི་དབང་དུ་མཛད་ནས་བཅོམ་ལྡན་འདས་ཀྱིས་དེ་བཞིན་གཤེགས་པ་རྣམས་བྱུང་ཡང་རུང་མ་བྱུང་ཡང་རུང་ཆོས་རྣམས་ཀྱི་ཆོས་ཉིད་འདི་ནི་གནས་པ་ཉིད་དོ་ཞེས་རྒྱས་པར་གསུངས་པ་ཆོས་ཉིད་ཅེས་བྱ་བ་ནི་ཡོད་དོ། །ཆོས་ཉིད་ཅེས་བྱ་བ་འདི་ཡང་ཅི་ཞིག །མིག་ལ་སོགས་པ་འདི་དག་གི་རང་བཞིན་ནོ། །དེ་དག་གི་རང་བཞིན་ཡང་གང་ཞིག་ཅེ་ན། དེ་དག་གི་བཅོས་མ་མ་ཡིན་པ་ཉིད་དང་གཞན་ལ་ལྟོས་པ་མེད་པ་གང་ཡིན་པ་སྟེ་མ་རིག་པའི་རབ་རིབ་དང་བྲལ་བའི་ཤེས་པས་རྟོགས་པར་བྱ་བའི་རང་གི་ངོ་བོའོ། །ཇི་དེ་

> ཡོད་དམ་མེད་དོ་ཞེས་དེ་སྐད་སུ་སྨྲ། གལ་ཏེ་མེད་ན་ནི་ཅིའི་དོན་དུ་བྱང་ཆུབ་སེམས་དཔའ་རྣམས་ཕ་རོལ་ཏུ་ཕྱིན་པའི་ལམ་སྒོམ་པར་འགྱུར་ཏེ། གང་གི་ཕྱིར་ཆོས་ཉིད་རྟོགས་པར་བྱ་བའི་ཕྱིར་བྱང་ཆུབ་སེམས་དཔའ་རྣམས་དེ་ལྟར་དཀའ་བ་བརྒྱ་ཕྲག་རྩོམ་པ་ཡིན་ནོ་

ཞེས་མདོའི་ཤེས་བྱེད་དང་བཅས་པས་བསྒྲུབས་སོ། །འོ་ན་སྔར་ཆོས་ཐམས་ཅད་ལ་རང་བཞིན་གྲུབ་པ་མ་བཀག་གམ་སྙམ་ན། ནང་གི་བློས་བཏགས་པ་མིན་པའི་ཆོས་རྣམས་ལ་རང་གི་ངོ་བོས་གྲུབ་པའི་རང་བཞིན་ནི་རྡུལ་ཙམ་ཡང་མེད་དོ་ཞེས་ཁོ་བོ་ཅག་གིས་ལན་དུ་མར་མ་སྨྲས་སམ། དེས་ན་དེ་འདྲ་བའི་རང་བཞིན་དུ་ནི་ཆོས་གཞན་རྣམས་ལྟ་ཅི་སྨོས། ཆོས་ཉིད་དོན་དམ་པའི་བདེན་པ་དེ་ཡང་གྲུབ་པ་ཙུང་ཟད་ཀྱང་མེད་དེ། ཚིག་གསལ་ལས།

> དུས་གསུམ་དུའང་མེ་ལ་མི་འཁྲུལ་བ་གཉུག་མའི་ངོ་བོ་མ་བཅོས་པ་གང་ཞིག་སྔར་མ་བྱུང་བ་ལས་ཕྱིས་འབྱུང་བ་མ་ཡིན་པ་གང་ཞིག །ཆུའི་ཚ་བའམ་ཚུ་རོལ་དང་ཕ་རོལ་ལམ་རིང་པོ་དང་ཐུང་ངུ་ལྟར་རྒྱུ་དང་རྐྱེན [865] ལ་ལྟོས་པ་དང་བཅས་པར་མ་གྱུར་པ་གང་ཡིན་པ་དེ་རང་བཞིན་ཡིན་པར་བརྗོད་དོ། །ཅི་མེའི་རང་གི་ངོ་བོ་དེ་ལྟ་བུར་གྱུར་པ་དེ་ཡོད་དམ་ཞེ་ན་དེ་ནི་རང་གི་ངོ་བོས་ཡོད་པའང་མ་ཡིན་ལ་མེད་པའང་མ་ཡིན་ནོ། །དེ་ལྟ་ཡིན་མོད་ཀྱི་འོན་ཀྱང་ཉན་པ

> པོ་རྣམས་ཀྱི་སྒྲིབ་པ་སྤང་བར་བྱ་བའི་ཕྱིར་སྒྲོ་བཏགས་ནས་ཀུན་རྫོབ་ཏུ་དེ་ཡོད་
> དོ་ཞེས་བརྗོད་པར་བྱའོ།

།ཞེས་རང་བཞིན་དེ་ཡང་རང་གི་ངོ་བོས་གྲུབ་པ་བཀག་ནས་ཐ་སྙད་དུ་ཡོད་པར་གསུངས་སོ།

།གལ་ཏེ་ཉན་པ་པོའི་སྒྲིབ་པ་སྤང་བའི་ཕྱིར་དུ་སྒྲོ་བཏགས་ནས་བསྟན་པར་གསུངས་པས་ཡོད་པར་མི་བཞེད་དོ་སྙམ་ན་དེ་ནི་རིགས་པ་མ་ཡིན་ཏེ། དགོས་པ་དེའི་ཕྱིར་དུ་བཏགས་ནས་གསུངས་པ་ནི་ཆོས་གཞན་རྣམས་ཀྱང་ཡིན་པས་དེ་དག་ཀྱང་མེད་པར་འགྱུར་རོ། །གོང་དུ་དྲངས་པ་ལྟར་དོན་དེ་མེད་ན་ཚངས་སྤྱོད་དོན་མེད་དུ་ཐལ་བའི་གནོད་པ་བརྗོད་ནས་བསྒྲུབས་ཤིང་། ཡང་འཇུག་འགྲེལ་ལས།

> རང་བཞིན་འདི་ནི་སློབ་དཔོན་གྱིས་ཞལ་གྱིས་བཞེས་པ་འབའ་ཞིག་ཏུ་མ་ཟད་
> ཀྱི། གཞན་ཡང་དོན་འདི་ཁས་ལེན་དུ་གཞུག་པར་ནུས་པས་རང་བཞིན་འདི་ནི་
> གཉིས་ཀ་ལ་གྲུབ་པ་ཉིད་དུའང་རྣམ་པར་བཞག་གོ

།ཞེས་གསུངས་པའི་ཕྱིར་རོ། །གཞན་དུ་ན་དབུ་མ་པའི་ལུགས་ལ་གྲོལ་བ་ཐོབ་པ་མི་སྲིད་པར་འདོད་དགོས་ཏེ། མྱ་ངན་ལས་འདས་པ་ཐོབ་པ་ནི་མྱང་འདས་དེ་མངོན་སུམ་དུ་བྱས་པ་ཡིན་ལ། མྱང་འདས་དེ་ཡང་འགོག་པའི་བདེན་པར་བཤད་ཅིང་དེ་ཡང་དོན་དམ་པའི་བདེན་པར་གསུངས་པའི་ཕྱིར་དང་དོན་དམ་པའི་བདེན་པ་མེད་པའི་ཕྱིར་རོ། །མྱང་འདས

ཐོབ་པའི་ཚེ་ནི་དོན་དམ་[866]པ་འགོག་པའི་བདེན་པ་མངོན་སུམ་དུ་བྱ་དགོས་པར་རིགས་པ་དྲུག་ཅུ་པའི་འགྲེལ་པར་འབད་པ་དུ་མས་བསྒྲུབས་སོ།

།དེ་ལྟར་ན་མིག་ལ་སོགས་པའི་འདུས་བྱས་འདི་དག་ནི་རང་གི་ངོ་བོས་གྲུབ་པའི་རང་བཞིན་དུའང་མ་གྲུབ་ལ། ཆོས་ཉིད་ལ་རང་བཞིན་དུ་བཞག་པ་དེར་ཡང་མ་གྲུབ་པས་རང་བཞིན་གང་དུའང་མ་གྲུབ་པ་དང་དོན་དམ་པའི་བདེན་པ་ནི་ཆོས་ཉིད་ལ་རང་བཞིན་དུ་བཞག་པ་དེར་གྲུབ་ཀྱང་རང་བཞིན་དེར་འཛོག་བྱེད་བཅོས་མ་མིན་པ་དང༌། གཞན་ལ་མི་ལྟོས་པ་ནི་རང་གི་ངོ་བོས་གྲུབ་པའི་རང་བཞིན་དེར་ཅུང་ཟད་ཀྱང་མེད་པས་ཐ་སྙད་དུ་གྲུབ་པ་ཙམ་མོ། །བཅོས་མ་ནི་སྔར་མེད་གསར་དུ་འབྱུང་བའི་བྱས་པ་དང་གཞན་ལ་ལྟོས་པ་ནི་རྒྱུ་རྐྱེན་ལ་ལྟོས་པའོ། །གཟུགས་སོགས་རྣམས་རང་བཞིན་གཉིས་གང་དུའང་མ་གྲུབ་པས་ཆོས་ཉིད་ལ་རང་བཞིན་དུ་བྱས་པའི་རང་བཞིན་དེ་བལྟ་བའི་ཕྱིར་དུ་ལམ་སྒོམ་པས་ན་ཚངས་སྤྱོད་ཀྱང་དོན་མེད་དུ་མི་འགྱུར་བར་གསུངས་ཤིང༌། ཆོས་རྣམས་ལ་རང་གི་ངོ་བོས་གྲུབ་པའི་རང་བཞིན་གཏན་མི་འདོད་པ་དང་གློ་བུར་དུ་རང་བཞིན་ཁས་བླངས་པ་གཉིས་མི་འགལ་བར་བཤད་དེ། འཇུག་འགྲེལ་ལས།

ཀྱེ་མ་མ་ལ་གང་ཞིག་དངོས་པོ་ཅུང་ཟད་ཀྱང་མི་འདོད་ཅིང་གློ་བུར་དུ་
བཅོས་མ་མ་ཡིན་པ་དང་གཞན་ལ་ལྟོས་པ་མེད་པའི་རང་བཞིན་ཡང་
འདོད་པ་ཁྱོད་ནི་ཕན་ཚུན་འགལ་བའི་དོན་བརྗོད་པ་ཞིག་གོ། བརྗོད་པར་བྱ་སྟེ།
ཁྱོད་ཀྱིས་བསྟན་བཅོས་ཀྱི་དགོངས་པ་མ་རིག་པ་ཞིག་སྟེ་འདི་ཡི་དགོངས་པ་ནི་

གལ་ཏེ་མིག་ལ་སོགས་པ་རྣམས་ཀྱི་རང་གི་ངོ་བོ་རྟེན་ཅིང་འབྲེལ་བར་འབྱུང་བ་[867] བྱིས་པ་སོ་སོའི་སྐྱེ་བོས་གཟུང་བར་བྱ་བ་གང་ཡིན་པ་འདི་ཉིད་དེ་རྣམས་ཀྱི་རང་བཞིན་ཡིན་ན་ནི། རང་བཞིན་དེ་ཕྱིན་ཅི་ལོག་ཏུ་གྱུར་པས་ཀྱང་རྟོགས་པའི་ཕྱིར་ཚངས་པར་སྤྱོད་པ་དོན་མེད་པར་འགྱུར་ན་གང་གི་ཕྱིར་འདི་ཉིད་རང་བཞིན་མ་ཡིན་པ་དེའི་ཕྱིར་དེ་བལྟ་བའི་དོན་དུ་ཚངས་པར་སྤྱོད་པ་དོན་དང་བཅས་པར་འགྱུར་རོ། །དེ་ཡང་བདག་གིས་ཀུན་རྫོབ་ཀྱི་བདེན་པ་ལ་ལྟོས་ནས་བཅོས་མ་མིན་པ་དང་གཞན་ལ་མི་ལྟོས་པ་ཉིད་དུ་བརྗོད་དོ། །གང་ཞིག་བྱིས་པའི་སྐྱེ་བོས་བལྟ་བར་བྱ་བ་མ་ཡིན་པ་དེ་ཉིད་ནི་རང་བཞིན་ཡིན་པར་རིགས་ལ་དེ་ཙམ་གྱིས་དོན་དམ་པ་དངོས་པོ་མ་ཡིན་ཞིང་དངོས་པོ་མེད་པའང་མ་ཡིན་ཏེ་དེ་ནི་རང་བཞིན་གྱིས་ཞི་བ་ཉིད་ཡིན་པའི་ཕྱིར་རོ།

།ཞེས་གསུངས་སོ། །འདིར་དངོས་པོ་ཡོད་མེད་ནི་སྔར་གཉིས་སུ་སྨྲ་བའི་སྐབས་སུ་བཤད་པ་ལྟར་རང་གི་ངོ་བོས་ཡོད་པ་དང་ཡེ་མེད་ཡིན་ནོ། །ད་ལྟ་ཆོས་རྣམས་ལ་རང་གི་ངོ་བོས་གྲུབ་པའི་རང་བཞིན་དུ་གྲུབ་པ་རྡུལ་ཙམ་ཡང་མེད་པར་གཏན་ལ་ཕབ་པའི་རང་བཞིན་གྱིས་སྟོང་བའི་སྟོང་ཉིད་ནི། གཟུགས་སོགས་ཀྱི་ཆོས་འདི་དག་ཁྱད་གཞིར་བྱས་པའི་སྟེང་དུ་ཁྱད་ཆོས་སུ་ཡོད་པས་བློ་གཅིག་གི་ཡུལ་ན་དེ་གཉིས་ཀ་ཡོད་པ་མི་འགལ་ཞིང་གཉིས་སྣང་དེ་མ་ལོག་པས་སྟོང་ཉིད་དེ་དོན་དམ་བདེན་པ་བཏགས་པ་བར་འགྱུར་རོ། །གང་གི་ཚེ་རང་བཞིན་མེད་པར་རྟོགས་པའི་ལྟ་བ་དེ་ཉིད་གོམས་པས་དོན་དེ་མངོན་སུམ་དུ་རྟོགས་

པའི་དོར་ནི་རང་བཞིན་མེད་བཞིན་དུ་རང་བཞིན་དུ་སྣང་བའི་ [868] འཁྲུལ་སྣང་ཐམས་ཅད་ལྡོག་པས་ན་ཆོས་ཉིད་དེ་མངོན་སུམ་དུ་བྱས་པའི་ཤེས་པས་ཆོས་ཅན་གཟུགས་སོགས་དེ་མི་དམིགས་པས། དེ་ལྟ་བུའི་ཆོས་ཉིད་དང་ཆོས་ཅན་གཉིས་བློ་དེའི་དོན་མེད་པས་དེ་གཉིས་ཆོས་ཉིད་དང་ཆོས་ཅན་དུ་འཇོག་པ་ནི་ཐ་སྙད་པའི་བློ་གཞན་ཞིག་གི་ངོས་ནས་བཞག་དགོས་སོ། །དེ་ལྟར་ན་དོན་དམ་པའི་བདེན་པ་ནི་རང་གི་ངོ་བོས་གྲུབ་པའི་སྤྲོས་པ་ཐམས་ཅད་ཞི་བའི་སྟེང་དུ་རང་བཞིན་མེད་བཞིན་དུ་དེར་སྣང་བའི་འཁྲུལ་སྣང་གི་སྤྲོས་པ་ཐམས་ཅད་ཀྱང་རྣམ་པར་ལོག་པ་ཙམ་ལ་འཇོག་པས་དེ་ཁས་བླངས་ཀྱང་རང་གི་ངོ་བོས་གྲུབ་པའི་རང་བཞིན་ཁས་བླང་ག་ན་དགོས། ཚིག་གསལ་ལས་ཀྱང་།

དངོས་པོའི་རྣམ་པ་མ་རིག་པའི་རབ་རིབ་ཀྱི་མཐུས་དམིགས་པ་ནི་
མ་གཟིགས་པའི་ཚུལ་གྱིས་བདག་ཉིད་གང་གིས་འཕགས་པ་
མ་རིག་པའི་རབ་རིབ་དང་བྲལ་བ་རྣམས་ཀྱི་ཡུལ་དུ་འགྱུར་ཏེ་ངོ་བོ་
དེ་ཉིད་དེ་དག་གི་རང་བཞིན་དུ་རྣམ་པར་བཞག་གོ།

ཞེས་དང་།

དངོས་པོ་རྣམས་ཀྱི་རང་བཞིན་དུ་གྱུར་པ་སྐྱེ་བ་མེད་པ་དེ་ཡང་ཅི་
ཡང་མ་ཡིན་པ་ཉིད་ཀྱིས་དངོས་པོ་མེད་པ་ཙམ་ཡིན་པས་ངོ་བོ་
མེད་པའི་ཕྱིར་དངོས་པོའི་རང་བཞིན་དུ་ཡོད་པ་མ་ཡིན་ནོ།

།ཞེས་གསུངས་སོ། །གང་དག་དོན་དམ་པའི་བདེན་པ་དགག་བྱ་བདག་གཉིས་ལ་སོགས་པའི་སྤྲོས་པ་རྣམ་པར་བཅད་པ་ཙམ་ལ་མི་འཇོག་པར་སྟོང་སེར་ལ་སོགས་པ་ལྟར། ཡིན་ལུགས་རྟོགས་པའི་བློ་མ་འཁྲུལ་བའི་ཡུལ་དུ་རང་དབང་དུ་གྲུབ་པའི་ཚུལ་གྱིས་འཆར་བ་དང་དེ་ལྟར་ཡོད་པར་ངེས་པ་ནི་ཟབ་མོའི་དོན་རྟོགས་པའི་ལྟ་བ་ཡིན་པར་འདོད་ཅིང་། སེམས་[869]ཅན་རྣམས་ཀྱིས་གང་ལ་བདག་གཉིས་སུ་ཞེན་པའི་གཞི་ཕྱི་ནང་གི་ཆོས་འདི་རྣམས་རང་བཞིན་མེད་པར་རྟོགས་པ་ནི། ཡང་དག་པའི་ལྟ་བའི་གོལ་སར་འདོད་པ་ནི་ཐེག་པ་ཆེ་ཆུང་གི་གསུང་རབ་ཐམས་ཅད་ལས་ཕྱི་རོལ་ཏུ་གྱུར་པ་ཡིན་ཏེ། སེམས་ཅན་ཐམས་ཅད་འཁོར་བར་འཆིང་བའི་རྩ་བ་བདག་ཏུ་འཛིན་པ་ལྡོག་དགོས་པར་ནི་འདོད་ལ། དེས་བདག་ཏུ་བཟུང་བའི་གཞི་དེ་རང་བཞིན་མེད་པར་རྟོགས་པས་དེ་མི་ལྡོག་པར་དེ་དང་འབྲེལ་མེད་ཀྱི་ཆོས་གཞན་ཞིག་བདེན་པར་ཡོད་པར་རྟོགས་པས་བདག་ཏུ་འཛིན་པ་ལྡོག་པར་འདོད་པའི་ཕྱིར་རོ། །འདི་ནི་དཔེར་ན། ཤར་ཕྱོགས་ན་སྦྲུལ་མེད་བཞིན་དུ་ཡོད་པར་བཟུང་ནས་སྐྲག་སྟེ་སྡུག་བསྔལ་བར་གྱུར་པའི་སྡུག་བསྔལ་ལྡོག་པ་ལ་ཤར་ཕྱོགས་སུ་སྦྲུལ་ཙུང་ཟད་ཀྱང་མ་གྲུབ་པོ་སྙམ་དུ་བཟུང་བས་སྦྲུལ་འཛིན་དེ་མི་ལྡོག་གི། ནུབ་ཕྱོགས་ན་ཤིང་སྡོང་ཡོད་དོ་སྙམ་དུ་ཟུངས་ཤིག་དང་དེས་སྦྲུལ་འཛིན་དང་སྡུག་བསྔལ་དེ་ལྡོག་པར་འགྱུར་རོ་ཞེས་ཟེར་བ་དང་ཁྱད་པར་ཅི་ཡང་མི་སྣང་ངོ། །དེ་ལྟར་ན་བདག་ལེགས་སུ་འདོད་པ་དག་གིས་ནི་དེ་འདྲ་བ་དེ་རྒྱང་རིང་དུ་སྤངས་ནས་འཁོར་བར་འཆིང་བྱེད་རྒྱུད་པ་ཐམས་ཅད་ཀྱི་རྩ་བ་མ་རིག་པའི་འཛིན་སྟངས་སུན་འབྱིན་པའི་ཐབས་ངེས་པའི་དོན་གྱི་

གསུང་རབ་དང་། དེའི་དོན་གཞན་དུ་དྲང་དུ་མི་རུང་བར་ངེས་པ་གཏིང་ཚུགས་པར་བྱེད་པའི་རིགས་པའི་ཚོགས་རྒྱ་ཆེ་བ་གསལ་བར་གསུངས་པའི་འཕགས་པ་ཀླུ་སྒྲུབ་ཡབ་སྲས་ཀྱི་གཞུང་ལ་བརྟེན་ནས་སྲིད་པའི་རྒྱ་མཚོའི་ཕ་རོལ་ཏུ་འགྲོ་བར་ [870] གྱིས་ཤིག །དགག་བྱ་ལ་ལོག་རྟོག་འགོག་པ་དེ་དག་ནི་དབུ་མའི་ལྟ་བ་རྙེད་པའི་གོལ་ས་གཅོད་པ་ལ་ཤིན་ཏུ་གནད་ཆེ་བ་ཡིན་པས་སྤྲོས་ཏེ་བཤད་པ་ཡིན་ནོ།།